Buddha Śākyamuni

GURU PADMASAMBHAVA

Longchen Rabjam Drimé Özer

༄༅། །རྒྱལ་བ་སྐྱོང་ཆེན་རབ་འབྱམས་ཀྱིས་མཛད་པའི་
གནས་ལུགས་རིན་པོ་ཆེའི་མཛོད་ཀྱི་རྩ་བ་དང་
ཁ་སར་རིན་པོ་ཆེ་བསྟན་པའི་དབང་ཕྱུག་གིས་མཛད་པའི་
འབྲུ་འགྲེལ་དཔལ་ལྡན་བླ་མའི་ཞལ་ལུང་ཀུན་མཁྱེན་
དགྱེས་པའི་མཆོད་སྤྲིན་ཞེས་བྱ་བ་
བཞུགས་སོ།།

པདྨ་ཀུ་རའི་སྒྲ་བསྒྱུར་མཐུན་ཚོགས་ནས
སྒྲ་བསྒྱུར་ཞུས།

The Padmakara Translation Group gratefully acknowledges the generous support of the Tsadra Foundation in sponsoring the translation and preparation of this book.

The Precious Treasury of the Fundamental Nature

Longchenpa

WITH A COMMENTARY BY
Khangsar Tenpa'i Wangchuk

TRANSLATED BY THE
Padmakara Translation Group

SHAMBHALA

Shambhala Publications, Inc.
2129 13th Street
Boulder, Colorado 80302
www.shambhala.com

© 2021 by the Padmakara Translation Group

Cover art: Longchenpa Drime Ozer (1308–1363)
Tibet; 19th century
Pigments on cloth
Rubin Museum of Art
Gift of Shelley & Donald Rubin Foundation
F1998.9.2 (HAR 631)
Cover design: Kate E. White

9 8 7 6 5 4 3 2 1

First Edition
Printed in the United States of America

♾ This edition is printed on acid-free paper that meets
the American National Standards Institute Z39.48 Standard.
♻ This book is printed on 30% postconsumer recycled paper.
For more information please visit www.shambhala.com.
Shambhala Publications is distributed worldwide
by Penguin Random House, Inc., and its subsidiaries.

LIBRARY OF CONGRESS CATALOGING-IN-PUBLICATION DATA
Names: Klong-chen-pa Dri-med-'od-zer, 1308–1363, author. |
Bstan-pa'i-dban-phyug, Khan-sar Rin-po-che Dbon-sprul, 1938–
writer of commentary. | Comité de traduction Padmakara, translator.
Title: The precious treasury of the fundamental nature / Longchenpa;
with a commentary by Khangsar Tenpa'i Wangchuk; translated by the
Padmakara Translation Group.
Description: Boulder: Shambhala, 2021. | Includes index.
Identifiers: LCCN 2020044701 | ISBN 9781611809336 (hardback)
Subjects: LCSH: Rnying-ma-pa (Sect)—Doctrines. | Rdzogs-chen.
Classification: LCC BQ7662.4 .K567 2021 | DDC 294.3/42—dc23
LC record available at https://lccn.loc.gov/2020044701

CONTENTS

FOREWORD

From the very first moment that I heard about Khangsar Tenpa'i Wangchuk Rinpoche and his commentary on Longchenpa's *Precious Treasury of the Dharmadhātu*, I felt a deep yearning to receive his teaching and blessing. I mentioned this to my brother Pema Wangyal Rinpoche and was delighted to hear that a student of Tenpa'i Wangchuk Rinpoche had asked whether it would be possible for Padmakara to translate his writings into English and other Western languages.

Happily, as the situation unfolded, we had the tremendous good fortune to receive the precious reading transmission of the entire published collection of Tenpa'i Wangchuk's works directly from the mouth of his own nephew and lineage holder, Khenpo Tsultrim Zangpo Rinpoche, who came to Dordogne in the autumn of 2019. This was in fulfillment of a prediction that his uncle's teachings would be transmitted to the West. I am immensely grateful to him for his kindness in making the long journey to France in order to teach us—with such compassionate grace, such profound ease and simplicity. His visit to La Sonnerie in Dordogne was a truly wonderful and profoundly moving occasion.

The translation of Tenpa'i Wangchuk Rinpoche's writings has now begun. We have started, in the present volume, with his commentary on *The Precious Treasury of the Fundamental Nature*. It is a direct introduction to the view of the Great Perfection, a point of entry into the profound teachings of Longchenpa.

We can read in the biography of Tenpa'i Wangchuk that he had direct visions of buddhas and bodhisattvas, ḍākas and ḍākinīs, as also wisdom Dharma protectors. We may thus be sure of the authenticity of his teachings. These, moreover, have the wonderful quality of expressing the most profound and intricate matters in clear and simple terms, in language that is very direct and accessible.

In this time of turmoil, it is an amazing good fortune even to hear the name of this book, let alone to be able to read, study, understand, and put it into practice. I am profoundly grateful not only to the inestimable author of these works but also to the kindness of his nephew Tsultrim Zangpo Rinpoche, to the translators, to our publishers, and to our most generous sponsors who have made this book possible. I pray that they will all live long and continue with their excellent work. On behalf of all the readers who will study and benefit from this book, I thank them with all my heart.

May the light of this text dispel the lies and falsehood of extremism, confusion, ignorance, and selfishness. May the truth be established and may beings flourish in the experience of it. May everyone be freed from suffering and from the virus not only of disease but of foolish opinions and beliefs.

Jigme Khyentse Rinpoche

TRANSLATORS' INTRODUCTION

This translation of Khangsar Tenpa'i Wangchuk's commentary on Longchenpa's *Precious Treasury of the Fundamental Nature* is the first step in a project to translate the collected works of this great modern Tibetan scholar. This ambitious task was entrusted to the Padmakara Translation Group by Tsultrim Zangpo Rinpoche, the abbot of Khangsar Taklung Monastery, and Yingrik Drubpa Rinpoche, both disciples of Tenpa'i Wangchuk (1938–2014) and trustees of his literary heritage. Aside from the autocommentary composed by Longchenpa himself in the fourteenth century, this is the first and only commentary ever to have been written on *The Treasury of the Fundamental Nature.*[1]

Unlike the general exposition, or "meaning commentary," provided by Longchenpa as an explanation of his own root text, the commentary of Tenpa'i Wangchuk is a "word commentary" and as such is of inestimable value to students and translators. Whereas meaning commentaries focus exclusively on the ideas expressed in a text, word commentaries are more elementary and didactic in style. They examine in fine detail the language of the root verses, every syllable of which (often indicated by typographical devices) is traditionally incorporated into the text of the commentary itself. Difficult terms and obscure, antiquated, or dialectal expressions are glossed with more common and up-to-date equivalents, and it is only then that the meaning of the text is explained. The purpose of the word commentary is thus to ensure that the reader understands as clearly as possible the meaning of the root verses themselves, which, even when they are accompanied by an autocommentary, are regarded as the principal expression of the author's message. The pedagogical advantages of such an approach are obvious, and it is hardly necessary to add that for translators, commentaries of this kind are invaluable and often indispensable tools.

It is perhaps too much to say that autocommentaries (that is, commentaries written by authors on their own root texts) are invariably meaning commentaries, but this seems certainly to be the case for Longchenpa. His usual practice is to cite sections of his own verses and then to enlarge on their meaning in general terms. His autocommentary, in other words, runs parallel to his root text, and he is rarely detained by simple considerations of vocabulary or the explanation of metaphor or other poetic devices. This is perhaps because he himself found the meaning of his text obvious and perhaps also because the poetry of his text resisted pedestrian analysis. Sometimes Longchenpa simply repeats in prose what he has already said more lyrically in the root text. At other times he expands on its meaning with more lengthy explanation, supporting it with voluminous citations from the scriptures. At yet other times he digresses into detailed and lengthy discussions of connected topics. On these occasions, it is as if the root text serves as a catalyst for the autocommentary, which then becomes the principal and often massive vehicle of his thought. So it is that whereas interesting ideas may well be picked up and elucidated, it quite often happens that difficult words and obscure poetic expressions in the root text are passed over in silence—much to the dismay of the translators, whose task it is, come what may, to discern the meaning of the root text and to render it intelligibly in another language.

When these and similar problems occur in the writings of other authors, students and readers are usually able to turn hopefully to the detailed word commentaries of third-party commentators. In the case of Longchenpa, however, it is here that we encounter a serious problem, for there are no third-party commentaries on his writings.[2] Perhaps because of their difficulty, perhaps because of the intense veneration with which they were and continue to be universally regarded, or perhaps out of diffidence and fear of censure, no one down the centuries has dared to produce written explanations of Longchenpa's works—even though, of course, the oral lineage of explanation has been maintained unbroken.

In recent times, this extraordinary situation has begun to change. With the easing of the political situation in the eastern provinces of Tibet during the final decades of the twentieth century, many monasteries have been restored, new centers of learning have been founded, and great efforts have been made to recover and protect the ancient traditions of study and practice. In institutions belonging to the Nyingma school—for example, in Khenpo Jigme Phuntsok's vast establishment at Serta Larung Gar or in the monasteries rebuilt by Khenpo Tenpa'i Wangchuk at Khangsar Taklung and Panak in Golok—this has led to the energetic revival of the teaching and practice of the Great Perfection and in particular to the study of the works of Longchenpa. As part of this wonderful initiative, Tenpa'i Wangchuk himself composed a large collection of writings. In response to enthusiastic interest and doubtless with the wish to preserve a tradition the fragility of which had been demonstrated all too clearly by the persecutions of the twentieth century, he produced several texts on the Great Perfection teachings of a kind, it is said, that had never been attempted before. It was his lot, so his biography tells us, to do what no other scholar had done before him: to express in writing something of the explanation lineage of Longchenpa's thought. It is thus that, among other things, Khangsar Khenpo Tenpa'i Wangchuk composed unprecedented commentaries on two of Longchenpa's Seven Treasuries: *The Treasury of the Dharmadhātu* and *The Treasury of the Fundamental Nature*. Furthermore, these two commentaries are, to our great good fortune, word commentaries: detailed explanations of Longchenpa's actual text. Celebrated for their clarity and ease of expression, they have been specially devised to provide the aspiring student with a means of access to Longchenpa's sublime teachings.

As Tenpa'i Wangchuk says in his preamble to the second of these commentaries, translated here, Longchenpa's *Treasury of the Fundamental Nature* "establishes the definitive view of the secret class of pith instructions" of the Great Perfection. Correctly implemented, it has the power to bring those endowed with the necessary karmic fortune to the highest accomplishment in a single life. "Happy indeed," Tenpa'i Wangchuk says, "are those who even see, hear, recall, or touch this text."

THE SEVEN TREASURIES

Because of the similarity of their names, Longchenpa's Seven Treasuries are often spoken of, for the sake of convenience, as if they were parts of a single integrated collection. A closer examination reveals, however, that there is little basis for this assumption and certainly no evidence to suggest that Longchenpa himself thought of them in this way. In the partial catalog drawn up at Tharpa Ling in Bhutan, Longchenpa mentions six of the Seven Treasuries—all except *The Treasury of the Fundamental Nature*—in a disconnected manner according to their subject matter without any indication of a significant relationship between them.

Only four of the Seven Treasuries clearly identify the place of their composition as Gangri Thökar, Longchenpa's hermitage in the mountains above the valley of the Tsangpo River. None of the Seven Treasuries is dated, and but for sparse internal evidence,[3] it is impossible to establish conclusively the order in which they were composed. Given, however, that Longchenpa left for Bhutan in 1350 at the age of forty-two in order to evade the hostility of the then overlord of Tibet, Tai Situ Changchub Gyaltsen, it is generally thought that all Seven Treasuries, with the probable exception of *The Treasury of the Fundamental Nature*, were composed while Longchenpa was still a young man—illustrating the fact that he was a prodigious scholar and master of high realization of an almost miraculous precocity.

An oral tradition states that all Seven Treasuries were composed in Bhutan but were lost in a catastrophic accident during Longchenpa's return from exile in the early 1360s, when his library and many of his compositions were swept away in a river. The Seven Treasuries, so the story continues, had to be rewritten in Gangri

Thökar. There are, however, several reasons for doubting the historicity of this legend, not least of them being that Longchenpa died in 1364, little more than three years—three intensely active years—after his return home. Barring the assistance of supernatural agencies, it is scarcely credible that they could have been composed anew in the time available. Even the ten years of Longchenpa's sojourn in Bhutan seem all too brief a period for the composition of the Seven Treasuries, some of which are of considerable length and complexity, especially in view of all the other things that Longchenpa is said to have accomplished during that time.[4]

Of greater immediate interest in the present context is the fact that *The Treasury of the Fundamental Nature* is not mentioned in the Tharpa Ling catalog, which was compiled at some point during the seven years between the construction of this temple hermitage in 1353 and Longchenpa's return to Tibet in 1360. And given that its colophon states that it was written at Gangri Thökar, it is not unreasonable to infer that the last of the Seven Treasuries was composed after Longchenpa's return from exile and therefore figures among his final works.

In view of the apparently unconnected nature of the Seven Treasuries (but for the similarity of their titles) as well as our inability to date them and thus establish an order of composition, it is hard to imagine that they were envisaged as a single collection drawn up by their author according to some preconceived plan. This does not mean, however, that it is impossible to see any order at all in these extraordinary compositions.

Khenpo Jigme Phuntsok, who regularly expounded the Seven Treasuries in an extended curriculum to thousands of students, discerned within them a natural teaching order irrespective of the dates of their composition.[5] For teaching purposes, he arranged them in a gradual order according to subject matter, beginning with the texts that deal principally with general sutra topics and progressing through to those that focus exclusively on the teachings of the Great Perfection. According to this scheme, he would first expound *The Treasury of Wish-Fulfilling Jewels* and *The Treasury of Tenet Systems,*[6] which are general and philosophical in character. These would be followed by a study of *The Treasury of Essential Instructions,*[7] which is a large collection of six-line aphorisms covering a wide range of doctrinal topics drawn from sutra, tantra, and Great Perfection teachings. A direct introduction to the Great Perfection would follow with an exposition of *The Treasury of the Dharmadhātu* and *The Treasury of the Fundamental Nature,*[8] two beautiful, poetic texts designed to bring students into direct and inspiring contact with the Great Perfection view of primordial purity and the practice of *trekchö,* or "cutting through." Finally, the cursus of study would conclude with a reading of *The Treasury of the Supreme Vehicle* and *The Treasury of Words and Meanings,*[9] scholastic expositions of the theoretical basis of the Great Perfection that are among Longchenpa's most difficult and demanding compositions.

THE TREASURY OF THE FUNDAMENTAL NATURE

In the early pages of his commentary on *The Treasury of the Fundamental Nature,* Tenpa'i Wangchuk mentions its close relationship with *The Treasury of the Dharmadhātu.* Both texts, he says, are distillations of the teachings of all three classes of the Great Perfection (the mind class, the space class, and the pith instruction class) and contain crucial points for the understanding of the view and practice of trekchö, the teaching on primordial purity.

These two works are said, moreover, to complement each other in terms of theory and practice. Theoretically, *The Treasury of the Dharmadhātu* establishes the nature of all phenomena of both samsara and nirvana not so much ontologically, in the sense of their being empty of real existence, but sapientially, as the creative expression of the vast expanse of the nature of the mind, "the great *dharmadhātu,* awareness alone." This is the characteristic note of the Great Perfection, where the ontological status of things as established in Madhyamaka is superseded by the vision of phenomena as being the display of awareness, primordially pure and spontaneously luminous. At the same time, however, Tenpa'i Wangchuk says that *The Treasury of the Fundamental Nature* differs from *The Treasury of the Dharmadhātu* in that it applies this understanding to the mind of the individual practitioner "in a systematic exposition in successive stages." It describes how practitioners who have entered the path of the Great Perfection are to understand and relate to phenomenal appearances themselves— both the apparently extramental world and the inner subjective states that apprehend it. Phenomena are thus presented in terms of four vajra principles (*rdo rje'i chings bzhi*): that is, their nonexistence (*med pa*), their evenness (*phyal ba*), their spontaneous presence (*lhun grub*), and their single nature (*gcig pu*). "If practitioners bring these same principles to bear on their own minds," the commentary goes on to say, "it will be easy for them to implement this teaching in a gradual and systematic way."

It is not perhaps immediately obvious how these principles are to be applied to the mind of the practitioner. *The Treasury of the Fundamental Nature* is in no sense a manual of practical instructions. Nevertheless, its description of the way phenomenal appearance is to be understood and related to introduces the student quite directly to the view and practice of trekchö. The four vajra principles are in fact the four *samayas* of nothing to keep, the four ways that qualified practitioners of the Great Perfection are to experience and understand the phenomena of the outer world detected by the senses as well as the subjective mental and emotional states that apprehend them. *The Treasury of the Fundamental Nature* is a profound and detailed exploration of these four samayas.

It must be understood that the word "samaya" is used here in a special sense. Generally speaking, on the level of the tantras, samaya is understood as a pledge and refers to the attitudes and behavior to which masters and disciples commit themselves once empowerment has been bestowed and received. In the present context, however, the four "samayas" are in fact four principles, four ways of understanding phenomenal appearance, that flow from the realization cultivated by the practitioner of the Great Perfection.

As Dilgo Khyentse Rinpoche once remarked, in such a context, "samaya" refers to the unmoving primordial wisdom of the ultimate expanse. And "since everything is the display of this wisdom, this samaya cannot be transgressed."[10]

The four samayas of nothing to keep are briefly referred to in Jigme Lingpa's *Treasury of Precious Qualities*, and a summary of their meaning can be found in Kangyur Rinpoche's brief but helpful commentary, which begins with a description of the kind of people to whom they apply—namely, those who are able to implement the Great Perfection teachings and for whom the four samayas are live issues. He says,

> Those who have been perfectly introduced to the nature of the mind, and are able to abide in it, realize that outer appearances are groundless and that inner awareness is object-free. Such people settle in the state in which they do not discriminate between what is to be accepted and what is to be rejected.[11]

Later he remarks,

> The samayas of "nothing to keep" refer to the way in which one remains in the fundamental nature of things, the vajra-like indestructible state, which is primordially free of defect, unsundered by duality. Mind and appearances are both overpowered by the primordial wisdom of the dharmakāya.[12]

These brief but loaded statements bring into focus the crucial point that the practice of the Great Perfection and specifically that of trekchö begins not with the intellectual understanding of a philosophical view, as is the case in the lower vehicles of Buddhist teaching, but with the recognition and stabilized experience of the nature of the mind—which in effect corresponds to the direct vision of the ultimate truth in itself. In other words, the starting

xxiii
point for the practice of the Great Perfection is not an intellectual understanding but a state of realization. Prior to the direct recognition of the nature of the mind, the intellectual study of the Great Perfection, the interest taken in it, and the practice itself all belong, strictly speaking, to the preliminary but crucially important path of aspiration.

The Treasury of the Fundamental Nature is an exhaustive presentation in which each of the four samayas of nothing to keep is explained in four successive stages. First, the meaning of the samaya in question (nonexistence, evenness, spontaneous presence, and single nature) is stated or revealed in a succession of key points. Second, phenomena are further explored and their nature is summarized or essentialized in terms of the samaya in question. Third, this same process is repeated but this time from the standpoint of the samaya itself, which is thus shown to include or subsume within itself the entire aggregate of phenomenal appearances. Finally, all these points are brought into focus so as to engender a state of decisive certainty.[13]

As a brief introduction of the four samayas, we tentatively suggest the following summary. We have indicated that the characteristic approach of the Great Perfection is not, as in Madhyamaka, to subject the phenomena of an apparently outer world to logical analysis as a means to undermine our clinging to it. Instead, the task is to recognize the nature of phenomenal appearance within the mind and to reach the understanding, or rather to see directly, that the phenomenal world is nothing but the display of awareness. To attain and rest in this recognition is liberation itself. For according to the teaching of the Great Perfection, it is precisely through the failure to recognize the nature of phenomena as the display of awareness, and through the belief instead that they are objectively existent, that beings wander through the hallucinatory experiences of samsara, deludedly thinking that they are real.

Longchenpa says that just as the universe, however vast it is, is contained within the abyss of space, so too the entire phenomenal field of both samsara and nirvana—everything that appears and is able to appear to the minds of beings—arises within the expanse of pure awareness. Phenomena have no existence outside awareness. And even within awareness itself, phenomena as mere appearances are without substantial reality. This is the samaya or principle of nonexistence (*med pa'i dam tshig*).

When the yogi settles in the recognition of the ultimate nature, in the understanding that phenomena are the unreal display of awareness, and when, in relation to these same phenomena, all sense perceptions are left open and free, without discrimination or qualitative assessment—when, in other words, phenomena are left just as they are without judgment, "decisively settled in the vast spaciousness of the ultimate nature," they are said to be "even." They all display the same seamless quality. This is the samaya of all-embracing evenness (*phyal ba'i dam tshig*).

When this evenness is taken a step further, we come to the samaya of spontaneous presence (*lhun grub kyi dam tshig*), which is perhaps the most difficult to grasp. In general, when things are said to be spontaneously present, it is understood that they do not arise through causes and conditions. They are simply "there." To explain this characteristic of phenomenal appearance, Longchenpa uses the example of dreaming. Even though the things experienced in dreams are—to the dreamer—indistinguishable from the things encountered in waking life, the fact is that they do not arise from the conjunction of causes and conditions, as do the things we encounter while we are awake. Having no existence outside the mind of the dreamer, dream visions arise simply "through the creative power of the state of sleep." They are "just there," spontaneously present. And just as dream visions appear through the creative power of sleep, in the same way, the phenomena of waking life arise through the creative power of awareness—beyond which they never stir.

Finally, one may further reflect that whatever phenomena are perceived, whether in terms of appearing objects or the subjective states that detect them—and regardless of their "coloring" in terms of being either positive or negative, good or bad—they all arise, endure, and subside within awareness. And in this sense they are simply the one awareness. This final samaya is the samaya of a single nature (*gcig pu'i dam tshig*).[14]

The Author of the Commentary

Khangsar Tenpa'i Wangchuk was born in 1938 in the Akyong Khangsar district of Golok, a remote region of eastern Tibet now included in the Chinese administrative province of Qinghai. Not long after his birth, which according to local report was accompanied by various preternatural signs, he was recognized by important lamas of different schools as the rebirth of Panak Öntrul Rigdzin Dorje, an emanation of Yudra Nyingpo, a disciple of the great eighth-century translator Vairotsana and one of the twenty-five disciples of Guru Padmasambhava. The detailed biography, which opens the first volume of Tenpa'i Wangchuk's collected works, describes his precocious intelligence and spiritual gifts. In 1952, he received his first monastic ordination at the age of fourteen from Akong Khenpo Lozang Dorje, the director of the *shedra*, or scriptural college, of Thösam Ling, who later instructed him in the three levels of Buddhist vows and gave him the transmission of Śāntideva's *Way of the Bodhisattva*. The following year, at the age of fifteen, Tenpa'i Wangchuk demonstrated his ability by giving a public teaching on the first two chapters of this same text. Not long afterward, he received from the throne holder of the monastery of Palyul Dimda. the transmission and explanation of the *Guhyagarbha Tantra*. Affiliated as he was to the Nyingma school, Tenpa'i Wangchuk's early studies were nevertheless wide-ranging and reflected the still surviving nonsectarian spirit of the *rime* movement. He studied numerous texts of the Geluk tradition, notably the textbooks of Jamyang Zhepa, the founder of the great monastery of Labrang Tashi Khyil in Amdo, and well as the foundational texts of collected topics, logic, and epistemology according to the Geluk curriculum. At the same time, he received the complete transmission of the works of Mipham Rinpoche. He began his study of madhyamaka and prajñāpāramitā at the age of sixteen and in the following year received the transmissions of the texts on these topics composed by the celebrated Jonang master Bamda Thubten Gelek.

At the age of eighteen, Tenpa'i Wangchuk consulted his teacher Palyul Choktrul Rinpoche and asked his permission to enter Labrang Tashi Khyil in Amdo. Palyul Choktrul, however, advised him to apply instead to Amchok Tsenyi, an important Geluk monastery also in Amdo but nearer to home, and wrote the letters of introduction himself. Tenpa'i Wangchuk spent two years at Amchok studying the great texts on logic and epistemology. He flourished and distinguished himself on the debating ground, so much so that it was said of him that if he were to remain there, he would doubtless become a great *geshe*. He nevertheless returned home to Khangsar a young scholar of great promise. By that time, the biography records, he was already showing signs of being a *tertön*, or discoverer of spiritual treasures.

Within a year of Mao Tsetung's accession to power in 1949, the Chinese army invaded Tibet and in a single advance reached as far as Chamdo, quickly defeating the vestigial Tibetan army in October 1950. Amdo, Golok, and much of Kham immediately fell under Chinese control, and communist land reform and social restructuring were at once imposed. This involved the wholesale confiscation of land and property that had previously belonged to the monasteries and the Tibetan nobility for redistribution to the former serfs. The traditional Tibetan way of life was abolished. Monasteries and temples were attacked and destroyed. And in a bid to break the traditional loyalties of the feudal past, infamous *thamzing*, or "struggle sessions," were organized in which former landowners, whether monks or laypeople, were singled out for punishment and public humiliation at the hands of their former employees, who were forced to participate in this exercise in class warfare on pain of similar treatment if they refused. On these traumatic occasions, the designated victims were reviled, beaten, maimed, and often killed. By 1956, rebellion erupted throughout

Amdo and Kham supported by the fighters of the nascent Tibetan guerrilla army, the legendary Chushi Gangdruk.

Tenpa'i Wangchuk was inevitably caught up in this period of unrest and danger: an evil time, as his biography describes, when out of sheer terror parents would turn on their children and children would betray their parents, and when the sacred bonds between teachers and disciples were shattered. As a monk and incarnate lama, Tenpa'i Wangchuk was in the front line of attack. His biography states that between the ages of twenty-seven and thirty, he was forced to partake in various "sinful activities," which eventually resulted in serious illness. The exact nature of these activities is not specified, but it probably involved the killing of animals and insects. Amid all these adversities, Tenpa'i Wangchuk remained unflinching and grew in courage and moral stature. He continued his studies, consulting various teachers of the region and requesting instruction, notably from Domtsa Tertön Dudul Wangdrak Dorje and his elder brother Domtsa Namgyal. It was at that time also that Tenpa'i Wangchuk secretly received important teachings of the Great Perfection, such as the *Tantra of the Self-Arisen Fundamental Nature*[15] and the *Refinement of Perception*[16] of Dudjom Lingpa.

In 1969, during what were to be the final, terrible years of the Cultural Revolution, several important lamas in Golok and Kham were arrested and subjected to struggle sessions. In a bid to escape similar treatment, Tenpa'i Wangchuk and several companions fled to the mountains. The period of respite was short-lived, however. Signs received from Tenpa'i Wangchuk's Dharma protectors indicated that he would soon be taken prisoner, and sure enough, after a few months he was captured, put on trial, and sentenced at the age of thirty-one to twelve years in prison.

The biography tells us that, undaunted by all the torments and privations reserved for monks and lamas like himself, Tenpa'i Wangchuk was able to implement fully the *lojong*, or mind training, teachings, bringing onto the path whatever hardships he encountered without falling into despair or losing the fundamental

attitude of love and compassion for the denizens of his prison—
guards and fellow prisoners alike.

The year 1971 marked an important change in Tenpa'i Wangchuk's fortunes when, at the age of thirty-three, he was sent to
Thangkarma, a gulag that, amazingly, counted among its prisoners
no fewer than fifty highly accomplished masters and *tulkus* taken
from all over Tibet. To his delight, he found himself in the presence of a host of realized beings, many of whom had preserved in
their memories vast treasuries of doctrine and indeed entire texts
that they knew by heart. It was thus that amid all the dreadful
hardships of prison life, he was able to complete his education,
secretly receiving essential instructions from many of the masters
he met there. For example, it was in Thangkarma that he met the
great Geluk master Alak Yongdzin Lozang Khedrub Gyatso from
Labrang Tashi Khyil. Feeling an instinctive devotion for this great
master of the Kadam tradition, Tenpa'i Wangchuk received from
him Tsongkhapa's *Three Principal Aspects of the Path* and essential
instructions on the *Stages of the Path*, as well as the crucial points
of the five great texts of the traditional curriculum of the Geluk
school.

Of the many great lamas imprisoned at Thangkarma, the most
important for Tenpa'i Wangchuk was Akyong Togden Lodrö
Gyatso of his own Nyingma school. Before imprisonment, this
extraordinary master, a great scholar gifted with a prodigious memory, had lived the life of a wandering hermit. Like Patrul Rinpoche
before him, he had been a vagabond, homeless and completely without possessions. Used to living in caves and makeshift shelters, he
had become utterly inured to physical hardship. He ate only what
he happened to find or what was offered to him, had little more
than an old leather shirt to cover his back, and was used to going
barefoot in the snow. One imagines that the physical hardships of
the gulag would have scarcely impinged on such a yogi, who was in
any case a master of mind training. For him, as well as for Tenpa'i
Wangchuk and for the other great masters in the gulag, the prison
guards, their tormentors, were never anything other than objects

of compassion and supports for the practice of patience. And in accordance with the principle that bodhisattvas bring benefit even to those who harm them, Tenpa'i Wangchuk's biography tells us that through these masters' perfect practice, the jailers were themselves brought to the threshold of liberation.[17]

Lodrö Gyatso was revered as an emanation of Vairotsana, the most eminent of Tibet's early translators. The meeting between him and Tenpa'i Wangchuk (who, it will be recalled, was an incarnation of Vairotsana's great disciple Yudra Nyingpo) awakened the ancient connection between the two masters. And although there was between them an age difference of only eight years, Tenpa'i Wangchuk looked upon Lodrö Gyatso as his long-lost teacher and received from him many transmissions and essential instructions. This process was greatly facilitated from 1973 onward, when Lodrö Gyatso, Tenpa'i Wangchuk, and several other prisoners were transferred to another gulag in which the regime was more relaxed and the prisoners were allowed occasional rest days. It was on these occasions that Tenpa'i Wangchuk received from Lodrö Gyatso the transmission of many of the works of Longchenpa, Jigme Lingpa, and others. In particular, he twice received oral instructions on *The Treasury of the Fundamental Nature*, on the basis of which he would eventually compose his commentary.

After his release from prison, Tenpa'i Wangchuk made his way back to Khangsar, where he devoted the rest of his life to teaching. The monasteries of Khangsar Taklung and Panak, which he restored, grew into immense establishments eventually housing thousands of students.

Tenpa'i Wangchuk, as an incarnation of Yudra Nyingpo (one of Guru Rinpoche's twenty-five closest disciples), was a tertön. The tradition of *terma*, or spiritual treasures—that is, teachings that Guru Padmasambhava is said to have concealed in the deepest levels of the minds of his disciples, to be revealed by their later incarnations at propitious moments in the future—is a characteristic mainly of the Nyingma school.[18] The manner in which these treasures manifest is complex and mysterious. They arise in three ways: as mind termas, directly in the mind of the treasure revealer; as earth termas, in the form of physical objects concealed in specific locations, the sight of which awakens in the mind of the tertön the memory of Guru Rinpoche's original instructions; or as pure visions.[19] The biography indicates that the ability to reveal treasure teachings awoke in Tenpa'i Wangchuk's mindstream when he was a young man. Many treasures appeared to him in the form of mind termas or pure visions, which he felt compelled to write down but which were lost in the course of time. Some were left unfinished and were eventually burned by Tenpa'i Wangchuk himself. Following his imprisonment, however—when the circumstances were more favorable—Tenpa'i Wangchuk revealed several important cycles of practice, either as mind termas or earth termas. These were committed to writing and are preserved in his collected works. In the case of earth termas, the discovery of physical objects miraculously concealed by Guru Rinpoche within, as it is said, the "essence of the elements" is usually performed in conditions of the strictest secrecy. On occasion, however, and no doubt as a means of inspiring faith in his disciples, Tenpa'i Wangchuk performed this extraordinary act in the presence of large crowds.

A tireless and skillful teacher, Tenpa'i Wangchuk was also a prolific writer and produced a series of important and fascinating works, some of which are still being edited. At the moment of writing, the collection comes to eight Tibetan *pecha* volumes or five Western-style books. As part of the enormous effort made to rekindle the practice of Buddhism in Tibet, Tenpa'i Wangchuk saved many teachings that might otherwise have been lost. He committed to writing in clear and accessible form many essential instructions pertaining to both the sutras and tantras and most especially to the teachings of the Great Perfection. These include expositions of Jigme Lingpa's *Unsurpassed Wisdom*[20] and of Mipham Rinpoche's *Beacon of Certainty*.[21] And as we have already mentioned, perhaps most extraordinary of them all are his completely unprecedented commentaries on two of Longchenpa's Seven Treasuries: a vast exposition in 450 pages of *The Treasury of the Dharmadhātu* and the shorter explanation of *The Treasury of the Fundamental Nature* translated here.

THE GREAT PERFECTION, TRANSLATION, AND SECRECY—A WARNING TO THE READER

Toward the end of *The Treasury of the Fundamental Nature*, Longchenpa gives a fairly brief description of the kind of people for whom his text was composed—those whom he considered able to understand and implement the four samayas of nothing to keep. He discusses the requisite qualities of teachers and students and, with regard to the latter, pointedly distinguishes those to whom the teachings should be given from those to whom they should be denied. Khenpo Tenpa'i Wangchuk comments on these issues at some length, describing the need and reasons for the secrecy surrounding the teachings of the Great Perfection.

In the broader tantric context, several reasons are traditionally given for secrecy, the concealing of the teachings from unsuitable recipients and from the general, uninitiated public. It is said that the purpose of secrecy is to maintain the integrity of the teachings themselves and to preserve the purity and potency of the lineages of blessing or spiritual power, which are an integral feature of the tantric vehicle of skillful means. In addition—a point that Tenpa'i Wangchuk emphasizes—secrecy is also seen as a means to protect the unqualified from doctrines that are potentially dangerous for them. In the present context, this refers to the apparently antinomian character of certain tantric doctrines—for example, statements to the effect that awareness transcends the workings of the karmic law of cause and effect, that from the point of view of awareness, phenomena whether "good" or "bad" are simply clear yet nonexistent appearances. For those who misunderstand this teaching and who are without the protection of the instructions and surveillance of a qualified teacher, the dangers are twofold.

First of all, the idea that good and bad are relative terms and that there is a level of understanding in which they are transcended may lead to what is traditionally known as the loss of one's conduct in the view. This arises through a failure to distinguish merely intellectual understanding from profound and authentic spiritual realization and leads to the mistaken idea that since all is emptiness, or merely the display of awareness, the moral quality of one's behavior is a matter of indifference and that, in practice, "anything goes." Mere intellectual understanding, however, does not abrogate the law of cause and effect. The karmic process of happiness and suffering continues on its course, and negative action, whatever ideas one may entertain about it, leads inescapably to moral and spiritual shipwreck. The teachings in fact repeatedly warn of these dangers. In an admonition to King Trisong Detsen on the practice of the Secret Mantra, Guru Rinpoche is reported to have said, "The view is attuned to the dharmakāya, but the conduct is in harmony with the way of the bodhisattva."[22] And on another occasion, he famously said, "My view is higher than the sky, but my attention to actions and their results is finer than flour."[23]

The second danger of speaking injudiciously of the tantras to general audiences is that those who are unprepared for their reception may be shocked and, as a result, may criticize and reject them. Thus breaking whatever links they may have had with such teachings, they will not encounter them again, and will wander in suffering, for many lifetimes to come. Again, this is a recurring theme in Buddhist teachings generally, where the danger of speaking of profound matters to the unprepared is clearly articulated.[24]

Referring to these dangers, Tenpa'i Wangchuk speaks in powerful and unequivocal terms of the need to keep the higher teachings secret from those who are unqualified for their reception:

> They should not even be spoken of in a wind that blows in their direction.... One should feel no inclination to explain the secret teachings to those who are unsuitable. One should not pronounce a single syllable to them. One should not put the texts into their hands. One must keep them secret.[25]

Reading such statements, the modern Western reader may well reflect ruefully that whatever the situation may have been in certain areas and in certain times in traditional Tibet, it is now far too late for such warnings. In today's world, any number of purportedly secret teachings have been translated and are available in the marketplace or for immediate download on one's personal computer. Advertisements in new age magazines may well contain announcements of high teachings open to anyone who has the time to spare and enough money to pay the subscription—of instructions in secret yoga, ranging from concentration on the subtle channels to meditations associated with the highest levels of Mahāmudrā and the Great Perfection.

Reacting to this fact of modern life, some Tibetan teachers have insisted categorically that certain texts should not be translated at all, or that if they are, they should not be published. Considering the traditional Tibetan approach to the reading of religious texts as contrasted with the attitude of free and open inquiry typical of a Western readership, this point of view is to some extent understandable. And yet careful reflection shows that a general prohibition of translation, and for that matter publication, is an inadequate response to the problem at hand and cannot possibly be the right answer. The role of translation is simply to extend into another language the propagation and the preservation of the teachings themselves. It is a service to the original authors proceeding from the same intentions that motivated the composition of their texts in the first place. Its purpose is to provide access to the Doctrine for those who wish to study it by removing the one insuperable obstacle that prevents them from doing so. The spread of the Buddhadharma down the centuries, throughout India and beyond, has been a history of translation. To oppose the translation of the texts seems oddly out of step with one of the fundamental characteristics of the Tibetan Buddhist tradition itself, which is founded, root and branch, on a vast body, exoteric and esoteric, of translated teachings.

Furthermore, it cannot be denied that once a translation has been made, the next task is to make it available to those who need it. This inescapably means publication in some shape or form. And this is, in effect, where the difficulties begin. For it is natural that translators of texts of the Great Perfection, for example, should be concerned that by making the texts available in the first place, they are contributing to the public diffusion of teachings that are intended only for a restricted group of recipients and are thus participating in the betrayal of the seal of secrecy. In order to safeguard against this, and as a means of ensuring that secret teachings find their proper destination and do not fall into the wrong hands, some have thought it expedient to create some sort of system of restricted distribution. Experience shows, however, that such schemes are only effective on a small scale within the confines of a fairly limited group of students whose identities are known and who belong to an organization where records are kept of the teachings and empowerments that have been given. It is possible that in such environments, the distribution of texts can be effectively monitored. In the case of the whole community of English-speaking Buddhists, however, the situation is quite different. Given the realities of modern publishing and the marketing practices that make it possible and given also the nature of the internet where so much material is pirated and may be dishonestly downloaded, the effectiveness of such schemes of restricted distribution is very questionable.

Recently consulted on this seemingly intractable problem, Alak Zenkar Rinpoche (who has done perhaps more than anyone living to preserve the Tibetan literary heritage from oblivion through his untiring work of finding, editing, and publishing Buddhist texts on a large scale) replied that in the case of the translation and dissemination of texts, the principal factor is motivation. If one translates and disseminates the esoteric teachings of the tantras and the Great Perfection indiscriminately as a means of livelihood or as a way of enhancing one's reputation—if, in other words, one knowingly contravenes the intentions of the author and the demands of the tradition—then one's actions are certainly wrong. If, on the other hand, translations are made in obedience to the instructions of one's teacher and with the sincere intention of making indispensable texts accessible to those who need them and who will practice them, it is clear that one is serving the tradition and the mission of the original authors. And in that case, Alak Zenkar remarked, how could there be a fault?

Is this a sufficient answer? From the point of view of the translator, and possibly also the publisher, it must be admitted that it is probably the only possible answer. Nevertheless, with regard to the prospective reader, there is perhaps something more to be said. Compared with the problems that face the translators of esoteric texts, the predicament of the Buddhist practitioner is different. For even if translators can appeal to the purity of their own intentions, it is still true that through the premature reading of texts and the possible misunderstandings that may result from this, the readers themselves may be at risk and therefore remain an object of concern. The only recourse is to be tediously explicit and to appeal to the intelligence and integrity of all readers of good faith. The secret teachings are indeed open to anyone who is willing to follow the traditional path of initiation, instruction, preliminary practices, and the maintaining of the samaya pledges.

Those who have already received instruction in a traditional setting will not need to be reminded of the importance of empowerment, transmission, and oral instruction—the three requirements for all tantric practice. Moreover, whatever may be the complexity of the problems just described, it remains true that on the level of individual behavior, it is still possible and completely necessary to behave in the ways prescribed by the tradition. Serious practitioners of Tibetan Buddhism, who have the good fortune to be connected with authentic teachers through the reception of empowerment and oral instructions, do indeed maintain the secret. They do not, as a matter of fact, mention or discuss openly the teachings they have received or the meditations in which they are engaged. On this level, the practice remains a matter of inviolable secrecy.

For those who are beginning on the path, however, and may be unaware of this aspect of Tibetan Buddhism, and who out of a laudable curiosity may have purchased this book and have read thus far, it is important to stress that the reception and practice of the tantric teachings generally and of the Great Perfection in particular should be pursued only in the context of a relationship with a qualified teacher. If this connection is lacking, then it is better to read no further. It is preferable to keep the book safely and respectfully until the proper connections have been made and the requisite teachings and empowerments have been received. It is important to remember that the transmission of blessing power mediated through a living tradition of realized masters is an indispensable component of the Great Perfection method, without which the introduction to the nature of the mind does not take place. Finally, it should also be remembered that the Tibetan authors of Great Perfection texts invariably place their work under the guardianship of powerful spirit protectors with the result that the misuse of texts and teachings is liable to attract misfortune. It is possible, perhaps probable, that certain modern readers will be inclined to dismiss these warnings as folkloric superstition. It is nevertheless our duty to make them clear and to repeat the traditional admonition that from a self-contrived practice pursued privately without reference to the tradition, accomplishment is not to be expected.

ACKNOWLEDGMENTS

In the autumn of 2019, Tsultrim Zangpo Rinpoche, the nephew and spiritual heir of Kyabje Tenpa'i Wangchuk and abbot of Khangsar Taklung Monastery, visited Dordogne, France in the company of Yingrik Drubpa Rinpoche and several other lamas. Having formally asked Padmakara to translate the collected works of Tenpa'i Wangchuk, Tsultrim Zangpo Rinpoche was in turn requested to come to Dordogne and grant the necessary transmissions. It is therefore our first duty to express our profound gratitude to him and to Yingrik Drubpa Rinpoche, the main instigator of the project, for their kindness in making the long and arduous journey to France and for the patience and graciousness with which Tsultrim

Zangpo Rinpoche bestowed the empowerments, reading transmissions, and oral commentaries over a period of several weeks.

We must then record our thanks to Jigme Khyentse Rinpoche and to Tulku Pema Wangyal Rinpoche, who, having accepted Tsultrim Zangpo Rinpoche's request, received him and his entourage at La Sonnerie in Saint Léon-sur-Vézère, Dordogne. And as for the work that lies ahead, we would like in particular to thank Pema Wangyal Rinpoche for his unfailing inspiration and for insistently reminding us that in the face of a long and seemingly endless task of apparently impossible difficulty, the first step is that of aspiration. Finally, we acknowledge with immense gratitude the assistance of Khenchen Pema Sherab of the monastery of Namdroling in India, who clarified many difficult points and without whose help the translation of this present text could not have been done. Last but by no means least, we confess whatever mistakes have been made in the translation, imploring the indulgence and patience of the *ḍākinīs* and Dharma protectors.

This translation was made by Helena Blankleder and Wulstan Fletcher of the Padmakara Translation Group.

PART ONE

THE PRECIOUS TREASURY OF THE FUNDAMENTAL NATURE

Homage

Homage to glorious Samantabhadra!

Buddha from the first,
The ground of actual enlightenment,
Beyond all change and present of itself,
The space of adamantine essence, indestructible—
This is the nature of the mind,
The natural great perfection.
Nothing do I take and nothing do I cast aside—
Nothing comes and nothing goes.
Thus it is that I bow down in homage.

The expanse of the nature inexpressible of all phenomena,
The culmination of all views and different from them all,
The all-transcending meaning of the Great Perfection
I shall now explain according to my realization.
Listen!

The ultimate and quintessential view
Belonging to the mind, space, pith instruction classes
Lies in nonexistence, evenness,
Spontaneous presence, single nature.
Each of these four has in turn four aspects:
Their key points are revealed, essentialized, subsumed,
A clear conviction is then gained in their regard.

1. NONEXISTENCE

1. First, I demonstrate the principle of nonexistence.
Nonexistence means the absence of intrinsic being.
In the great expanse of the enlightened mind, which is like space,
Whatever may appear has no intrinsic being.

2. In the vast expanse, the womb of space,
The universe, the beings it contains,
And the four elements in constant flux
Are simply empty forms without intrinsic being.
The things appearing in the enlightened mind
Are just the same.

3. Illusory reflections, however they appear,
Are unreal, empty by their nature.
Likewise, all things in phenomenal existence,
In the very moment of appearing,
Never stir from the enlightened mind.
They have no real existence.

4. Dream visions, never stirring from the state of sleep,
In the very moment they are seen, are utterly unreal.
Likewise, all phenomenal existence,
Both samsara and nirvana,
Never stirs from the enlightened mind.
It is unreal, devoid of features.

5. Although phenomena appear within the mind,
They are not the mind and are not separate from the mind.

They are nonexistent
And yet, like illusions, clearly appear.
They are ineffable and inconceivable.
They defy expression.
Understand therefore that all phenomena
Appearing in the mind are nonexistent
In the very moment that they are perceived.

6. Just as apparent objects are by nature nonexistent,
So too the subject, the enlightened mind,
Like space, has no existence by its nature.
Ineffable and inconceivable and inexpressible—
It's thus that you should understand it.

7. Because in self-arisen primal wisdom,
Ultimate quintessence,
There is neither cause nor fruit,
Samsara's vast abyss is crossed.
Because there is no good or bad,
Samsara and nirvana are the same.
Because there is no deviation and no obscuration,
The three existences are clearly understood.

8. In the nature of the mind, enlightened, similar to space,
There are no sides and no directions, no duality.
Therein there is no view, no meditation,
And no pledges to observe.
There is in it no effortful activity;
There are no veils obscuring primal wisdom.
There is no training on the grounds, no path to be traversed.
There is no "subtle thing";
Since [gross and subtle] are not two,
There is no link between them.
Ascription of existence and denial are both transcended;
Thus there is no good or bad.

All is an expanse in which, as on a golden isle,
There is no differentiation.
The self-arisen nature of the mind,
Like space without existence,
Defies description and expression.

9. Since the ultimate quintessence—
Awareness, open, unimpeded—
Cannot be contrived,
It is not improved by virtue.
It is unchangeable,
So evil does no harm to it.
Since there's neither action nor its fruit,
There is no ripening of joy and sorrow.
Since in it there is no good or bad,
There's nothing to be taken or rejected—
No samsara, no nirvana.
Since there is no thought and no expression,
Awareness is a space devoid of such elaborations.
Since there are no past or future lives,
A line of incarnations is but imputation.
What birth is taken? Who is born and where?
What action is there? What is its maturing fruit?
Everything is similar to space.
Think about this and reflect on it.

10. Even though you may investigate with reasoning,
Pondering, reflecting time and time again,
The parts of things have no reality.
For not a single particle is found.
There is no partless instant;
There is no apprehended and no apprehender.
In this very moment, everything abides
Within the quintessential fundamental nature.
When examined, things have no existence.

Likewise, when left unexamined,
They have no existence either.
Even on the level of conventionality,
Since nothing can be found,
Phenomena in all respects and always
Are without existence.
Understand that they resemble magical illusions,
Lacking all reality.

11. In the very moment they encounter
Dreams and magical illusions,
Childish beings ignorantly cling
To their supposed existence
And are taken in by them.
But those who understand their nature
Cannot be deceived thereby.
In just the same way, those who do not know
That things have no existence
Cling to all such things as real,
And caught by them, they circle in samsara.
Yogis skilled in understanding suchness
Resolve that things lack true existence
In the very moment they perceive them.
Therefore, they find freedom
In the space of *dharmatā* beyond the law
Of karmic cause and fruit.

12. The enlightened nature of the mind
Is neither permanent nor discontinuous.
It is the natural dwelling place of primal wisdom
Devoid of apprehender and an object to be apprehended.
Awareness, naked and devoid of causes and effects,
Is the abode of that one sphere
Wherein there is no virtue and no sin.
Awareness, open, unimpeded, free of center and periphery,

Is the natural dwelling of the wisdom mind
Of the dharmakāya Samantabhadra.
The essential core of nonexistence,
Awareness, self-cognizing and enlightened,
Is clearly revealed.
It is completely pure and objectless,
The primal wisdom of Victorious Ones.

13. In the case of yogis of illusion,
The self-experience of awareness
Arises as the ceaseless show of things without existence.
Such yogis are convinced that in the moment of appearing,
Phenomena have no existence.
They therefore do not make the slightest effort—
Accepting some, rejecting others.
With spacious minds relaxed without a care,
They rest within the state of leaving
Everything just as it is.

14. Childish beings, taken in by nonexistent things,
Resemble thirsty animals that look for water in a mirage.
Expecting to find truth in false, mistaken theories,
They are deceived by different tenets,
Assuming their reality.
Now if this error of the common intellect,
Belonging to the gradual vehicles, eight in all,
Is not removed, the ultimate quintessence is not seen.

15. Atiyoga is the ultimate expanse,
Transcending every category.
There is nothing whatsoever—just a space-like nature.
In this very instant there is not the slightest movement
From the fundamental stratum of the dharmakāya.
When you rest in the primordial expanse,
The natural great bliss is present of itself.

16. If awareness, wisdom's secret state,
You do not realize,
You will not find freedom
Through the virtuous deeds that you may fabricate.
Don't you understand?
Conditioned things all pass,
Are destined to disintegrate.
How can this tight knot
Of body, speech, and mind
Come into contact with
The ultimate and indestructible quintessence?

17. So if you wish to realize
The sublime fundamental nature of phenomena,
Leave aside all things that are like childish games,
That fetter and exhaust you
In your body, speech, and mind.
The state of nonexistence, the expanse devoid
Of mind's activity, is the nature of phenomena.
It is the dharmatā, the dwelling place
Of natural great perfection.
Within this all-pervading state devoid of action,
Which goes beyond all thoughts,
Behold the great and uncontrived equality.
Decisive certainty will come that it transcends
Causality and striving.

18. In awareness, there's no outer object to be apprehended;
There's no inner apprehending subject.
In awareness, there is neither time nor place.
Awareness is beyond phenomena that arise and cease.
It is pure like space—
No vehicles can guide you to it.
All thoughts about it are mistaken,

For they invest phenomena with an identity.
Cast away this ground for deviation and obscuring veils.
Be convinced that everything without distinction
Has the nature of Samantabhadra,
The great and all-pervading state of emptiness.
Keep to the state of dharmatā
Beyond all change and movement.
By doing this you soar amid the sky-like spaces of the view,
The primordial expanse that rests in no extreme.
All the key points of the nonexistence of phenomena
Are herein set forth.

* * *

19. The key points of the nonexistence
Of phenomena are thus revealed.
Subsequently, in the state that's free of meditation,
Where all is left alone and uncontrived, just as it is,
A state without acceptance or rejection of whatever happens,
These same points are essentialized within awareness:
The equality, the evenness of the vast expanse of mind.

20. Natural great bliss,
The vajra space that's indestructible,
Is supreme absorption that is present of itself
Without the need for cultivating it.
It is there at all times like a flowing river.
If you stay in evenness, within a state
That's free of all contrivance,
It clearly and naturally manifests.

21. When you settle properly in space-like dharmatā,
There is no change or movement.
Therefore, there's no wandering and no absence of the same.
This ultimate expanse, supreme and infinite,

Is inseparably present in all things.
It is not some sphere that words can indicate.
Those whose wisdom has burst forth,
Those for whom awareness comes unprompted,
Those whose minds are unencumbered,
Even though they have engaged in study—
Yogis who experience the ineffable and inconceivable—
Are completely certain that this state
Transcends both indication and non-indication.
They find neither meditation
Nor anything on which to meditate.
And thus they need not slay
The foes of lethargy and agitation.

22. Appearances and mind
Are free and open from the outset—
Nonexistence is their essence.
Hallucinatory appearances
Have as their natural state
The vast expanse of evenness, the dharmatā.
They constantly subsist within the dharmakāya,
Seamlessly arising and subsiding,
Remaining in the one expanse of bliss.
Arising, they arise spontaneously,
Keeping their own nature.
Remaining, they remain spontaneously,
Keeping their own nature.
Subsiding, they subside spontaneously,
Keeping their own nature.
They arise, remain, subside
Within the vast expanse of dharmatā.
They come from nowhere else,
Being simply the display of dharmakāya.
They are the empty forms

Of the self-experience of awareness.
They are not different from each other;
They are neither good nor bad,
Abiding in their ultimate quintessence.

23. Whatever may arise, whatever may appear,
Whatever states of movement or of stillness may occur—
Five poisons and the rest,
Arising from awareness's creative power—
When their nature is detected in their moment of arising,
These same displayed appearances arrive at their exhaustion.
They vanish without leaving any trace.
When the mind perceives its objects,
The key point is to leave all as it is
In its equality.
The key point is to leave all without trace—
Just like the flight path of a bird—
Within primordial wisdom, self-arisen.
The key point is that all things
And the ultimate expanse are one,
Like water and its waves.
All things are, from the very first, essentialized
Within this one key point of the great secret.
Simply knowing this brings freedom,
For it is simply the nature of phenomena.

24. Constantly within the great expanse,
Awareness, self-cognizing,
All arises equal and as equal dwells.
All is equal in subsiding, neither good nor bad.
There's nothing that's not equal to awareness,
Nothing that does not abide,
And nothing that does not subside therein.
All things are essentialized

As being the immense primordial expanse
Of the enlightened state.

25. Within awareness, uncreated and spontaneously present,
The view of the immense and natural state
Arises without effort.
The key point of the enlightened mind,
Which lies beyond the causal law,
Transcending sin and virtue,
Is essentialized as the unchanging dharmatā.

* * *

26. Nonexistence, which is space-like in its nature,
Subsumes within it everything without exception.
Just as space subsumes the world and its inhabitants,
Phenomena, the experience of ordinary mind,
Are all subsumed in great primordial emptiness.

27. Samsara is a mere name.
It is beyond the causal process,
Beyond all effort and all undertaking.
Good and evil neither help nor harm;
They are the state of emptiness.
Liberation too is just a name,
And there is no nirvana.
There's nothing to be gained or worked for
By means of the ten elements.

28. Constantly to strive in what can only bring fatigue
Is to be like children building castles in the sand.
All is destined to collapse. All causes and effects,
All virtue and nonvirtue, and all striving and exertion—
Things are from the outset all subsumed in nonexistence.

29. Yogis of the quintessential Atiyoga
Should be convinced that teachings based upon causality,
Designed to guide the simple,
Constitute the way for those of lesser fortune,
Who progress upon the upward path in stages.
They should subsume the nature of their mind,
Transcending all phenomena,
Into the space-like absence of all action.

30. Beings are misled by action—
Look at the deceptive seemings of samsara.
Beings are affected by their efforts—
Think of the turning wheel of suffering.
From sin and virtue comes a ceaseless
Stream of pain and happiness.
Through their actions, beings wander
In samsara high and low.
No occasion do they have to flee
The ocean of existence.

31. If you break the stream of virtue and nonvirtue
And dwell within the dharmatā and never part from it,
You are a yogi of the ultimate great secret.
Free of effort and of striving, you will reach
The primal ground and take the royal seat
Of ever-present dharmakāya.

32. In the very moment things appear,
They are beyond all misconception
And all language that expresses name and meaning.
All acts and all exertion based on cause and its result,
Adoption of the good, rejection of the bad—
All are nonexistent things
And nonexistent actions, just like space.

Whoever knows this has subsumed
All things within the state of nonexistence.

* * *

33. The clear conviction that phenomena are nonexistent
Is reached essentially as follows.
Because phenomenal existence,
All things in samsara and nirvana,
Is without intrinsic being,
It transcends the status of existence.
Since it is unceasing in the way that it appears,
It transcends the state of nonexistence.
Not existent and not nonexistent,
It transcends the state of being both.
Not being both,
It goes beyond the state of being neither.
Being neither both nor neither,
Its ultimate quintessence
Is beyond all thought and word,
Beyond all indication.

34. The nature of phenomena is primordially pure,
But childish beings, ignorant of this,
Adopt some things, and others they reject.
Clinging to their various views, they're permanently fettered.
Clinging to the features they perceive, how pained they are!
Clinging to a self in what is nonexistent, how they are deluded!
Clinging to the aspects of the aspectless, how they tire themselves!
Drifting in samsara constantly, how pitiful they are!

35. The sun of ultimate reality, awareness, self-arisen,
Is covered by white clouds of virtue
And black clouds of sin.
And it is overwhelmed by lightning bolts:
Passionate endeavor in adopting and rejecting.

Beings thus are drenched in pouring rains,
The false appearances of happiness and sorrow.
These bring samsara's seeds to ripeness
As the crop of six migrations.
Beings are tormented, and how pitiful they are!

36. Just as ropes and golden chains bind equally,
Virtuous and unvirtuous states
Bind equally the ultimate, definitive quintessence.
Clouds, black and white, enshroud the sky in equal measure.
Likewise, virtue and nonvirtue equally obscure awareness.
It is crucial thus to understand
That yogis who have realized suchness
See beyond the causal law of virtue and of sin.

37. Self-arisen wisdom wells up from within.
The dark night of causality is scattered.
The massing clouds of good and evil melt away.
The sun of ultimate luminosity
Shines in the sky of dharmadhātu—
You gain a clear and final certainty.
You come to this conviction
Without need of the ten elements.
All the causal vehicles are surpassed thereby.

38. You reach a clear conviction
That awareness—self-cognizing, open, unimpeded,
Free of all appearance,
Beyond all concentrated meditation on an object,
Devoid of all conceptual construction—
Is the state wherein phenomena are all exhausted.
They are all exhausted in awareness.
Awareness, too, as a phenomenon,
Itself comes to exhaustion.
"Exhaustion," "non-exhaustion"—

Yogis understand them both to be unreal.
They are convinced beyond all doubt
That things transcend existence, nonexistence,
Definition, and expression.
Without a point of reference, thinking "It is this,"
Yogis are enveloped in an all-pervading vastness.
For them phenomena are all exhausted,
The ordinary mind is passed beyond.
And for such yogis what a joy this is,
A joy that is a seamless state of dharmatā!
In this, the yogis of the past, the future,
And the present time are merged
With the single ultimate expanse of wisdom mind.
The realization of such yogis equals
That of buddhas and *vidyādharas*.

39. This same expanse, unchanging,
Unconditioned, indivisible,
Is the space of self-arisen primal wisdom
That transcends all effort and all striving.
It is the same expanse wherein phenomena
Transcend mere names,
All thought and all expression.
In this dimension of Samantabhadra,
Which is free of action,
Everything that there appears
Is nothing but Samantabhadra's vast expanse.
And in Samantabhadra's ultimate expanse,
There are no appearances; there's no emptiness;
There is neither good nor bad.
When what does not exist is taken as existent,
Identifying labels are affixed
To what is but a false hallucination.
But even as the labeling takes place,
There's no hallucination and no absence of the same.

A clear conviction thus is reached
That phenomena transcend all names.
Such is the fundamental nature
Of the natural great perfection.

40. Thus you're clearly certain that all things
Within phenomenal existence, samsara and nirvana,
Are neither hallucinations nor are they not hallucinations,
And that nirvana is not gained by shunning of samsara.
You are certain that phenomena are neither born nor unborn.
All the objects that you clung to—origin, cessation,
Existence, nonexistence—all are now transcended.
Convinced that things are neither pure nor impure,
You see them as a space of evenness,
As neither good, to be adopted,
Nor as bad, to be rejected.
You reach a clear conviction that all things
Are within Samantabhadra's vast expanse.

2. EVENNESS

When the fundamental nature of phenomena—
Their nonexistence—is correctly grasped,
The nature of their evenness is understood.
According to the precepts of the Atiyoga
Summit of all vehicles,
Samantabhadra's vast and spacious mind,
The greatest of the great,
Is like the sky, beyond both center and circumference.
It has the character of unbroken great equality.

1. The fundamental nature, as it is,
Of things belonging to phenomenal existence
And of the enlightened mind devoid of form
Is never parted from the state
Of freedom from conceptual construction.
Here there is no center, no periphery, no thought—
Its evenness subsists
Within a vast, uninterrupted state.

2. All things that appear as objects of the senses,
In the instant of appearing,
Are free of substance, free of parts—
A state of infinite and all-embracing evenness.
Neither can the mind, awareness, self-cognizing,
Be divided into instants, earlier and later.
It is a space-like state
Of infinite and all-embracing evenness.
The past is gone, the future not yet born.

The present moment does not stay.
All is groundless in the enlightened mind,
All is rootlesss, without substance,
Beyond the reach of indication.
By nature it's a state of utter evenness,
The vast immensity of space.

3. In the ultimate quintessence free of all extremes,
Not falling to one side or to another,
No view is found and no empowerment,
No mandala, no mantra recitation.
There are no grounds, no paths, and no samaya;
There is no training and no progress on the path.
All are groundless. In the vast space [of awareness],
They are an endless, all-embracing state of evenness.
They all subsist in dharmatā, the enlightened mind.

4. Inasmuch as it is understood that all things,
In whichever way that they appear,
Are by their nature without origin,
Without abiding or cessation,
They are all spontaneously present.
They are not existent and not nonexistent;
They are beyond the reach of all conceptual fixation.
They are completely pure, and in the dharmatā,
The great perfection,
They are an endless, all-embracing evenness.

5. Awareness, the enlightened mind,
Ultimate and quintessential,
Is not seen in the extremes;
It is beyond distinctive features.
Words and logic do not serve to prove it.
It is beyond the reach of symbols.
It has neither growth nor diminution.

It is neither permanent nor discontinuous.
It neither comes nor goes.
Within the vast expanse of its spontaneous equality,
All is utterly immaculate—
An unbroken evenness
Devoid of limitation and of falling to one side.

6. There is neither hope nor fear
Regarding the bestowal of wisdom.
Thus, no matter what arises,
All is but unbroken, endless, all-embracing evenness.
In seamless, self-arising, unimpeded openness,
There is never any risk of being caught
Within the cage of clinging.

7. All phenomena sink back
Into the state of evenness.
Their nature is beyond the frontiers
Of adoption and rejection.
Just as the universe and its inhabitants
Are empty in the vast immensity of space,
Adoption and rejection, craving and aversion,
All dissolve in the primordial expanse.
Nowhere else do they depart.
When thoughts that leave no trace behind
Become the state of infinite and all-embracing evenness
Within awareness seamless and unbroken,
The frontier of one's clinging
To both hope and fear is crossed.
The tethering peg—the object to be apprehended
And the apprehender—is torn out.
The city of samsara's false appearances is emptied.

8. All apparent extramental things,
Together with all inner mental states,

Are manifested as the play
Of mind's creative power.
Those who understand that everything
Is from the outset emptiness and evenness
Reveal the key point of phenomena:
They are all even.

*   *   *

9. All aspects of the nature of phenomena are essentialized
As your awareness, luminous and empty,
Primordial wisdom, evenness.
The latter is not bound—restricted—by an apprehender.
It transcends all objects to be apprehended.
Within it there is nothing that might
Act as target, nothing to refer to.
Alert and wakeful, open, undistracted,
It is the state of wisdom where mentation is exhausted—
The sky-like, endless, all-embracing state of evenness,
Transcending meditation and the absence of the same:
The great space of Samantabhadra's wisdom.

10. In this vast expanse of empty, luminous awareness,
The varied features of phenomena
Unceasingly arise.
Sense faculties perceive them in their freshness;
Awareness, nature of phenomena, is clearly present.
Appearance is untrammeled.
However it arises,
The mind is in a state of bliss.
The six gatherings of consciousness are all relaxed.
This expanse of self-arising primal wisdom,
Open, spacious, neither outside nor within,
Is the state of luminosity. It is present of itself within
The supreme natural state devoid of all contrivance.

11. When your consciousness is carefree,
Like a person who has nothing more to do,
And, not tense or loose,
Your mind and body rest at ease,
Awareness, endless, all-embracing evenness,
Immaculate as space,
Rests in the dharmadhātu,
Never to be parted.

12. When dharmatā is realized, luminous and empty,
Every bond subsides in its expanse.
Awareness is revealed
As evenness, unbroken, all-embracing.
Unfettered by fixation, it transcends all thought.
All is gathered in the single
And completely even space of wisdom.
The blissful mind is mingled with the bliss of peace—
The state of the enlightened mind
Where outside and within are of a single taste.
The fundamental nature then is seen,
The dharmatā where all comes to exhaustion.

13. In the instant when the object,
Faculty of sense, and mind's intent all meet,
In the evenness of mind,
Appearances are vast and blissful.
In this naturally luminous and limpid state,
Unfettered by fixation and by clinging,
The key point of phenomena
Is essentialized as an unbroken evenness.

* * *

14. In the space whence objects, mind, and clinging
Have been cleared away,

Awareness, free of memory and thoughts,
Self-seeking, and aversion,
Is subsumed within the pristine clarity of evenness.
It is the vajra dance of unconfined, unbroken dharmatā—
Expanse of suchness, primal wisdom of equality—
Marked from the outset with the seal
Of the wisdom of Samantabhadra.

15. Just as various dreams are all subsumed in sleep
And are the empty, false perceptions of the mind,
Just so, the universe and beings—
All within samsara and nirvana—
Are subsumed within the mind.
They appear within the mind's expanse;
They have no real existence.

16. Just as in the bosom of the vast expanse,
The universe and beings it contains,
In all that great immensity,
Are an unbroken evenness
Beyond both center and periphery,
So too within the reaches of awareness,
All appearances of things and minds—
Everything both outside and within—are even:
All the mind's perceptions are subsumed in emptiness.
This demonstrates that all phenomena
Are subsumed within the enlightened mind—
That evenness falls neither to one side nor to another,
For it is free of apprehender
And of objects to be apprehended.

17. The enlightened mind subsuming all phenomena
Is itself subsumed within great evenness,
Devoid of all extremes and falling to one side.

Like space's vast immensity,
Containing both the universe and beings,
It has no center, no periphery.
It is beyond both thought and all expression.

18. Awareness is the great condition of equality,
Free from all extremes.
All things of phenomenal existence,
Samsara and nirvana,
Ceaselessly arise therein.
But in the moment they appear,
The mind and all phenomena
Are indefinable as this or that.
They are subsumed within the evenness of
    dharmatā.

19. The seal of the enlightened mind,
Beyond which none can go,
Is set primordially upon phenomena
By the vast expanse, Samantabhadra.
It is subsumed within the wisdom of the teacher,
Lord of beings, lord of Dharma.
This primordially awakened state
Is sealed with the signet of the vajra essence.
The final meaning of the mighty secret
Lies beyond the scope of everyone
Except for those of highest fortune.
The principle of the vajra peak,
Beyond all change and movement—
The great space of awareness, self-cognizing,
The state of luminosity—
Is hard to realize, though it lies within yourself.
Only through the kindness of the glorious master,
Teacher, lord of Dharma, is it seen.

Thus all phenomena are said to be
Subsumed in an unbroken evenness.

* * *

20. A clear conviction then is gained:
The ultimate quintessence of phenomena
Is evenness.
All outer things are empty and unborn.
They do not stay; they do not come or go.
They are beyond all indication and expression.
All inner states arising seamlessly subside.
There is no finding them—
Like paths of birds that fly across the sky.

21. Just like phenomena and mental states,
So too awareness self-arisen
Has no existence even as a simple name.
It is beyond all indication and expression,
All conceptual elaboration.
Since like space it does not act,
It is a state of emptiness.
Free of action, free of all exertion,
It transcends both good and bad, all virtue and all sin.
It is beyond the causal law;
Ten elements of tantra have no place in it.[26]
It is a vast, completely even space
Beyond all indication and expression.
Within awareness, virtue and nonvirtue
Are primordially empty; they have never been.
A clear conviction thus is reached
That this nature, inconceivable and inexpressible,
Is the great perfection
Beyond the reach of ordinary mind.

3. Spontaneous Presence

---

1. And now the nature of spontaneous presence is revealed.
It abides, not made by anyone, from the beginning.
Like an all-providing jewel, the enlightened mind
Is ground and source of all things in samsara and nirvana.

2. The things appearing in phenomenal existence
Are all manifest in space.
Likewise, both samsara and nirvana
Ceaselessly appear in the enlightened mind.
Just as various dreams occur while beings sleep,
The six migrations and the three worlds
Manifest within the mind.
All things, in the very instant of arising,
Subsist within awareness.
They are the great appearances of the ground,
Empty yet spontaneously present.

3. The ground and the appearances arising there
Are not identical and yet are not distinct.
The ground's appearances are from the first
Spontaneously present—
Arising through the portal of awareness.
Nirvana and samsara, the display of its creative power,
Appear distinctly: pure or else impure.
But in the very moment of appearing,
They are neither good nor bad:
They are a single ultimate expanse.

4. When five lights shine unhindered
From a crystal sphere,
These same lights are perceived
According to their different colors.
Neither good nor bad,
They are the display
Of the single crystal sphere.
The ground, awareness, self-cognizing,
Is like this crystal sphere.
Its emptiness is dharmakāya,
Its radiant luminosity is the sambhogakāya,
And its unobstructed ground for the unfolding
Is nirmāṇakāya.
The three *kāyas* in the ground's expanse
Are all spontaneously present.

5. When appearances arise within the ground—
The three pure kāyas, the buddhas' self-experience,
As well as the impure phenomena
Of both the universe and beings—
Are all by their nature
Empty, luminous, and manifold.
All are the display of dharmakāya,
Of sambhogakāya, and nirmāṇakāya.
The displayed appearances of the ground (the triple kāya)
Are all spontaneously present—
Awareness that experiences itself.
Do not seek for them elsewhere.
When this analysis is understood correctly,
All phenomena in both samsara and nirvana
Will be realized as the pure field of the triple kāya,
Spontaneously present in the enlightened mind.

6. The kāyas and the wisdoms
Of the buddhas of the triple time,

The body, speech, and mind
Of beings of the triple realm,
And karma and defilement—
Everything belonging to phenomenal existence—
Are not other than enlightened mind.

7. Within spontaneous presence's expanse
Is found the ground whence everything arises.
All that has appeared as form—
The outer world and its inhabitants—
Lists to neither one side nor another.
All arises as the wheel of ornaments
Of the enlightened body.
Sounds and languages,
Excellent, indifferent, or inferior,
List to neither one side nor another.
All arises as the wheel of ornaments
Of the enlightened speech.
Ordinary mind and primal wisdom,
Realization and the lack of it,
List to neither one side nor another.
All arises as the wheel of ornaments
Of the enlightened mind.
Likewise, enlightened qualities and deeds
List to neither one side nor another.
Thus the dharmadhātu is a precious jewel
Fulfilling every wish.
There is no need to strive,
For everything arises naturally.
This is why it has been called
Primordial wisdom, self-arisen and spontaneously
    present.

8. The ground, spontaneously present,
Of the various array of things

Is the enlightened mind,
Ever and spontaneously present.
Therefore, there's no need
To look for the three kāyas,
For you have them naturally within yourself.
In the causal law concerning good and ill,
There is no need for you to strive.
Resting in the natural state,
You will be called a yogi free of action,
Free of effort in adopting or rejecting.
The vast space of spontaneous presence
Is yours from the beginning.
Therefore, make no effort now in dharmatā!

9. Even the enlightenment
Of all Victorious Ones, past, present, and to come,
Is spontaneously present
As the great bliss of the natural state.
Therefore, do not have recourse
To teachings on the causal law
Designed for those of lesser fortune,
But watch the nature that, like space,
Transcends intended action.

10. Suchness as it is
Has now no need to be accomplished.·
Within spontaneous presence,
Primordial and uncontrived,
Abandon hope and fear within your mind
Concerning the transmission and reception
[Of the teacher's blessing power.]
Just recognize the ultimate expanse
That is spontaneously present
And thus need not be sought.

11. Just as each and every thing
Is the display of dharmakāya,
Sambhogakāya, and nirmāṇakāya
(The triad uncontrived
Of nature, character, and knowing power),
So too samsara and nirvana are themselves the triple kāya,
The expanse of the enlightened mind,
Spontaneously present as a great and uncontrived equality.
Samsara, thus, is not to be abandoned,
Nirvana likewise not to be achieved.
Ascription and denial in their regard subside.
Samsara and nirvana
Dwell within the ultimate quintessence.
This reveals the key point:
Phenomena subsist within the enlightened mind,
Spontaneously present from the first.

* * *

12. All things are now essentialized
As spontaneous presence.
The five great elements,
The appearing world and its inhabitants,
Arise as teachers, all spontaneously present,
In a state that, from the first,
Is free of all discursive thought.
When there is no thought of self and other,
They are themselves intrinsically pure.
They are essentialized as your own mind,
Free of all activity and effort.
Do not block appearances,
But leave the six sense consciousnesses
In a state of relaxation.

13. Awareness, spontaneous presence,
Luminously radiant,

Is the fundamental source of all.
The key point is to leave
The five sense doors unmodified
And to be without the to-and-fro of thoughts.
Recognize the dharmakāya state,
Spontaneously present, aware and empty.
Be certain of it; leave it free
Of all conceptual movement.

14. In the vast and pure expanse
Of uninhibited awareness, self-cognizing,
All appearances—objects, mental states—
Are an unbroken state of evenness.
They are all essentialized
As a seamless and spontaneous presence,
A natural meditative absorption.
At all times like the current of a mighty stream,
Primordial wisdom,
Not cultivated through one's meditation
But spontaneously present, is unceasing.
The essential core of all phenomena
Is the expanse, primordial, self-arisen,
That in its full measure corresponds
To Samantabhadra's actual wisdom mind.

15. The root of all phenomena
Is the enlightened mind,
Which is like space—
The all-applicable analogy.
All things are contained in the abyss of space,
And all is pure by nature
Without striving or exertion.
Likewise, in the state beyond intended action,
Beyond the reach of ordinary mind,
Where all things that appear

Are left just as they are—
It's here that is essentialized
The key point of phenomena,
Spontaneously present
Both outside and within.

16. In suchness there's no origin, no ending,
No going and no coming (and the rest).
Therein the wisdom mind
Of the Victorious Ones is gathered—
The pure unwavering concentration
Of spontaneous presence.
In this state, transcending action,
Phenomena are all essentialized.

* * *

17. All things are subsumed within spontaneous presence.
All phenomenal existence, spontaneously present,
Is the self-experience of awareness.
Samsara and nirvana,
Spontaneously present, are awareness's display.
Also, the enlightened mind is, from the very first,
Spontaneously present.
All phenomena are nothing other
Than spontaneous presence.

18. Spontaneously present
Is the nature of the mind.
And thus the ground or root,
The essence [of phenomena],
Is gathered in the enlightened mind.
No need is there to seek it out
By means of the ten elements.
It is spontaneously present;
There is no need to strive for it

By means of view and meditative concentration.
There is no need to gain it by extraneous means,
As in the systems of causality.
There is no need to be preoccupied
With hope and fears regarding it.
For right now in the present time,
Spontaneous presence is primordial dharmakāya.

19. The nature of the mind is an immense expanse
Of space beyond all change.
From this expanse of the three kāyas,
Samsara and nirvana spontaneously arise,
Although they never stir from it.
Indefinitely various is its display:
A treasure of illusory appearances
Of cognitive power
Arising solely as spontaneous presence:
Samantabhadra.
He is thus the master of samsara and nirvana—
For they have never strayed elsewhere
From this, the ultimate expanse.
Samantabhadra thus is everything;
Nothing is there that could not be so.
All is the expanse, spontaneously present,
Of the vajra essence.
All things are primordially subsumed
Within spontaneous presence.

* * *

20. A clear conviction thus is reached
About their nature of spontaneous presence.
Within spontaneous presence,
Which transcends all boundaries,
Outside and within,
All things are but the self-experience of awareness.

They neither go nor come;
They lie beyond affirming and negating.
All things are an all-encompassing expanse
Devoid of all directions, up and down.
Completely indeterminate, completely unconfined,
Inconceivable and inexpressible,
They cannot be identified.

21. Because phenomena are,
By nature, pure from the beginning,
Because, by character, they are spontaneously present,
They are free of all extremes:
Existence, nonexistence, permanence, discontinuity.
This is the nature of nondual, enlightened mind.

22. By nature, primal purity
Does not exist as anything at all.
Its character is similar to space
And pure from the beginning.
In itself, spontaneous presence
Has not been made by anyone.
Its arising is unceasing,
And anything may manifest.
It is the source of both samsara and nirvana.
It had no beginning in the past,
And in the future it will have no end.

23. Indeterminate, unborn, spontaneous presence
Is the ultimate ground. The way that things arise,
Beginningless and endless,
Cannot be arrested.
The way things are—without intrinsic being—
Cannot be identified.
The way that things subside—without inherent character—
Cannot be interrupted.

Clear conviction thus is reached
That subsequently also
All things dwell within the ground
From which they have arisen.
This is called the "dissolution in the dharmakāya,
Exhaustion in the ultimate expanse."

24. Like clouds that melt into the sky from whence they came
And like the crystal's lights withdrawn into the crystal,
Samsara and nirvana
(The ground's appearances
Arisen from the ground)
Keep to their primordial, pure nature
In the ultimate ground.
A clear conviction is acquired
That all phenomena are gathered
In the expanse of the fundamental stratum
Of spontaneous presence.
All mental movement naturally dissolves
In the expanse devoid of cognitive activity.

25. When all the things that now appear—
All objects of the six sense consciousnesses—
Dissolve into the fundamental stratum, dharmakāya,
You will be utterly convinced
That both the outer and the inner blend together
In the vast expanse: spontaneous presence.
You will be utterly convinced
That both samsara and nirvana,
Self-experience of awareness,
Are the enlightened mind, devoid of form,
The state of manifest awakening.
Likewise, if you leave appearances and mental movement
In their natural state, the space of luminosity,
Not making differences between them,

Keeping to a natural flow without conceptual elaboration,
You will be utterly convinced
That they are the empty, luminous radiance
Of awareness, present and immediate.
This is called the "firm abiding in the precious sphere."

26. If now you lack a clear conviction
In the fundamental stratum of the ultimate expanse,
It is not later that you'll find
Your freedom in the primal ground.
If freedom in the ground expanse you fail to gain,
Your rigid meditation will not lead to liberation
But to high celestial states.
So now it is of great importance
To embrace with clear conviction
The kind of concentration
Where you're naturally at rest
Within the pristine inner ultimate expanse.

27. You will come to clear conviction
That all things are awareness,
Spontaneous presence.
You will come to clear conviction
That spontaneous presence
Is the fundamental stratum
Of primordial purity.
You will come to clear conviction
That primordial purity is free
From reference, thought, expression.
This is the clear, definitive conviction
Of spontaneous presence.

4. Single Nature

1. And now the one sole nature [of phenomena] is shown.
The one awareness is the ground of all phenomena.
However many they may seem,
They do not waver from their one sole nature.
So it is said. Their one and only root
Is primal wisdom self-arisen.
In certain situations, from a single gem,
Fire and water, different and distinct, may both emerge.
And yet their root is one, the pure and precious lapis lazuli.
Likewise, even though from one awareness, self-cognizing,
Nirvana and samsara both arise,
Their root is one, the ultimate enlightened mind.
The difference that divides them is illusory,
Deriving from the recognition or nonrecognition of awareness.

2. Phenomenal existence, samsara and nirvana,
All things appearing in awareness,
In the moment of their being perceived,
Have but the nature of emptiness alone.
They are like magical illusions, dreams,
Like moons reflected in the water.
Wholly empty and primordially empty,
Beyond conceptual elaboration,
They dwell within awareness,
Space-like, insubstantial,
The ground of their appearance.
Since all is, in the one expanse,
Primordially pure,

There is no dualism, no "two."
All is gathered in a single sphere,
The dharmakāya without edges, without corners. *Émaho!*

3. That which appears as the five elements—
That very thing is the enlightened mind.
It does not stir from the one state: unborn equality.
The appearances of animate existence
Are but the empty forms of six migrations.
The appearances of the ground do not depart
From the condition of awareness.
Happiness and woe may both appear,
And yet they are the single essence,
The enlightened mind.
They do not waver from the one and only
Primal wisdom self-arisen.
So it is that you should understand
Phenomena are but a single ultimate expanse,
The state of emptiness.
They are the unborn, the enlightened mind.

4. Within this ultimate dimension,
The vast expanse of awareness, self-cognizing,
There dwells the one sole wisdom
Of Victorious Ones, past, present, and to come.
Do not think of it as manifold,
For it transcends all thought of having parts.
It is the palace of the essence
Of unwavering enlightenment,
Where nothing but primordial wisdom, self-arisen, dwells.

5. It is the wish-fulfilling, jewel-like
Treasury of all phenomena,
The buddha field of the three kāyas,
Spontaneously present.

6. The one sole great expanse
Was made by none.
All things without exception
That emerge from it
Are the single fundamental ground
From which they came.
For to its cause does the result return.
This ground is the immensity
Of luminous and empty dharmatā.
It exceeds all limits, all directions;
It is everywhere—like pure, unsullied space.

7. The maker of all things, samsara and nirvana,
Is one and self-arisen.
Yet this root, awareness, none has made.
Beyond all action and exertion, it abides like space.
The example and the thing exemplified concur—
It is a single vast expanse
Where all ascriptions and denials are stilled.

8. Within the ultimate quintessence
Transcending being and nonbeing,
Whatever things appear displayed unceasingly,
Their nature is an inconceivable and inexpressible expanse
Beyond conventions of both speech and language.

9. In the enlightened mind,
The quintessence whence all things have sprung,
There's no duality and yet uncountable variety.
Buddhas, beings, phenomenal existence,
The world and its inhabitants are clearly present.
Yet they do not stir from suchness, dharmatā alone.

10. All things are connected to this one and only thing
In which they're perfectly included.

This is the supreme quality of the enlightened mind.
From the very instant that a thing appears in it,
The misconception that it differs from it
Is to be eliminated.
It should be understood that outer things
Are but the empty radiance
Of the nondual nature of the mind,
While things within the mind
Are just awareness bare and open,
Neither one nor many.
The realization that their nature
Is the single, ultimate expanse
Reveals a key point of awareness.

* * *

11. In one taste all things are essentialized.
All appearing objects are illusions;
They are the state of emptiness.
However they appear,
Rest without contrivance in the one awareness.
No matter what appears,
The one sole empty luminosity arises.

12. Thoughts, the mind's appearances,
Fade naturally away.
Whatever movement comes
Within the state of emptiness,
Just rest within the natural flow, relaxed.
Through the movement and proliferation of your thoughts,
The wisdom of the dharmatā will clearly appear.

13. When you see that objects of the senses
And the mind are seamlessly the same,
When, free of focus and of reference,
You rest within the state of traceless natural purity,

Within its very radiance there manifests
The primal wisdom of deep insight.

14. Essentializing into one quintessence
These three key points—
That realization and non-realization
Are both primordially equal,
That mind and object indivisible
Are the equality of dharmakāya,
That faults and obscurations are inseparable
From the equality of dharmatā—
You continually keep to ultimate reality.
Without rejecting or adopting, you will find
The ultimate quintessence.
Not coming and not going, you abide
Within the realization of the dharmatā.
All is gathered in this state
Wherein both change and movement are transcended.

15. Space-like is the vast immensity,
The mind of the Victorious Ones.
Beyond elimination and atttainment,
It is the great expanse, the one sole sphere.
Freedom in itself, it is beyond the states
Of realization and non-realization.
The place of the exhaustion of phenomena is reached
In all-embracing evenness beyond the ordinary mind.
Above the summit of the victory banner, never to be lowered,
The sun and moon illuminate a myriad worlds.

*   *   *

16. All things are subsumed
Within awareness, one and self-cognizing.
All things of phenomenal existence,
All samsara and nirvana,

Infinitely, endlessly appear
Arising from the ultimate expanse.
Therefore, the expanse whence they emerge
Subsumes them.

17. Even now, when various things appear,
They do not from awareness stray elsewhere.
Appearances are thus subsumed
Within the vast expanse, awareness self-arisen.

18. Seamlessly arising and subsiding,
They dissolve into the ultimate expanse.
Appearances are not other than
The enlightened mind.
All things are subsumed within
The one primordial dharmatā,
The ground of their exhaustion.

19. Subsumed into the one and sole awareness,
Phenomena have never left awareness,
Essence of enlightenment,
Beyond all change and movement.
They are subsumed within the ultimate quintessence;
They dwell in the expanse, unchanging, uncompounded.

*　*　*

20. A clear conviction is attained
That all phenomena are the one, sole,
Self-arisen primal wisdom,
The ultimate expanse,
Beginningless and endless.
All is there contained.
All movement of the mind subsides,
And all abides within the dharmatā,
The ultimate quintessence.

21. Outer objects, therefore, and the inner mind,
Phenomena of both samsara and nirvana—
When gross are analyzed into the subtle,
No notion of a part remains.
Thus you are clearly convinced
That they are but the vast expanse,
Empty from the outset, similar to space.

22. Enlightened mind, when analyzed,
Is found to be devoid of substance.
It has no source, no dwelling place;
It does not come or go.
It eludes all indication and expression.
You reach a clear conviction
That it is the space of wisdom
That transcends the ordinary mind.
It's not an entity with features,
Definable as this or that.
Not known through words,
It cannot be described.

23. You reach a clear conviction
That all things in phenomenal existence
Belonging to samsara and nirvana
Are the vast expanse,
Devoid of mental movement and of naming.
You reach a clear conviction
That all things are the vast expanse,
Awareness, empty and unborn,
Primordial wisdom self-cognizing.
You reach a clear conviction
That all things arising from enlightened mind
Are but the vast expanse
Beyond both knowing and not knowing.
You reach a clear conviction that all phenomena,

Primordially empty and completely empty,
Constitute the vast expanse,
Unmoving and unchanging in the triple time.

5. THOSE TO WHOM THIS TEACHING MAY BE GIVEN

1. This essence of the vehicle most profound
Should be revealed exclusively
To those who clearly have
Both supreme fortune and intelligence.
It should be withheld
From those who bigotedly cling
To lesser vehicles and to the causal principle,
From those who are of lesser fortune and intelligence.

2. From those who criticize their teacher,
Who show aggression to their vajra kindred,
Who betray the secret, speaking of it openly,
Faithless and tightfisted, of an evil disposition,
Who are engrossed in temporal things—
From all these keep the teachings secret.

3. Those of highest caliber, endowed with fortune,
Are the proper vessels for the Great Perfection.
They respect their teachers and possess great knowledge.
They are joyful and broad-minded,
Faithful friends and generous.
They are without ambitious thoughts
And have but little clinging.
They give up all preoccupation for this present life
And are intent on winning their enlightenment.

Endowed with faith and diligence,
They are able to maintain the secret.
These are those to whom
The teachings should be given.

4. With presents they should please their teachers,
And in a spirit of commitment
They should wholeheartedly request instruction.
When the teaching has been granted,
They should practice it correctly
And reach the level of exhaustion of phenomena
In the fundamental nature.

5. Teachers should be very learned,
Possessing all required qualities.
They should examine their disciples
And gradually bestow on them the key instructions.
But they should keep these teachings
From unsuitable recipients.
They should mark them with the seal of secrecy
And hide them with the seal of their entrustment.

6. To the children of the teacher's heart,
The fortunate of high capacity,
Essential teachings, definitive in meaning,
Should be granted.

7. And they in turn must not divulge to all
This essence, which is ultimate and free from all decline.
They must keep it undiminished
As the essence of their practice.
If the secret door is compromised,
Punishment is sure to come.
Through misinterpretation,

The essential teachings will recede.
Disciples therefore must maintain the secret
And keep their masters joyful company.
They will reach within this very life
The everlasting kingdom of the dharmakāya.

6. Conclusion

1. This teaching has disclosed
Directly, without hiding anything,
The view of the sublime and secret
Great Perfection.
May it naturally and without effort
Bring beings, leaving none aside,
To freedom in the space of the primordial ground.

2. This teaching, which completely covers
All the lower views,
Is the very peak of all the vehicles,
The vast space of the great *garuḍa* king.
May this teaching of the Atiyoga,
Superior to every other,
Be spread in all the ten directions.
May the banner of its victory be never lowered.

3. Three classes, nine expanses
All subsumed in the four principles.
The final view of all their sixteen sections
Is expounded in this *Precious Treasury*
Of the Fundamental Nature,
Which Longchen Rabjam Zangpo
Has perfectly composed.

4. The final view that is contained
In the five topics of *The Treasury*
Of the Fundamental Nature

Is perfectly adorned with riches,
Both profound and vast.
It is made beautiful with the splendor
Of its words and meanings.
Let a host of fortunate disciples
Take great joy therein.

This concludes *The Precious Treasury of the Fundamental Nature*. It was composed by Longchen Rabjam, a yogi of the supreme vehicle.

PART TWO

An Offering to Please the Omniscient Lord

The Instructions of My Glorious Teacher,
a Word Commentary on
The Precious Treasury of
the Fundamental Nature,
a Teaching of the
Great Perfection

KHANGSAR TENPA'I WANGCHUK

Textual Outline

PREAMBLE

In the pure field of the dharmadhātu,
You are the dharmakāya, Samantabhadra.
You are Vajrasattva, the sambhogakāya
Endowed with fivefold certainty,
And Garab Dorje, the nirmāṇakāya
And teacher of a host of different beings.
To you in whom the threefold kāya manifests,
To you, my teacher, I bow down.

Lord of Dharma entrusted to explain
The teaching in three classes
And the view of the most secret unsurpassed—
Supreme, omniscient master Matisara,
I pray that you will always rest within the lotus of my mind.

Orgyen Chökyi Dawa Palzangpo once said:

> Paṇḍita Lord of Sakya, sunlight of the teaching of five
> sciences,
> Tsongkhapa, wellspring of fine discourse on the sutras and
> the tantras,
> Longchenpa, sovereign lord of all the teachings—
> All three were truly Mañjughoṣa in the Land of Snow.

Now, as these words declare, one of the three direct manifestations of Mañjughoṣa in our snowy land of Tibet was the victorious Longchenpa, the great elucidator of the teachings of the Great Secret Essence. He was the author of the Seven Treasuries, which expound the vast cycle of teachings [belonging to the scholarly way] of paṇḍitas, and he compiled the Four Parts of the Heart Essence, which set forth the cycle of the profound teachings of yogis. In addition, he wrote *The Trilogy of Rest*, the definitive teachings that express without error the entire meaning of the teachings both profound and vast; and finally, he composed *The Trilogy on Natural Freedom*, the *Trilogy on Dispelling Darkness*, and a host of other works, all of them indistinguishable from the exalted speech of the victorious Vajradhara. Of these, the two most sublime and profound texts—which reveal all the crucial points of trekchö, the Great Perfection teaching on primordial purity—are *The Precious Treasury of the Dharmadhātu* and *The Precious Treasury of the Fundamental Nature*.

The Precious Treasury of the Dharmadhātu is a treatise that definitively establishes all phenomena of samsara and nirvana as the great dharmadhātu, awareness alone. *The Precious Treasury of the Fundamental Nature* applies this teaching to the mind of the individual practitioner in a systematic exposition in successive stages. An especially eminent instruction, it establishes four vajra principles: the nonexistence of phenomena, the evenness of phenomena, the spontaneous presence of phenomena, and the single nature of phenomena. If practitioners bring these same principles to bear on their own minds, it will be easy for them to implement this teaching in a gradual and systematic way.

The Precious Treasury of the Fundamental Nature comments generally on the three classes of the teachings of the Great Perfection: the outer mind class, the inner space class, and the secret pith instruction class. In particular, it establishes the definitive view of the secret class of pith instructions. Happy indeed are those who even see, hear, recall, or touch this text. And, if among those fortunate beings there are some who, endowed with the right karmic connection, implement its teachings, there is no doubt that they will attain the state of union in a single life.[27]

For this reason and to satisfy repeated requests, I shall write a brief word commentary on *The Precious Treasury of the Funda-*

mental Nature according to the oral instructions of my glorious and supreme master Lodrö Gyatso. To this end, I invoke and beg my teacher, my *yidam* deity, and the guardians and owners of this teaching—the ḍākas, ḍākinīs, and Dharma protectors—to grant me their permission and guidance.

The commentary is in four parts: first, an introduction to the treatise; second, an extensive explanation of the main body of the text; third, an instruction on the qualities of those who are able to grasp its meaning; and fourth, the conclusion of the treatise as a whole.

1. Introduction to the Treatise

The introduction comprises three sections: an explanation of the title of the treatise, Longchenpa's expression of homage, and his promise to compose the text.

1. The Title

The Sanskrit title of the text is *Tathātvaratnakoṣanāma*. The Tibetan title is *gnas lugs rin po che'i mdzod ces bya ba*.[28] Rendered word for word, *tathātva* (*gnas lugs*) means "fundamental nature," *ratna* (*rin po che*) means "precious," *kośa* (*mdzod*) means "treasury," and *nāma* (*ces bya ba*) means "name."[29]

"Fundamental nature" must be understood in the sense of "awareness"—the ultimate enlightened mind, the dharmakāya, which is beyond the reach of demonstration and refutation, beyond movement and change. It is the mode of being of all phenomena, their profound, secret, fundamental nature. It is beyond the karmic law of cause and effect, beyond effort and action.

This text is a "precious treasury" because, just as from a hoard of wish-fulfilling jewels there comes an endless stream of all that one could wish for, in the same way, if the fundamental nature of the mind, the ultimate truth and self-arisen primordial wisdom, is realized just as it is, the final and resultant state—the precious gems of the twenty-five qualities of the result, such as the four kāyas and the five primordial wisdoms—will effortlessly and spontaneously appear. The same description may also be applied to the ground, path, and result. Since the nature of the ground, the luminous character of the mind, is primordially and spontaneously endowed with all the excellent qualities of both existence and peace, the fundamental nature of the *ground* is also a precious treasury.

Similarly, in the present moment, at the time of the path, it is thanks to the ripening effect of the empowerment of the power of awareness and thanks to the liberating power of a teacher's essential instructions that the indwelling primordial wisdom is no longer concealed. It is awakened and appears nakedly in the mind of the fortunate disciple, who in that very moment realizes the fundamental nature just as it is. Accordingly, the luminous, fundamental nature of the *path* is also a precious treasury.

Finally, since immaculate self-cognizing awareness—the fundamental nature endowed with twofold purity—is the dharmakāya, sambhogakāya, and nirmāṇakāya, the result is not to be looked for elsewhere. It dwells unmoving and unchanging throughout the three times as awareness, the great fundamental stratum. And since this is like a hoard of precious things, the *result* too is a precious treasury.

1. Longchenpa's Expression of Homage

2. A Brief Homage

Homage to glorious Samantabhadra.

Samantabhadra is described as glorious because he attains the glory of the supreme dharmakāya for his own sake and without ever stirring from this ultimate expanse, he is in sovereign possession of the perfect glory of the supreme rūpakāya for the sake of others. And he is Samantabhadra because, the first of all buddhas, he is the "all-good" dharmakāya buddha. He is buddha before both the arising of any buddha endowed with equal realization and before the arising of sentient beings who are destitute of such realization.

How does this happen? Within the primordial expanse that is common to both samsara and nirvana, and stirred by the wisdom wind endowed with a network of five-colored light, awareness rises up from the ground and the appearances of the ground unfold. At that very moment, Samantabhadra sees that they are his own self-experience. And as it is said,

> In a single instant, their specific qualities he sees;
> In a single instant, he is perfect buddha.

It is thus that his buddhahood is endowed with six special features.[30] In the instant of a single perfect enlightened deed, this same primordial lord Samantabhadra—appearing as the teacher of both samsara and nirvana—is freed in the state of indwelling primordial wisdom. Samantabhadra is thus the perfect guide who, with magisterial authority, reveals the swift and profound path exactly as it is. To him, Longchen Rabjam, the author of this text, pays homage by resting in the view, the realization of the inseparability of their wisdom minds, a state elicited through his own unshakable faith.

The *ground Samantabhadra* is suchness, the ultimate reality of all things. The *ornament Samantabhadra* is the appearance aspect of spontaneous presence, which without stirring from the ground arises as the display of phenomena. *Awareness Samantabhadra* is self-arisen primordial wisdom, the ultimate enlightened mind; it is awareness, the *sugatagarbha*. The *path Samantabhadra* is the discovery of the fundamental nature just as it is, in other words, primordially occurring, self-arisen awareness and its actualization. To all of these, Longchenpa, the author of this text, pays homage with unshakable faith. This is the oral teaching of my own supreme and glorious teacher.

2. A Detailed Homage

> Buddha from the first,
> The ground of actual enlightenment,
> Beyond all change and present of itself,
> The space of adamantine essence, indestructible—

> This is the nature of the mind,
> The natural great perfection.
> Nothing do I take and nothing do I cast aside—
> Nothing comes and nothing goes.
> Thus it is that I bow down in homage.

Independent of any new causes and conditions, the fundamental nature of the ground is, from the very first, pure, primordial buddhahood. This is actual enlightenment, the great primordial openness and freedom of the ground.

Awareness, spontaneously present as unchanging primordial wisdom, immutable throughout the continuity of time, is self-arisen buddhahood. In the present context it is referred to as the ultimate expanse of the indestructible adamantine or vajra essence. It is established as dharmatā, ultimate reality, the unchanging ultimate vajra expanse. This same dharmatā, which is unconfined and leans to no extreme or side, is the nature of the mind endowed with the seven qualities of a vajra.[31] It is, in other words, the natural great perfection. It is to this that the author pays homage in the most superior way by resting in his realization of the view. This is an indication that the object of homage is awareness, self-arisen primordial wisdom, the ground for the unfolding of both samsara and nirvana.

How is such an homage expressed? When there is neither acceptance nor rejection, neither the projection nor the dissolution of thoughts, neither going nor coming, nothing stirs from the fundamental stratum of the dharmatā and the very face of awareness, dwelling as the ground, the dharmakāya, is actualized. In this context, to realize or experience this state is described as paying homage. The great primordial wisdom of equality, in which the three spheres of subject, object, and action are not found (for they are devoid of true existence) stands here for the person who is paying homage.

The first six lines of the above stanza refer to the ground: the self-arisen fundamental nature. The remaining three lines describe the path whereby one meditates upon this same ground. As for the result, since the stability gained in the fundamental stratum of the ultimate nature is simply a particular instance of stabilization within the ground, it should be understood that the ground, path, and result are awareness alone.

1. Longchenpa's Promise to Compose the Text

> The expanse of the nature inexpressible of all
>   phenomena,
> The culmination of all views and different from
>   them all,
> The all-transcending meaning of the Great
>   Perfection
> I shall now explain according to my realization.
> Listen!

The nature of absolutely everything in phenomenal existence, whether of samsara or nirvana, is the dharmatā, ultimate reality: inexpressible and inconceivable awareness. It is the ultimate enlightened mind, the luminous expanse of the great perfection. As the teachings say,

> Untouched by the eight vehicles' mind-made tenets,
> It is the very summit of the ninth, the view of Great
>   Perfection.

As the culmination of the views of the nine vehicles, the Great Perfection states that all together, the phenomena of samsara and nirvana are completely and perfectly included within the expanse of the one self-arisen primordial wisdom that transcends the causal process and effortful striving. It is different from all the other, mentally contrived tenets of the eight vehicles. All the qualities of the paths and results of these lower vehicles are its expression, contained and enhanced within it like a hundred streams that pass beneath a single bridge. This is the unique and defining feature of the vehicle of Ati. As it is said in *The All-Creating King*,

> If you understand the nature of myself, the all-creator,
> Everything is seen as my expression.

When awareness, which is beyond the causal process and active effort, is realized, it is seen to be superior to, or to transcend, all the teachings of the lower vehicles. It is beyond entities and their characteristics, beyond permanence and impermanence, beyond existence and nonexistence, sameness and difference, and so on. It lies beyond the scope of speech, conception, and expression. In saying that he will explain for the sake of his disciples, fortunate beings to be guided, this profound and vast teaching, just as he has realized it, the author of the text makes the promise to compose, exhorting all those who are proper vessels, endowed with superior abilities and the proper karmic disposition, to listen to him.

It is said in the great commentary on the *Prajñāpāramitā in Eight Thousand Lines*,

> Those who strive with great love for the sake of others
> Never slacken though their lives be threatened.
> Holy beings, shouldering their heavy burden,
> Never in despondency abandon it.

And,

> Holy beings do not promise much.
> But when they pledge themselves to a hard task,
> It is as if they carved it on a rock.
> Though they may die, they will not turn to something else.

As these texts say, holy beings never allow other things to deflect them from what they have promised.

Regarding the fourfold interrelated purpose of Longchenpa's treatise, its *subject* is awareness, the enlightened mind, which lies beyond the causal process and all effortful striving. Its *immediate purpose* is to enable beings of the highest capacity to acquire a perfect understanding of this. Its *ultimate purpose*, or finality, is— on the basis of the practice related to such an understanding—to enable yogis to attain its objective (namely, the fundamental nature) and thereby to gain liberation. The *connection* between these three elements refers to the fact that they are mutually consistent, with each element leading to the one that follows.

2. An Extensive Explanation of Longchenpa's Treatise

This consists of a brief presentation followed by a detailed exposition according to four vajra topics.

1. A Brief Presentation

> The ultimate and quintessential view
> Belonging to the mind, space, pith instruction
> classes
> Lies in nonexistence, evenness,
> Spontaneous presence, single nature.
> Each of these four has in turn four aspects:
> Their key points are revealed, essentialized,
> subsumed,
> A clear conviction is then gained in their regard.

This stanza demonstrates that the ultimate, quintessential view of the outer mind class, the inner space class, and the secret pith instruction class—that is, the view of the Great Perfection—is summed up in four great principles, or "samayas."[32] This view is like butter churned from the milk of the holy Dharma. First, phenomena are "nonexistent," for it is established that they are empty or devoid of self. Second, phenomena are "even" or equal, for they are unconfined and do not fall to one side or another. Third, phenomenal appearances are "spontaneously present," for they are uncontrived from the very first and are present in and of themselves. Finally, phenomena are of a "single nature" in that they are established as being none other than self-arisen awareness. In these four great samayas, the final view of the Natural Great Perfection[33] is gathered. Furthermore, each of these samayas displays four subsidiary aspects. First, their key points are "revealed," that is, they are extensively elucidated as being suchness. These same key points, extensively revealed, are then "essentialized" as ultimate, self-arisen primordial wisdom. They are then "subsumed" in unborn, thought-transcending awareness. And finally, a "clear conviction" or certainty is reached that phenomena are beyond causality and deliberate action and effort. The distinction of four particular instances for each of the four samayas means that this treatise is composed of sixteen sections of teaching.

In brief, all things in both samsara and nirvana are simply the display and creative power of the one, self-arisen, primordial wisdom. Not even a single infinitesimal particle exists apart from that. The creative power and display of self-arisen primordial wisdom arise as the ornament of this same wisdom. Whatever manifests is but the self-experience of primordial wisdom; it has no existence apart from this. By means of various examples that illustrate this truth, the key points of the four great samayas are "revealed" and explained. These same revealed points are then essentialized as self-arisen primordial wisdom, the fundamental stratum of equality. Whatever appears is then subsumed in the experience of the naked expanse of spontaneously present, self-arisen wisdom. Finally, a clear conviction is reached—in other words, it is decisively resolved—that spontaneously present appearances are none other than the one, self-arisen primordial wisdom. Although many such distinctions are made, they are in truth all gathered into the sphere of the one primordial wisdom. These four samayas may be clearly understood thanks to three factors: an example, its meaning, and an evidential sign. It is said in *The All-Creating King*,

> If you wish to understand with certainty this meaning,
> Take the sky as your example.
> The meaning is the unborn nature of phenomena.

The fact that mind is unobstructed is the evidential sign.
Thus space-like things are illustrated
By the sky, which acts as an example.

And,

All phenomena are the enlightened mind.
All things may be compared with space;
This too exemplifies the enlightened mind,
For in itself it has a sky-like nature.

As this text says, just as the universe and its inhabitants appear within the dimension of space, so too all things in both samsara and nirvana appear within the one expanse of self-arisen awareness—outside which not a single particle exists. All phenomena arise from within the ultimate enlightened mind. They appear in the mind; they are made by the mind; and yet this same enlightened mind is made by none. As *The All-Creating King* declares,

The enlightened mind made everything but is itself
unmade.

1. A Detailed Exposition

This text is structured according to the four vajra topics just mentioned: nonexistence, evenness, spontaneous presence, and single nature.

2. THE FIRST VAJRA TOPIC: NONEXISTENCE

We shall begin by establishing the first of the four topics, namely, that of nonexistence. The teaching itself, which concludes with a statement of the vajra topic's name,[34] has four sections: the key points [of the topic] are revealed, essentialized, and subsumed; and a clear conviction is then reached in their regard.

3. Section One: The Key Points Are Revealed

This consists of eighteen stanzas. First, phenomena are shown to be devoid of real existence and of characteristics.

> 1. First, I demonstrate the principle of nonexistence.
> Nonexistence means the absence of intrinsic being.
> In the great expanse of the enlightened mind, which
> is like space,
> Whatever may appear has no intrinsic being.

All things belonging to the sphere of phenomenal existence, samsara and nirvana, are the mere imputation of the deluded mind. Indeed, from the very first they have never existed; the text now demonstrates how this fundamental nature of theirs is established.

All phenomena are by nature primordially empty and devoid of self. All conceptual elaborations concerning them are stilled. Phenomena are unborn and the manner in which they are empty of intrinsic being is as follows. Within awareness, the state of equality, empty and self-cognizing, the ultimate enlightened mind similar to space, an open, all-embracing, unconfined expanse that falls neither to one side nor another, the endless phenomena of the outer universe and the beings that it contains are, in the very moment of their appearance, devoid of intrinsic being. They are a groundless, rootless display, a state of openness that is devoid of all objective reference. As Longchenpa will say later in the fifth stanza,

> Understand therefore that all phenomena
> Appearing in the mind are nonexistent.

Second, the nonexistence of phenomena is ascertained by means of an example and the meaning that it expresses.

> 2. In the vast expanse, the womb of space,
> The universe, the beings it contains,

> And the four elements in constant flux
> Are simply empty forms without intrinsic being.
> The things appearing in the enlightened mind
> Are just the same.

As this example shows, in the vast, womb-like expanse of space (without center, periphery, outside, inside, zenith, nadir), all the world systems of the great three thousandfold universe, the beings that inhabit them, together with the four elements, at first take shape and then subsist, only to be destroyed at length by seven fires and a single flood. In whichever period of the *kalpa* a universe happens to be (formation, duration, destruction, or void), the space that supports it is empty. It has no intrinsic being. Likewise, all phenomena, the universes and beings supported by this same space—all moving and evolving, all passing through the same periods of formation, subsistence, destruction, and the void—are also devoid of even the tiniest truly existent particle. The phenomena of both the support and the supported are without existence. They are empty. And just like these empty, nonexistent but appearing forms, all devoid of even the tiniest atom endowed with real existence, the whole of phenomenal existence—both samsara and nirvana, appearing in the expanse of the ultimate enlightened mind or self-arisen awareness—seems to be real but in fact has no existence.

As we find in *The All-Creating King*,

> Just as in phenomenal existence, the universe and beings,
> There is nothing that is not within the vast expanse of space,
> So too is the immense expanse of the enlightened mind:
> Buddhas, beings, universe and contents—all are there.
> All are present indivisible in this same pure nature,
> There being no ascription of existence or denial.

Third, the phenomena appearing in awareness are without intrinsic being.

>   3. Illusory reflections, however they appear,
>   Are unreal, empty by their nature.
>   Likewise, all things in phenomenal existence,
>   In the very moment of appearing,
>   Never stir from the enlightened mind.
>   They have no real existence.

A skilled magician, master of his craft, is able to produce for his spectators a magical display full of variety: the beautiful illusory appearance, wonderful to see, of the islands and lands of a vast universe together with all the beings that live in it: humans, horses, cattle, and so on. At the same time, he knows perfectly well that all these apparently real forms have never existed in truth and are by nature empty and without the slightest reality. In the same way, the things that manifest within the vast expanse of all-embracing self-cognizing awareness—the outer and inner things of phenomenal existence, samsara and nirvana— are all, in the very moment of their appearing, groundless and rootless. It is only because one clings to the phenomenal self (the cause) and to discursive thoughts (the condition) that entities appear separate from all-embracing awareness—that they seem to arise as something other, even though they are awareness experiencing itself.

Whatever manifests does not in the slightest way diverge from the ultimate enlightened mind, from open, unimpeded, self-cognizing awareness, the state of equality free of all conceptual construction. There is not even the tiniest atom of a so-called phenomenon endowed with characteristics, existing separate and distinct from self-cognizing awareness. As we find in *The All-Creating King*,

>   The world with its inhabitants, phenomenal existence—
>   Everything in both samsara and nirvana—
>   By nature, never stirs from the enlightened mind.

Fourth, phenomenal appearances do not stir from spontaneously present awareness.

4. Dream visions, never stirring from the state of
   sleep,
In the very moment they are seen, are utterly unreal.
Likewise, all phenomenal existence,
Both samsara and nirvana,
Never stirs from the enlightened mind.
It is unreal, devoid of features.

The objects seen in dreams: mountains, rocks, houses, and so on—the outer universe and the beings that inhabit it (oneself and others)—are perceived separately and distinctly, and [in the dream] give rise to feelings of happiness, sorrow, or indifference. One is deluded in grasping at them as if they were daytime appearances. Dreams arise within the sleeping state, in which they play themselves out and finally subside. Since they do not exist outside the sleeping state, it is hardly necessary to point out that the things one sees in a dream had no previous existence. Indeed, even in the present moment, when they appear to the sleeping person, they are utterly devoid of reality. It is just the same with the things of phenomenal existence, samsara and nirvana. They never stir from the ultimate enlightened mind, a state that is beyond all movement and change. All the things perceived by beings in the six migrations are never outside the expanse of awareness. The same is true of the phenomena of pure perception, the three kāyas, and so on. They never stir from the expanse of awareness, which is itself free from the fetters of an apprehender and an object to be apprehended. For this reason, they are not at all real entities in their own right, endowed with their own features. As it is said in *Meeting the Three Kāyas*,

> Beings of the six realms, born in the four ways,
> Originate within the dharmadhātu and return to it.
> Although the apprehender and the object to be
>   apprehended—
> Mind and object—both appear so clearly,

The dharmadhātu is the apprehender
And the dharmadhātu is the object to be apprehended.

Moreover,

All that the buddhas of the three times comprehend
Arises from the dharmadhātu and is known as
dharmadhātu.

Fifth, whatever appears as an outer object does not exist separately from the mind

5. Although phenomena appear within the mind,
They are not the mind and are not separate from the
mind.
They are nonexistent
And yet, like illusions, clearly appear.
They are ineffable and inconceivable.
They defy expression.
Understand therefore that all phenomena
Appearing in the mind are nonexistent
In the very moment that they are perceived.

The phenomena that are normally perceived as objects of the five senses—in other words, the universe and the beings it contains—appear distinctly in the minds of individual people. Nevertheless, these appearances are not their minds. Longchenpa said that if appearances were their minds, the unwanted consequence would be that if objects are perceived as having color and shape, their minds too would have a similar color and shape. For example, if a distant mountainside were to have a fire on it, it would follow that their minds would also be on fire. And if their minds were in movement, the mountain would move as well. Reasoning is able to adduce numerous refutations of this kind.

It is said in *The Mirror of Samantabhadra's Mind*, "Those who say that appearances are the mind are at variance with me." And we find in the *Tantra That Embodies the Definitive Teaching of the Great Perfection*,

> Fools who do not understand the final teaching
> Say that what appears is their own mind.
> But this is to take brass for gold.

It might be objected that this contradicts the scriptures in which it is said that phenomena are the mind. This, however, is not so, for when it is asserted that phenomena are the mind, the meaning is that they do no not diverge from the state of awareness. This is said in order to indicate that phenomena arise as the ornament of the display and creative power of awareness. This is like using the word *sun* to refer to the sunlight. Appearances are not the mind, but neither are they other than the mind. When their nature is decisively established, apparently extramental things are shown to be like magical illusions or dream visions. From their own side, they do not have the slightest existence independent of the mind. When phenomena, which seem different from the mind, are proven to be devoid of self, their infinitesimal partless particles are also disposed of. They are shown to be empty, and nothing is found. This, however, does not mean that phenomena are simply nothing at all, as when it is said that there is no tea, or there is no water, or when fire goes out and water dries up, or like a rabbit's horns, or the son of a barren women. On the contrary, phenomena appear clearly even though they are nonexistent. They are just like magical illusions. As it is said,

> The nature of emptiness is luminosity.
> The cognitive potency of luminosity is unimpeded.

Clearly appearing yet nonexistent, phenomena do seem to exist and to be genuinely real. And yet in truth, in the very moment of their appearing, they are but hallucinations, magical illusions. In the very moment that they seem to be truly existent, they are beyond the eight conceptual extremes.[35] They are ineffable, inconceivable, and inexpressible. They are groundless and rootless. They are just a state of openness devoid of all reference.

Now, when it is said that phenomena are neither the mind nor different from the mind, the mind in question should not be understood in the sense of the ultimate enlightened mind. This is clear from Longchenpa's teachings. He said, for example,

> Nowadays some people claim to understand the Great Perfection and say that appearances are the mind. This is an important mistake that comes from failing to make a proper distinction between the ordinary mind and the enlightened mind, which are not the same. The ordinary mind consists of the eight impure consciousnesses together with the mental factors that arise adventitiously within the three worlds. By contrast, the enlightened mind [the nature of the mind] is awareness itself, self-arisen wisdom, devoid of true existence, and without characteristics. It is the ultimate expanse of both samsara and nirvana. To say that the whole of phenomenal existence, arising as the creative power or display of the enlightened mind, *is* the enlightened mind is to give the name of the result to the cause. Having understood that the appearances of samsara and nirvana are the creative power of awareness, one understands that awareness does not exist *as* samsara or nirvana but is rather their unceasing ground of manifestation.

These are Longchenpa's own words.[36] And he continues,

> When one realizes that objects, clearly appearing and yet nonexistent, are neither the mind nor separate from the mind—that they are empty, luminous, groundless, and primordially pure—these same appearances subside.

At that moment, when the groundless creative power and display of awareness spontaneously vanish, it is as when one wakes from a dream. Self-cognizing awareness does not stir from the original fundamental stratum of unchanging dharmakāya, and one understands that entities and their characteristics are pure.[37] I am the only one these days who makes this distinction. No one else does. Some say that phenomena are the mind; some say that they are different from the mind. And apart from these two alternatives, nothing else is said.

Longchenpa also says in his *Treasury of the Dharmadhātu*,

> Some dumb oxen these days claim to practice Ati.
> They say that moving thoughts are the enlightened mind.
> These fools are in great darkness,
> Far from the Natural Great Perfection.
> If they do not know how the creative power differs
> From that which comes from this creative power,
> How can they know the enlightened mind?

In the autocommentary, this stanza receives the following explanation:

> Regarding the creative power of awareness, when, in brief, the appearance of an object arises bright and clear within awareness—like a reflection in a mirror—the creative power of cognitive potency is the kind of naked, limpid knowing that does not actively cognize objects. A creative power of this kind is necessarily unceasing. When the creative power arises and awareness does not move from its fundamental stratum of luminosity, the act of knowing does not stray into the object. The creative power is only spoken of from the point of view of its unceasing manifestation. In fact, creative power

and awareness are not two separate things. An act of knowing that strays into the object of creative power is explained as the display of that creative power. This, on the other hand, is not self-arisen primordial wisdom, because unless it is restrained by skillful means, it will produce karma and defilement, which lead to samsara. Moreover, this detecting and discerning act of knowing does not go beyond the samsaric state conditioned by an apprehender and an object to be apprehended. As it is said in *The All-Creating King,*

> Primordial wisdom, self-arisen, is primordial knowledge.
> But "primordial wisdom" that detects an object
> Arises from that object and is not self-arisen.

Moreover, in the common vehicle it is said,

> The mind and mental factors are cognitions
> That ascribe existence to the triple world.

And Dignāga has also said,

> Thought, this state of ignorance,
> Causes us to fall into the ocean of samsara.

In the autocommentary to *The Treasury of the Fundamental Nature,*[38] Longchenpa also says:

> "Creative power" is the power of awareness through which samsara and nirvana individually manifest. It is like the one light of the sun that by day causes the lotus blossom to open and the night-blooming lily to close. "Display" is simply awareness displayed through its own radiance in the same way that a flame is displayed through the light it sheds and the sun through

its own sunlight. "Ornament" refers to the fact that when anything appears and is perceived in its full array, this appearance is an adornment for awareness that is self-arisen. It is like a rainbow, the sun, the moon, the planets, and the stars, which are adornments for the sky itself.

For all these reasons, it should be understood that all phenomena appearing in the mind are nonexistent from the first moment of their being perceived.

Sixth, awareness does not exist as anything at all.

> 6. Just as apparent objects are by nature nonexistent,
> So too the subject, the enlightened mind,
> Like space, has no existence by its nature.
> Ineffable and inconceivable and inexpressible—
> It's thus that you should understand it.

Like the groundless, rootless, magical illusions of the universe and its living contents, the appearing objects of the six consciousnesses, which arise as the creative power of awareness, do not go beyond the state of nonexistence. The subject (the enlightened mind), which is itself the ground for the manifestation of phenomenal existence, samsara and nirvana, is just the same. It has no existence at all. It is like space. *The All-Creating King* declares,

> The enlightened mind is space-like in its nature,
> And all things are the enlightened mind.
> One example serves for all.
> Space-like also is the nature of phenomena.

As this text says, the enlightened mind is like space. It neither arises nor dwells nor ceases. It is beyond the eight conceptual extremes, the thirty-two misconceptions, and so on. It should be understood, therefore, that it is ineffable, inconceivable, and inexpressible.

Seventh, the way in which awareness is nonexistent.

> 7. Because in self-arisen primal wisdom,
> Ultimate quintessence,
> There is neither cause nor fruit,
> Samsara's vast abyss is crossed.
> Because there is no good or bad,
> Samsara and nirvana are the same.
> Because there is no deviation and no obscuration,
> The three existences are clearly understood.

The fundamental nature, the quintessential and ultimate luminosity, the open, unimpeded, luminous, naked awareness is self-arisen primordial wisdom. It is free of the conventional phenomena of causes and their effects, and like space it is free of all conceptual elaboration. This is why the abyss of the hallucinatory experiences, the joys and sorrows of samsara, is traversed from the very beginning. The appearances of samsara occur through the ceaseless manifestation of causes and effects. But since within the very nature of awareness there are no causes or effects to be found, there are no deviations, no obscurations, no good, and no bad. Consequently, no matter how the phenomena of samsara and nirvana appear, they are the same—they have an equal status—in the nature of awareness. As it is said in *The Direct Immediacy of Awareness*,

> In the ultimate expanse, real and unreal are the same.
> In the ultimate expanse, buddhas and beings are the same.
> In the ultimate expanse, relative and ultimate are the same.
> In the ultimate expanse, excellence and defects are the same.
> In the vast immensity of the ultimate expanse, high and low
> are just the same.

The appearances of samsara and nirvana have never at any time existed in any way. They are equal in their status. Consequently, however, they have arisen within awareness (which itself does not exist as anything at all), and however they remain therein, they do not exist; they are equal in their primordial openness and freedom. The state of abiding in such a condition of awareness is called buddhahood. This, however, does not imply that an improvement has occurred, for one never stirs from the ultimate space-like nature. Consequently, because no deviations or obscurations occur, all the hallucinatory appearances of the three levels of existence are clearly understood as the awareness alone, which is itself groundless and rootless. As it is said in *The All-Illuminating Sphere*,

> In the one sole sphere of great perfection,
> Deviation and non-deviation are not two different things.
> Deviation is completely pure by nature.

And,

> View, meditation, action, and result—
> All these four are from the very outset
> Self-arisen primal wisdom.
> There is no deviation and no obscuration
> Occurring through the gathering of causes and conditions.

Eighth, awareness transcends the teachings of the lower vehicles and is free of their conceptual features.

> 8. In the nature of the mind, enlightened, similar to
>   space,
> There are no sides and no directions, no duality.
> Therein there is no view, no meditation,
> And no pledges to observe.
> There is in it no effortful activity;
> There are no veils obscuring primal wisdom.
> There is no training on the grounds, no path to be
>   traversed.
> There is no "subtle thing";

Since [gross and subtle] are not two,
There is no link between them.
Ascription of existence and denial are both
    transcended;
Thus there is no good or bad.
All is an expanse in which, as on a golden isle,
There is no differentiation.
The self-arisen nature of the mind,
Like space without existence,
Defies description and expression.

Ultimate, self-arisen awareness transcends the teachings of the lower vehicles. In the abyss of space, there is no up or down, no center or periphery. In just the same way, the nature of the mind, the ultimate enlightened mind—being space-like—is devoid of conceptual construction. As we find in *The All-Creating King*,

My nature is like space,
The example that applies to everything.
In pure space there's no striving;
In pure space there is nothing to be striven for.
Space is utterly beyond all action, effort, and exertion.

As Palgyi Yeshe[39] said,

Awareness, self-cognizing and spontaneously present,
Is beyond the mind.
The nature of the mind
Is space beyond both center and periphery.
It cannot be cognized by the eight consciousnesses.
Such is the nature of awareness self-arisen.

As this indicates, the space-like ultimate enlightened mind is without sides or directions, without duality or nonduality, and so on.

It is free of all conceptual characteristics and has been so from the very beginning. *The All-Creating King* says,

> Because my form is all-pervading,
> There is, from the beginning, no so-called duality.
> Since I am self-arisen primal wisdom from the very first,
> There is nothing whereby I might be confirmed.

Similarly, the ultimate enlightened mind cannot be discerned through any view. It cannot be cultivated through any kind of [contrived] meditation. It is just as *The All-Creating King* declares,

> Likewise, I, the enlightened mind, the essence and the agent
>   in all things,
> Transcend all spheres and objects of experience.
> So, from the first, there is no seeing me
> And nothing to be meditated on.

Since, as these texts imply, awareness is without any existence, when the samayas of nothing to keep are actualized,[40] the generation and perfection stages endowed with characteristics are no more. There are no conceptual samayas to be observed, no activities to be implemented with strenuous effort. There is no result; no accomplishment bestowed. Other than awareness itself, there is no "good" primordial wisdom on the one hand, and no "bad" obscurations on the other. As *The All-Creating King* declares,

> This essence is spontaneously present from the very first,
> And so there is no need for striving or accomplishment.
> Since self-arisen primal wisdom is free of obscuration,
> Awareness, self-cognizing, is not rendered luminous.

Since the nature of awareness is free of conceptual elaboration, there is [in its regard] no training on the grounds and paths. Neither is there a path on which to progress through the gradual increase of good qualities. *The All-Creating King* says,

> Since everything abides upon my level,
> There are no grounds to scale by dint of training.

Since awareness is primordially free of the subtle and the coarse, that is, an apprehender and an object to be apprehended, it cannot now be described as "a subtle thing." And since "subtle" and "coarse" have no reality, either separate or together, how could there be a relationship between them? Again, in *The All-Creating King* we find,

> Since from the first I'm free of apprehender and something
>   to be apprehended,
> The label "subtle" cannot be applied to me.

Moreover, since awareness transcends every kind of ascription or denial through the incorrect conception of its being or not being this or that, phenomena are neither good nor bad. It is for this reason that whatever arises, whatever appears, does so as the self-experience of awareness—the display of primordial wisdom. As a means of bringing us to a clear conclusion that everything is primordially pure, the state of openness and freedom, Longchenpa gives the example of an island of gold. When one goes to such a place, no ordinary earth and stones can be found, for everything is perceived as gold without any differentiation. In just the same way, all appearances remain within the expanse of the great dharmakāya without ever straying from it. They remain in the primordial expanse of dharmatā, which is devoid of such distinctions as good or bad. In other words, they remain within awareness, the self-arisen nature of the mind, which, like space, is free of all extremes. In searching for the nature of the mind, one cannot use a method that is not open and free. One cannot seek for it by accepting this and rejecting that or through a deliberate practice of view, medita-

EXTENSIVE EXPLANATION — 91

tion, action, and result. It cannot be indicated by means of examples, expressed by words, and so on. It is beyond the reach of all such things. In *Meeting the Three Kāyas*, it is said,

> Beyond extremes of birth and of destruction,
> Free of all intentioned action is the great expanse,
> Free of variation like an isle of gold.
> The root of the elimination
> Of the darkness of extremes
> Is the enlightened mind.
> Within the enlightened mind,
> The four extremes are not avoided,
> Yet it is untouched by such extremes.
> Implicitly, therefore, it's free of deviation.

Ninth, awareness is beyond causality, transcending good and evil.

> 9. Since the ultimate quintessence—
> Awareness, open, unimpeded—
> Cannot be contrived,
> It is not improved by virtue.
> It is unchangeable,
> So evil does no harm to it.
> Since there's neither action nor its fruit,
> There is no ripening of joy and sorrow.
> Since in it there is no good or bad,
> There's nothing to be taken or rejected—
> No samsara, no nirvana.
> Since there is no thought and no expression,
> Awareness is a space devoid of such elaborations.
> Since there are no past or future lives,
> A line of incarnations is but imputation.
> What birth is taken? Who is born and where?
> What action is there? What is its maturing fruit?

> Everything is similar to space.
> Think about this and reflect on it.

The fundamental nature of all things, ultimate primordial wisdom, the vajra essence of luminosity, is open, unimpeded awareness, naked dharmakāya, the emptiness of emptiness. This great primordial emptiness cannot be contrived through causes and conditions, which is why goodness—the practice of the ten white virtuous deeds—does not improve it. Empty awareness is not made better by virtue; it is a totally free and open state of primal wisdom.

In the same way, empty awareness, primordial wisdom, which is all-pervading and unimpeded like space, cannot be altered even if the three worlds were to rise against it as an enemy. Whatever black negative actions are committed, they are unable to harm awareness, for it is the ultimate, indestructible vajra. One may gain confidence in this by means of the "twelve vajra peals of laughter," which are spoken of in *The Heap of Jewels Tantra* as follows:

> *Kyé!* O Essence of the Buddhas' Speech, behold the
> view: primordial wisdom, self-arisen. How marvelous
> it is! It transcends both sin and virtue, both view and
> meditation. The ground is unchanging. Whatever acts
> may be performed of body and speech, the ground itself
> is neither helped nor harmed. Ha ha!

Likewise, because past and future lives, as well as the karmic process of cause and effect, have no existence for primordial wisdom (which dwells in the ground of dharmakāya, empty, self-cognizing awareness, primordial wisdom that is completely open and free), neither is there any ripened result of happiness and suffering. However, for those who have not realized the nature of awareness, the karmic sequence of causes and their ripening effects of joy and sorrow does indeed exist. And it will continue to exist until the cessation of dualistic perception. On the other hand, for practitioners who have realized the "ultimate exhaustion" of phenomena in the empty, primordially pure dharmatā, there is no more karmic action, no causes, and no ripening effects of happiness and suffering. *The Heap of Jewels Tantra* says,

> Behold the fundamental way of phenomena! It is marvelous: appearances do not transform and their colors do not change. Whatever happiness or suffering is felt, in fact there is no change. Ha ha!

Since there are no conceptual elaborations within the secret, unimpeded space of awareness, beyond all benefit and harm, there are no buddhas, no sentient beings, or anything else. There is neither good nor bad. There is neither adopting nor rejecting. There are no characteristics at all—whether of samsara or nirvana. When it is understood that nothing can stain or blemish the nature of awareness and that the three worlds themselves are but great primordial purity, all phenomena become an inconceivable and inexpressible expanse beyond all conceptual construction. When practitioners who have attained this realization settle in the state of awareness, then no matter what actions they perform, whether positive or negative, these same actions neither benefit nor injure them in the slightest. For these practitioners are one with awareness. *The Heap of Jewels Tantra* says,

> Even if you were to seize a sharp weapon and slay every being in a single moment, this would not affect your mindstream in the slightest. Ha ha!

For practitioners with such a level of realization, there are no past or future lives. All the appearances of a series of lives are just a question of names, no more than an imputation. These beings realize that the three worlds of samsara are in fact great, primordial purity. They are said to "churn the depths of samsara into the dharmadhātu." Indeed, when primordial purity, the state of primordial openness and freedom, is actualized, what possible birth could be taken? For all the appearances and experiences of past and future lives subside into the expanse of dharmatā. [From this point of view,] what person is there and where would that person go? For without stirring from the ground, the place of transmigration and the being who transmigrates subside nondually into the ground. And since no actions, white or black, are performed, what ripening effects of these actions can occur? Everything subsides nondually into an expanse that is like the sky—the state of primordial openness and freedom, the state of equality devoid of conceptual elaboration. This is something that one should think about and reflect on, for it is thus that one will realize the true and fundamental nature of things.

Tenth, the indivisible particle of matter and the indivisible instant of consciousness are at all times nonexistent.

> 10. Even though you may investigate with reasoning,
> Pondering, reflecting time and time again,
> The parts of things have no reality.
> For not a single particle is found.
> There is no partless instant;
> There is no object to be apprehended and no
>   apprehender.
> In this very moment, everything abides
> Within the quintessential fundamental nature.
> When examined, things have no existence.
> Likewise, when left unexamined,
> They have no existence either.
> Even on the level of conventionality,
> Since nothing can be found,
> Phenomena in all respects and always
> Are without existence.
> Understand that they resemble magical illusions,
> Lacking all reality.

It has already been explained how there is no virtue and no vice, no cause and no effect. But yet again, through repeated investigation and reflection—as when one examines the three times, past, future, and so on—nothing is found. An analysis of phenomena in the outer, inner, and intermediate spheres reveals that nothing is found apart from the dharmatā, which is beyond all conceptual construction. Outer and inner phenomena (the universe and its inhabitants) are reducible to their parts, down to the infinitesimal particles. And even these particles can be shown to be unreal. So it is that so-called causes and their effects, virtue and vice, are shown to be without the tiniest fragment of true existence. They are empty of themselves. Apart from dharmatā—aware, empty, unconditioned, and free of all conceptual elaboration—there is nothing at all.

When the indivisible instant is subjected to logical analysis, it is not found. When one examines past, present, and future time, the past has ceased, the future is yet to be born, and the present moment of mind ceases on the instant. And between all such moments, there is no time; time is not found. Even if the indivisible moment of consciousness were to be logically established [as according to the Vaibhāṣika and Sautrāntika tenet systems], the so-called causal process of virtue and nonvirtue is not found. When the object to be apprehended and the mind that apprehends are analyzed, investigated, and pondered, nothing at all exists. Everything vanishes into the expanse of dharmatā, free from conceptual elaboration, the expanse of great equality. In this very moment, it dwells within awareness, the fundamental nature, the state of quintessential luminosity—and nowhere else.

When analyzed, investigated, and pondered, phenomena are found to be nonexistent. The same is true when they are not so analyzed, investigated, and pondered. For the things that are subjected to such an analysis are primordially nonexistent. They are groundless and rootless. They are a non-referential, all-encompassing dimension of openness.

Phenomena are not only without existence on the ultimate level. Even conventionally, not even a single partless particle exists. For example, even if an illusory man appears to be acting virtuously or sinfully, the illusory man will not himself experience the ripened effect of his actions because an illusory man is not a real man. Therefore, while there is no such thing as a truly existent ripening of the causal process of virtue and nonvirtue for anyone, the yogi will not think of it even in terms of an illusion. For at all times [on both the ultimate and relative levels], the phenomena of samsara and nirvana are in every respect unreal. Because all phenomena are without true existence and are like magical illusions, they do not exist as real things. It should be understood that they are the expression of one great emptiness, the state of one great emptiness, the all-encompassing dimension of one great emptiness.

Eleventh, freedom comes from realizing the nonexistence of phenomena.

> 11. In the very moment they encounter
> Dreams and magical illusions,
> Childish beings ignorantly cling
> To their supposed existence
> And are taken in by them.
> But those who understand their nature
> Cannot be deceived thereby.
> In just the same way, those who do not know
> That things have no existence
> Cling to all such things as real,
> And caught by them, they circle in samsara.
> Yogis skilled in understanding suchness
> Resolve that things lack true existence
> In the very moment they perceive them.
> Therefore, they find freedom
> In the space of dharmatā beyond the law
> Of karmic cause and fruit.

The things seen in dreams and magical illusions are empty and have no existence, but when various illusory experiences occur, ignorant children think that they are real. They are deceived by them and

EXTENSIVE EXPLANATION — 97

cling strongly to their supposed existence. Older people, on the other hand, knowing that magical illusions are false, are not taken in by them. In the same way, even though the phenomena that appear to us are nonexistent, the ignorant do not understand that the phenomena that they clearly perceive are in fact illusory, empty forms. They do not realize that phenomena are nonexistent. They cling to their putative identity, or "self," and are deceived. They take phenomena as real. And because of their ignorance and delusion, they circle in samsara.

Skilled yogis, on the other hand, understand and realize such-ness, the fundamental nature of phenomena. They are convinced of the utter nonexistence of the things of the phenomenal world, of samsara and nirvana, which in the very moment of their being perceived, are nothing but empty forms, clearly appearing and yet illusory. It is said in *The Precious Tala Sutra*,

> All phenomena are like the *sugatas.*
> Those who have the minds of children
> Cling to them as real
> And therefore, in the various worlds,
> Experience things devoid of all existence.
> Those trained in the view, however,
> Understand the nature [of these things].

Garab Dorje said in *The Natural Subsiding of Characteristics*,

> The dharmatā, the nondual, open nature of samsaric things,
> Is not envisaged in the lower vehicles;
> But mountain goats can scale a cliff with ease—
> A feat not possible for other beasts is possible for them.

Those who have realized the dharmatā, the fundamental nature of things, have realized the nonexistence of the phenomena that make up the causal process: happiness and suffering as the ripened effect of action and so on. They have gained freedom in the fundamental nature—in the expanse of dharmatā, which is free from conceptual elaboration. Primordial wisdom stands fully revealed for them, and they can never again be deluded.

Twelfth, the essential core of nonexistence is shown.

> 12. The enlightened nature of the mind
> Is neither permanent nor discontinuous.
> It is the natural dwelling place of primal wisdom
> Devoid of apprehender and an object to be
> apprehended.
> Awareness, naked and devoid of causes and effects,
> Is the abode of that one sphere
> Wherein there is no virtue and no sin.
> Awareness, open, unimpeded, free of center and
> periphery,
> Is the natural dwelling of the wisdom mind
> Of the dharmakāya Samantabhadra.
> The essential core of nonexistence,
> Awareness, self-cognizing and enlightened,
> Is clearly revealed.
> It is completely pure and objectless,
> The primal wisdom of Victorious Ones.

Awareness—open and unimpeded, beyond the causal process of good and evil—is not permanent. For it is empty; it does not exist as anything whatsoever. But neither is it discontinuous, for it knows distinctly and illuminates all things of phenomenal existence, which are its own display. In the 119th chapter of the *Tantra That Embodies the Definitive Teaching of the Great Perfection*, we find,

> It is not discontinuous; it is luminous, aware.
> It is not permanent; it has no real existence.
> It is not two; it has no counterpart.
> It is not one; for it is all-pervading.

Any object of apprehension appearing within the fundamental nature of the mind—that is, suchness, the ultimate enlightened mind—subsides nondually within the expanse of awareness. Likewise, all the mind's cognitions and excogitations (the apprehender) naturally arise and subside therein. The object to be apprehended and the apprehender blend indivisibly in the one great state of equality. It does not happen in any other way. The apprehender and the object to be apprehended are naturally and evenly immersed in the state of self-cognizing primordial wisdom. They never fall outside this vast expanse. When extracted from the covering of thoughts of past, present, and future, awareness—naked and unclothed, devoid of the characteristics of the causal process and of effortful action—is not something that can be either enhanced by virtue or damaged by sin. It is an unimpeded, open state free of mental elaboration, a state that is unencumbered by the corners and edges of ordinary cognition and thought. The phenomena of samsara and nirvana both dwell in a nondual manner within the single expanse of awareness. As Vairotsana has said,

> Awareness, inexpressible and unimpeded—
> A thought-transcending state
> Wherein defilement of the mind is purified—
> Is indeed primordial self-arisen wisdom.
> Everything occurring there arises
> As the dharmakāya's ornament.

To remain therein without stirring is to abide in space-like, unimpeded awareness beyond zenith and nadir, beyond center and periphery. This is what [to rest within] the wisdom mind of dharmakāya Samantabhadra means. To abide naturally in this way within this fundamental dharmatā means none other than to have a decisive certainty in it. Langdro Könchok Jungne[41] said,

> There is within the mind
> An inconceivable experience,

> Naked, self-illuminating.
> It embraces all samsara and nirvana.
> It is the wisdom mind of the Victorious Ones,
> Past, present, and to come.

Although phenomena such as the karmic process—virtue and non-virtue and their ripened effects, together with their accompanying habitual tendencies—are empty and beyond all reference, they are not completely nothing, like a rabbit's horns. The essential core of [their] nonexistence is in fact awareness—the ultimate enlightened mind. And it is in the expanse of this ultimate enlightened mind that all phenomena are purified into an objectless, open, unimpeded state. It is in this same expanse that the primordially pure dharmadhātu—the wisdom mind of the Victorious Ones, past, present, and to come, transcending all the concepts and excogitations of the ordinary mind—stands fully revealed. It is as Palgyi Yeshe, one of the twenty-five disciples of Guru Rinpoche, said,

> Awareness, self-cognizing and spontaneously present,
> Is beyond the mind.
> The nature of the mind
> Is space beyond both center and periphery.
> It cannot be cognized by the eight consciousnesses.
> Such is the nature of awareness self-arisen.

Thirteenth, this is what it means to realize nonexistence.

13. In the case of yogis of illusion,
The self-experience of awareness
Arises as the ceaseless show of things without
  existence.
Such yogis are convinced that in the moment of
  appearing,
Phenomena have no existence.
They therefore do not make the slightest effort—

Accepting some, rejecting others.
With spacious minds relaxed without a care,
They rest within the state of leaving
Everything just as it is.

For yogis who have realized that phenomena are the illusion-like self-experience of awareness, whatever appears—the objects of the six consciousnesses, which are no more than awareness experiencing itself—arises in the very moment of its being perceived as the display of what does not exist. Such yogis are completely and absolutely certain that such things are without existence. Phenomena, however, are not simply a blank nothing (as when we say "there is no tea; there is no water"). Nonexistent phenomena can appear in every possible way. They arise unceasingly. And yogis simply leave the manifested display just as it is, without contrivance. They place upon [such appearances] the primordial seal [of nonexistence]. Owing to their decisive conviction that phenomena, in the very moment that they appear, are without existence, these yogis do not make any deliberate effort to accept some and reject others. They have no hope or fear in their regard; they do not affirm some and deny others. Those for whom whatever appears is simply a display of what does not exist remain within the great state of leaving everything just as it is—with minds completely spacious, carefree, and relaxed. They are immersed in awareness, self-arisen primordial wisdom. This is so for those who have realized the fundamental nature as it actually is and are therefore carefree and relaxed. By contrast, those who have no such realization and who merely say and pretend to place the seal of nonexistence on appearances—or again, those who merely wonder about the existence or nonexistence of phenomena—have fallen into the snare of mere cleverness. They do not rise above the level of ordinary beings. *The Great Garuḍa Tantra* says,

Those who fall into the trap of cleverness
Fail to pass beyond the triple world.

But those who rest
Relaxed in their perceptions, simple, uncontrived,
Dwell neither in samsara nor nirvana.

Fourteenth, the failure to realize the nonexistence of phenomena is the defect of the lower vehicles.

14. Childish beings, taken in by nonexistent things,
Resemble thirsty animals that look for water in a
mirage.
Expecting to find truth in false, mistaken theories,
They are deceived by different tenets,
Assuming their reality.
Now if this error of the common intellect,
Belonging to the gradual vehicles, eight in all,
Is not removed, the ultimate quintessence is not
seen.

Because they do not realize the fundamental nature of phenomena (that is, their nonexistence), foolish, childish beings, taken in by the illusion of an apprehender and things to be apprehended, are like the deer on the great northern plain. When the latter see a mirage, they mistake it for water and run after it tirelessly hoping to quench the thirst that torments them. It is thus that childish beings take all the conventional phenomena that they are able to apprehend as things that truly exist. They cling strongly to mistaken theories and expect them to express the fundamental nature. So it is that they are deceived by the eight lower vehicles, assuming that they are really true. Afflicted in this way, they are unable to attain the true and ultimate fundamental nature of phenomena.

The error of the ordinary mind consists in adhering strongly—as though to the final truth—to the intellectually contrived doctrines of view, meditation, action, and result, propounded in the eight successive vehicles. If this error is not eliminated, it is impossible to realize the fundamental nature, the ultimate quintessence, the genuine, uncontrived view of the resultant doctrine of Atiyoga. Longchenpa says in his autocommentary,

> In this regard, the personal self refers to the thought processes of the ordinary mind, which automatically assume the reality of the object and the subject of apprehension and of attachment and aversion. The phenomenal self is a reification of what does not exist. It also includes the powerful, impure adherence to the view, meditation, action, and result of various doctrines intellectually devised and taken to be the final truth.

Fifteenth, nonexistence is shown to be the actual nature.

> 15. Atiyoga is the ultimate expanse,
> Transcending every category.
> There is nothing whatsoever—just a space-like
>   nature.
> In this very instant there is not the slightest
>   movement
> From the fundamental stratum of the dharmakāya.
> When you rest in the primordial expanse,
> The natural great bliss is present of itself.

Atiyoga, the Great Perfection, transcends all categories: existence and nonexistence, duality and nonduality, permanence and discontinuity, being or not being something, sameness and difference, and so on. It is the great, all-pervading, ultimate expanse of equality, empty and aware. Within it, there is nothing whatsoever—neither cause nor effect, neither virtue nor nonvirtue, neither acceptance nor rejection. The Great Perfection has the nature of space. As it is said in *The Heap of Jewels Tantra*,

> Here, there's neither out nor in,
> No place to look, above, below.

> In all the cardinal and intermediate directions,
> There is not the slightest thing that anyone may grasp.

And,

> Therein is nothing done
> And nothing is perfected there.
> It is beyond to stay or not to stay;
> To come or not to come.
> It dwells in great primordial, empty suchness.

If one remains, never parting, in the space-like dharmadhātu, then in this very instant one does not move from the fundamental stratum of the dharmakāya. This fundamental stratum must be understood in terms of resting in great primordial purity, the primal, ultimate expanse. In other words, if one dwells in the state of self-arisen primordial wisdom, which does not exist as any thing, and is the state of empty but luminous spontaneous presence, one merges inseparably with the fundamental stratum of the dharmakāya. And when one settles in this expanse, without stirring from it, this state is described as resting in the primordially empty dharmatā, the primal, ultimate expanse. *The Heap of Jewels Tantra* says,

> You do not settle now, but from the first
> You rest in the foundation that was ever thus—
> Those who take this for their dwelling place
> Are lauded secretly by all the buddhas.

And,

> This is the abode of the nonabiding primal wisdom
> Of primordial buddha from the very first.

So it is that one should remain in this primordial expanse: the fundamental stratum of the dharmakāya. If now one leaves self-cognizing awareness in its natural state without contrivance—if one rests in the state of natural great bliss—duality and nonduality will automatically coalesce into a single taste, as when one pours water into water.

Sixteenth, buddhahood cannot be attained through a process of fabrication.

> 16. If awareness, wisdom's secret state,
> You do not realize,
> You will not find freedom
> Through the virtuous deeds that you may fabricate.
> Don't you understand?
> Conditioned things all pass,
> Are destined to disintegrate.
> How could this tight knot
> Of body, speech, and mind
> Come into contact with
> The ultimate and indestructible quintessence?

The profound, secret state of dharmakāya wisdom—in other words, self-cognizing awareness—is beyond the range of intellectual examination and of effortful practice. It must be realized directly. One can never be freed through fabricated virtue—through the deliberate efforts of thought, word, and deed and by means of the purification of obscurations. Haven't we understood, Longchenpa asks us, that conditioned things are impermanent and momentary—like pillars and pots—and subject to disintegration? This is something that we must understand. On the other hand, awareness, the secret state of wisdom, is not something fabricated by causes and conditions, whereas all virtue is a product of physical, verbal, and mental construction. "Fabricated" is the contrary of "unfabricated." If something is fabricated, it is necessarily "destructible." If it is unfabricated, it is beyond the conventional distinction of destructible and indestructible.

Now, if the three spheres (of subject, object, and action) are considered to be truly existent, whatever positive actions of body, speech, and mind are performed, they will only give a temporary result: the happiness of the divine and human realms. The state of dharmakāya, freedom from samsaric existence, will not be achieved. Moreover, all compounded or conditioned virtue, produced through the efforts of body, speech, and mind, is a tight knot whereby awareness, the dharmakāya, is fettered. How could it possibly attain to the indestructible luminous quintessence, which is beyond birth and death and, like space, free of every obscuration? It is completely impossible. As it is said in *The All-Creating King*,

> Even all unerring thoughts are powerless to produce it.
> Owing to the knot that tightly binds both word and deed,
> It's very hard to reach the dharmatā.

Seventeenth, we are admonished not to stir from the fundamental stratum of nonexistence.

> 17. So if you wish to realize
> The sublime fundamental nature of phenomena,
> Leave aside all things that are like childish games,
> That fetter and exhaust you
> In your body, speech, and mind.
> The state of nonexistence, the expanse devoid
> Of mind's activity, is the nature of phenomena.
> It is the dharmatā, the dwelling place
> Of natural great perfection.
> Within this all-pervading state devoid of action,
> Which goes beyond all thoughts,
> Behold the great and uncontrived equality.
> Decisive certainty will come that it transcends
> Causality and striving.

If therefore one wishes to nurture one's experience of the supreme fundamental nature as expounded in the luminous Great Perfection and if one wishes to seize the kingdom of the dharmakāya in this very life, [one should understand] that all actions of adopting and rejecting and every kind of effortful striving—such as the performance of virtue and the refraining from negative deeds of body, speech, and mind—achieve nothing but one's own exhaustion and fatigue. These indeed are the things that hamper awareness. Like the silkworm imprisoning itself with its own saliva, all action of the three doors, performed in the hope of actualizing awareness, the state beyond all such deliberate action, succeeds only in binding awareness and fails to assist it in any way. It is like sweeping the debris on the ground in the hope of clearing the sky of clouds. The activities and efforts of the three doors are never ending, and the fatigue that they produce is all to no avail. They are just like the games that children play. One should abandon them completely.

Phenomena are by their very nature nonexistent. They are an expanse of emptiness devoid of mental activity; they are beyond the law of cause and effect. They are beyond acceptance and rejection, beyond effortful action and thought. One should be like an old person sitting comfortably in the sun, leaving things to themselves just as they are. One should rest in the great bliss of the dharmatā, the state of the natural great perfection.

When one rests in this way, in the knowledge that self-arisen awareness in its present immediacy is beyond deliberate action and thought, one will, in that space-like all-pervading state, behold the uncontrived, natural, and intrinsic equality of samsara and nirvana. A certainty will arise from within that this self-arisen awareness transcends causality and is beyond all activity and effort.

Eighteenth, the explanation of the key points of the nonexistence of phenomena is brought to a conclusion.

> 18. In awareness, there's no outer object to be apprehended;
> There's no inner apprehending subject.
> In awareness, there is neither time nor place.
> Awareness is beyond phenomena that arise and cease.
> It is pure like space—

No vehicles can guide you to it.
All thoughts about it are mistaken,
For they invest phenomena with an identity.
Cast away this ground for deviation and obscuring
　　veils.
Be convinced that everything without distinction
Has the nature of Samantabhadra,
The great and all-pervading state of emptiness.
Keep to the state of dharmatā
Beyond all change and movement.
By doing this you soar amid the sky-like spaces of
　　the view,
The primordial expanse that rests in no extreme.
All the key points of the nonexistence of phenomena
Are herein set forth.

No matter how apprehender and objects to be apprehended—
the inner and outer phenomena of the universe and beings (samsara
and nirvana)—may appear, the fact is that in the very moment of
their appearance, they are but the empty forms of the mind's subjective experience. They are completely without existence. Their
nature is self-arisen awareness, which is beyond both time and
location.

As it is said in *The Six Expanses*,

There is no dwelling place; there is not even emptiness.
There are no skillful means, nor any audience of hearers.
There are no objects and no present, past, or future.

Awareness transcends all phenomena that arise and cease. It is pure
like the sky, limpidly clear, and devoid of center and circumference.
Therefore, one cannot be led to it by means of [the teachings of]
the provisional vehicles. In this context, not even the names of the
various tenet systems are found. As it is said, "No assertions are
there, and no tenet systems."

Deluded thoughts fail to realize this ultimate way of being of things just as it is and take for an existent thing that which is without existence, investing it with an identity. This is the basis and foundation of all deviation and obscuration. Casting all such thoughts away in the unborn, ultimate expanse, which is empty but aware, one should be utterly convinced that the universe and beings, samsara and nirvana, are undifferentiated in terms of purity and impurity and that they never stir from the dharmadhātu, the mind of dharmakāya Samantabhadra, the expanse of all-pervading emptiness. If one keeps within this very place and if one rests with utter assurance in the dharmatā (awareness beyond all mental activity, beyond any movement and change), Longchenpa says that one "will soar in the sky-like spaces of the view," the expanse of the great primordial emptiness that does not dwell in any extreme. There arises a decisive conviction that all appearances are empty, that they are nonexistent phenomena. And the key points of their nonexistence are all revealed in the fact that in their condition of clear appearances they are groundless and rootless.

3. Section Two: The Key Points of Nonexistence Are Essentialized

This consists of seven stanzas. First, awareness evenly pervades the state of nonexistence.

> 19. The key points of the nonexistence
> Of phenomena are thus revealed.
> Subsequently, in the state that's free of meditation,
> Where all is left alone and uncontrived, just as it is,
> A state without acceptance or rejection of whatever
>   happens,
> These same points are essentialized within
>   awareness:
> The equality, the evenness of the vast expanse of
>   mind.

The key points of the nonexistence of the phenomena of samsara and nirvana, the universe and beings, have been revealed in the preceding stanzas. One should now understand that everything that arises, everything that appears, is—in the very moment of its being perceived—groundless and rootless. And one should relax in a state that is free of thought, free of meditation, free of any care, without altering or manipulating anything, without accepting or rejecting anything. One should leave everything just as it is. It is important to essentialize the key points of nonexistence as being the single expanse of awareness—open, unimpeded, and empty.

It is thus that—without accepting some appearances and rejecting others—one essentializes the key points of the nonexistence of all appearances in the fact that they are awareness alone, the state of equality. It is then that both appearances and the mind blend into one—the great expanse of the mind's equality and evenness. Everything remains evenly in the vast expanse of equality. It is said in *The Great Garuḍa Tantra*,

> The ground of utter openness and freedom,
> Free from the first of all specific features,
> Effortlessly cancels, in a way that's free of action,
> The sticking point that is the ordinary mind.
> Regarding objects of the three encounters—
> The key to this display is not to push away whatever may
>   appear
> But to bind the objects and the mind as one.

Second, the natural, spontaneously present meditative absorption is set forth.

20. Natural great bliss,
The vajra space that's indestructible,
Is supreme absorption that is present of itself
Without the need for cultivating it.

It is there at all times like a flowing river.
If you stay in evenness, within a state
That's free of all contrivance,
It clearly and naturally manifests.

When the three doors of body, speech, and mind are left relaxed in an uncontrived state, the primordial wisdom of natural great bliss, the indestructible vajra space symbolized by the seven qualities of a vajra, appears.[42] This is the object of meditation. It is awareness as the ultimate nature,[43] dharmatā, the genuine condition of all phenomena. It is the mother-like ground luminosity. Awareness, which is great indwelling primordial wisdom, is spontaneously present from the very beginning without the need for cultivating it. The supreme meditative absorption of greatly blissful self-cognizing awareness is at all times present and does not arise anew through deliberate effort and practice. It may be exemplified by a flowing river and is consequently said to be the "continuous river-like concentration free of meditation."

The "meditator" is the path luminosity [of the yogi]. It is awareness as cognitive potency.[44] It is the childlike luminosity. When it rests evenly in the great natural state free of all contrivance, its [luminous] character becomes clearly, spontaneously manifest. And the meditator—namely, awareness as cognitive potency—attains the object of meditation, the state of awareness as ultimate nature. It is said that these two luminosities, mother and child, must mingle together indivisibly. As we find in *The All-Illuminating Sphere*,

> Meditation and non-meditation—these conventionalities—
> Are completely cleansed, and nondual bliss abides within
>   one's nature.
> Effortlessly resting there, one never parts from it.
> It is unbroken like the Ganges river.

Third, natural meditative absorption is essentialized as the absence of deviation and obscuration.

21. When you settle properly in space-like dharmatā,
There is no change or movement.
Therefore, there's no wandering and no absence of
    the same.
This ultimate expanse, supreme and infinite,
Is inseparably present in all things.
It is not some sphere that words can indicate.
Those whose wisdom has burst forth,
Those for whom awareness comes unprompted,
Those whose minds are unencumbered,
Even though they have engaged in study—
Yogis who experience the ineffable and inconceivable—
Are completely certain that this state
Transcends both indication and non-indication.
They find neither meditation
Nor anything on which to meditate.
And thus they need not slay
The foes of lethargy and agitation.

When awareness, which does not stir from its fundamental stratum, is seen, and when one settles in it correctly, the natural meditative absorption of space-like ultimate reality is discovered. At that moment, whatever arises does so without ever changing or moving from the fundamental stratum of meditative absorption. This occurs, moreover, without any kind of deliberate focusing. Thus, there is neither distraction nor the absence of distraction, neither arising nor the absence of arising. When something arises, the mind is luminous. When there is stillness, the mind is concentrated. Calm abiding and deep insight are united. There is no need to banish lethargy, agitation, or any other deviation or obscuration with respect to meditative absorption. For they are all automatically purified right where they stand. Whatever is seen is inseparable from the great expanse of primordial purity, and the infinite, supreme ultimate space is now revealed. This is something beyond the power of words to describe; it is beyond the learning and explanations of scholars, trained as they are in conventional language.

On the contrary, this is the domain of those for whom the wisdom that beholds the actual and ultimate nature of things bursts forth from within, thanks to a karmic fortune based on training in their past lives. Or again, it is the sphere of fortunate disciples who are introduced to self-arisen awareness through the blessings of the realized masters who are their teachers. Or again, it is the domain of those who have attained to the furthest limit of a vast erudition regarding the ultimate quintessence, who are now released from all mental fixation and analysis, and who have minds that are free of hope and fear. In brief, yogis who have experience of the ineffable and inconceivable are completely certain that this state is wholly beyond indication and non-indication, whether through symbol, meaning, or sign. They find neither meditation nor an object on which to meditate. It is as Shabkar[45] says,

> What cannot be meditated on
> Transcends meditation: meditation brings you trouble.
> What you cannot watch transcends the view,
> For what is there to watch?

So it is that such practitioners have no need to slay the enemies of dullness, lethargy, and drowsiness or of the agitation of proliferating thoughts. Arising and subsiding within the expanse of awareness, thoughts naturally vanish. As it is said in the text *The Direct Immediacy of Awareness*,

> Those who have great learning and whose minds are yet
>   untrammeled,
> Those who have a wisdom that has burst forth from within,
> Those in whom awareness has spontaneously arisen—
> All such yogis who have realization in the space of the
>   ineffable . . .

Since this citation resembles Longchenpa's root text, one might suppose that Longchenpa has simply copied it. This is not so, however. Similar cases can be found elsewhere. For example, the homage that we find in *The Root Stanzas of the Middle Way* also figures in *The Ratnakūṭa Sutra*, and the lines in *The Treasury of Abhidharma* that begin "to have a physical body like that of a previous existence" can be found in *The All-Illuminating Sphere Tantra*. Moreover, in Haribhadra's short commentary [on the *Prajñāpāramitā in Eight Thousand Lines*] called *The Clear Meaning*, the lines that begin with "Alas, different scriptural traditions" are also found in the *Illumination of the Prajñāpāramitā in Twenty Thousand Lines*, the commentary by Vimuktasena. Such texts, which are said to be harmonious both in meaning and word, inspire confidence regarding certain profound topics and are therefore used as textual embellishments.

Fourth, it is demonstrated that all things dwell constantly in the expanse of the dharmakāya.

> 22. Appearances and mind
> Are free and open from the outset—
> Nonexistence is their essence.
> Hallucinatory appearances
> Have as their natural state
> The vast expanse of evenness, the dharmatā.
> They constantly subsist within the dharmakāya,
> Seamlessly arising and subsiding,
> Remaining in the one expanse of bliss.
> Arising, they arise spontaneously,
> Keeping their own nature.
> Remaining, they remain spontaneously,
> Keeping their own nature.
> Subsiding, they subside spontaneously,
> Keeping their own nature.
> They arise, remain, subside
> Within the vast expanse of dharmatā.

They come from nowhere else,
Being simply the display of dharmakāya.
They are the empty forms
Of the self-experience of awareness.
They are not different from each other;
They are neither good nor bad,
Abiding in their ultimate quintessence.

Appearances (the object) and the cognitive activity of the mind (the subject) are both open and free from the very beginning. They dwell within great emptiness, which is the fundamental nature that does not exist as anything at all and is their ultimate quintessence. All the hallucinatory appearances that are now occurring arise, abide, and subside, spontaneously and uninterruptedly within the natural spaciousness of awareness, the vast expanse of the equality of the dharmatā. They subsist within the dharmakāya and never stir from it. All appearances that arise within the vast expanse of awareness subside therein. And primordially subsiding [meaning that they are primordially free and open], they arise.[46] The arising and subsiding of these appearances form a seamless process. They are encompassed by ultimate space, the vast expanse of great bliss.

When appearances arise, they arise naturally within the expanse of awareness. And even as they are arising—without ever stirring from the expanse of awareness—they necessarily keep their own nature. Similarly, even as they abide—since appearances abide within the expanse of awareness without stirring from it—they necessarily keep their own nature. Finally, even as they subside— since they spontaneously subside within the expanse of awareness, without stirring from it—they inevitably do so while keeping their own nature. All this is illustrated by examples of the reflections in a mirror, the stars and planets in the sky, and the waves on the ocean. Although they seem to arise [as something separate] from their respective grounds—the mirror, the sky, the ocean—in fact, they arise, subsist, and subside within these same grounds of their appearance. Regardless of the form in which they occur (reflections, stars, or waves), they never stir from their respective grounds as things that are separate from them. Consequently and in a similar fashion, appearances have no existence beyond the ground of their appearing. As it is said in *Meeting the Three Kāyas*,

> However it may rest, it rests within its nature.
> However it may move, it moves within its nature.
> By nature, in the enlightened mind,
> There is no going and no coming.

All appearances arise, dwell, and subside within the expanse of ultimate reality, that is, awareness. These three aspects—arising, dwelling, and subsiding—all partake of a state of openness and freedom. They arise as the creative power of awareness within the expanse of ultimate reality. Without arising or moving from anywhere else, they simply manifest as the display of the creative power of the dharmakāya.

The arising, dwelling, and subsiding of outer appearances within the expanse of awareness seem to be distinct from each other yet never stir from the empty ground. Likewise, although the factors of arising, dwelling, and subsiding of mental states within the expanse of awareness also seem to be distinct from each other, one should nevertheless be certain that they never stir from the ground, the expanse of awareness itself. All appearances are but the self-experience of awareness. They occur within the expanse of awareness, and their arising and subsiding are seamless. Just like reflections in a mirror, they arise as the empty forms of the self-experience of awareness. Within the expanse of ultimate reality or awareness, appearances are neither good nor bad to the slightest degree. This corresponds to their fundamental nature, their innate condition. Once it is understood that they abide in their ultimate quintessence, one inevitably comes to the conclusion that they are but the single expanse of awareness. This constitutes the fourth essentialized key point.

Fifth, the meeting between appearances and the mind leaves no trace.

> 23. Whatever may arise, whatever may appear,
> Whatever states of movement or of stillness may
>   occur—
> Five poisons and the rest,
> Arising from awareness's creative power—
> When their nature is detected in their moment of
>   arising,
> These same displayed appearances arrive at their
>   exhaustion.
> They vanish without leaving any trace.
> When the mind perceives its objects,
> The key point is to leave all as it is
> In its equality.
> The key point is to leave all without trace—
> Just like the flight path of a bird—
> Within primordial wisdom, self-arisen.
> The key point is that all things
> And the ultimate expanse are one,
> Like water and its waves.
> All things are, from the very first, essentialized
> Within this one key point of the great secret.
> Simply knowing this brings freedom,
> For it is simply the nature of phenomena.

The appearing and arising of every state of thought proliferation— that is to say, the inner mental experiences of the five senses making contact with the five outer objects occurring within the expanse of awareness (as well as all perceptions, pure or impure, such as the five poisons or defilements) together with the state of mental stillness—all proceed from the creative power of awareness. If one recognizes their nature in the very moment that they arise in relation to an object and if one maintains the recognition that these same appearances are of the nature of the creative power of awareness, they come to exhaustion in the ground. They subside within it; they vanish without leaving any trace.

More specifically, the mind projects and withdraws whatever thoughts arise regarding objects as they variously appear. But, if, in that very moment, one leaves whatever arises as it is without contrivance and if one leaves the mind spacious and relaxed in regard to it—if, in other words, one essentializes the key point concerning the arising [of appearances] as being the state of equality that is awareness—one will lay hold of the fundamental stratum of the dharmakāya.

Just as birds leave no trace as they fly through the sky, whatever appearances, pure or impure (belonging to the subjective experience of the mind) arise, the key point about them is that they are essentialized as the expanse of self-arisen primordial wisdom, wherein they are groundless and rootless. Whatever phenomena of samsara or nirvana occur within the expanse of awareness, they are one with that same expanse and have no existence otherwise. It is just as with the waves that arise in the ocean—the key point about them is that they are at one with the water of the ocean and have no existence otherwise. In short, all things belonging to phenomenal existence, to samsara and nirvana, are primordially essentialized in the key point of the great, secret, all-penetrating expanse. And this occurs through the recognition of their nature and the exhaustion of these displayed appearances, which vanish without trace. The simple understanding of this key point brings freedom, for it corresponds to the very nature of things.

Sixth, phenomena are essentialized as being the vast expanse of awareness.

> 24. Constantly within the great expanse,
> Awareness, self-cognizing,
> All arises equal and as equal dwells.
> All is equal in subsiding, neither good nor bad.

There's nothing that's not equal to awareness,
Nothing that does not abide
And nothing that does not subside therein.
All things are essentialized
As being the immense primordial expanse
Of the enlightened state.

The arising, remaining, and disintegration of the universe and beings, as well as the ensuing period of voidness, all occur within the expanse of space. The universe and the beings that it contains never diverge from the vast abyss of space. Similarly, for a yogi who succeeds in essentializing both samsara and nirvana as being the one expanse of awareness, the phenomena of samsara and nirvana at all times arise equal, remain equal, and subside equal with the ground, the vast expanse of self-cognizing awareness. In fact, without being either good or bad in the slightest way, they are merely the expression of the one awareness, they are the state of the one awareness, they are the display of the one awareness. Other than this, there is not a single thing that is not equal to awareness and that does not abide or subside within it. Therefore, all phenomena, whether of samsara or nirvana, are essentialized as being the ultimate enlightened mind: the vast, primordially empty expanse that is like space. It is important to understand that phenomena never move from empty, open, and unimpeded awareness. As it is said in *The Direct Immediacy of Awareness*,

When they arise, they arise as equal;
They are neither good nor bad.
When they remain, they remain as equal;
They are neither good nor bad.
When they subside, they subside as equal;
They are neither good nor bad.
Although they may arise unequal,
They arise from the vast space of equality.
Although they may abide unequal,

They abide within the vast space of equality.
Although they may subside unequal,
They subside within the vast space of equality.

Seventh, awareness transcends causality.

> 25. Within awareness, uncreated and spontaneously
>   present,
> The view of the immense and natural state
> Arises without effort.
> The key point of the enlightened mind,
> Which lies beyond the causal law,
> Transcending sin and virtue,
> Is essentialized as the unchanging dharmatā.

When one remains in meditative equipoise within the ultimate expanse of spontaneously present awareness that has not been created with effort (through a process of cause and effect), the view of the natural state, vast and even, arises without any need for it to be produced through the effortful contrivance of a focused mind that adopts or rejects. When this is actualized through the occurrence of an inner experience, yogis should remain in it. Similarly, the most important point is to essentialize all phenomena as awareness (the enlightened mind that lies beyond the causal law, transcending sin and virtue)—in other words, as the unchanging dharmatā, the single sphere of great equality.

Once again, when the very essence of all phenomena—awareness, the enlightened mind that transcends the impurity[47] of the causal law and the practice of meditation and diligent effort—is realized, this same awareness is indeed found to be beyond causality, all effort, and all striving. As we find in *The All-Creating King*,

> I, the all-creator, am beyond the causal law.
> Beyond the causal law, I am beyond the field of action.

All-transcending dharmatā is the enlightened mind.
The enlightened mind is the essence of all things.

3. Section Three: All Phenomena Are Subsumed in the State of Nonexistence

This consists of seven stanzas. First, all phenomena are subsumed in primordial emptiness, which is pure from the beginning.

> 26. Nonexistence, which is space-like in its nature,
> Subsumes within it everything without exception.
> Just as space subsumes the world and its
>   inhabitants,
> Phenomena, the experience of the ordinary mind,
> Are all subsumed in great primordial emptiness.

Nonexistence, space-like in its nature, must be understood in terms of the mind of all the enlightened ones. It is the great equality of the dharmadhātu, the one expanse of Samantabhadra, uncontrived awareness, the state of space-like equality. Within this expanse, the great pristine state of emptiness, all phenomena of samsara and nirvana are subsumed without exception. It is just the same with the vast abyss of space in which all the phenomena of the universe and its inhabitants are subsumed without merging, without being confused or destroyed. Likewise, it should be understood that all phenomena, the appearances that constitute the subjective experience of the ordinary mind—such as the five outer sense objects and all mental cognitions as these arise and subside—are subsumed in primordial emptiness, the great wisdom mind of Samantabhadra. It is said in *The Six Expanses*,

> All phenomena, however many they may be,
> If briefly told, are but the dharmatā.
> All are but the mind of me, Samantabhadra.

Second, the fact that the causal process of samsara and nirvana is transcended is also subsumed in the nonexistence of phenomena.

> 27. Samsara is a mere name.
> It is beyond the causal process,
> Beyond all effort and all undertaking.
> Good and evil neither help nor harm;
> They are the state of emptiness.
> Liberation too is just a name,
> And there is no nirvana.
> There's nothing to be gained or worked for
> By means of the ten elements.

In terms of the fundamental nature as set forth in the Natural Great Perfection, samsaric existence is no more than a name. In truth, it is beyond the causal process as well as any kind of effortful undertaking. Indeed, in the space-like fundamental nature, the all-pervading dharmadhātu, which transcends the karmic law of good and evil, virtue brings no benefit and evil does no harm. For they never stray from wakeful, open, and unimpeded emptiness, which is beyond the causal process of good and bad.

In the same way, even liberation is no more than a name, and the phenomena of nirvana have no existence. This is why they cannot be achieved by striving in the ten elements of tantra as set forth in Mahāyoga, the first of the three inner tantras of the Secret Mantra. These ten items are: the view, samaya, empowerment, mandala, the grounds and paths, activities, primordial wisdom, result, dharmatā, and so on.[48] These constitute a great method of teaching and training, but to understand that they are without existence is the extraordinary view of the path of the Great Perfection. As it is said in *The All-Creating King*,

> In ultimate reality, the space-like nature of the mind,
> There is no view to meditate and no samaya to observe.

There's no activity in which to strive, no wisdom that has
been obscured.
There is no training on the grounds, no paths on which to
travel.

Third, it is shown that the ultimate result comes without the
need of action.

28. Constantly to strive in what can only bring fatigue
Is to be like children building castles in the sand.
All is destined to collapse. All causes and effects,
All virtue and nonvirtue, and all striving and
exertion—
Things are from the outset all subsumed in
nonexistence.

However much one may strive and persevere in what can only bring
exhaustion to one's body, speech, and mind, all one's efforts are
futile. To act in this way is to be like children who are excited and
happy building castles in the sand and cry when they fall down.
All samsaric phenomena, produced by causes and conditions, are
impermanent and liable to destruction. They do not transcend the
four conditions.[49] The view and meditation that belong to systems
relying on mental concentration, as well as the conceptual mind
itself, do not even come close to the profound view of the Natural
Great Perfection, which is beyond deliberate action, effort, and
intellect.

Knowing, therefore, that cause and effect, virtue and sin,
and everything contrived with persevering effort are actually
nonexistent—like space, which is beyond the scope of action—one
should understand that all the phenomena of samsara and nirvana
are subsumed, from the very first, in the state of nonexistence. They
are beyond the qualifications of bondage and freedom. As it is said
in *The Great Garuḍa,*

No need to strive with speech, reciting mantra.
No need to use your hands in making mudras.
When the mind is without movement,
Projecting or withdrawing,
When it stays within its nature,
The unmoving state is present of itself.

Fourth, the law of cause and effect and effortful action are subsumed in nonexistence.

29. Yogis of the quintessential Atiyoga
Should be convinced that teachings based upon causality,
Designed to guide the simple,
Constitute the way for those of lesser fortune,
Who progress upon the upward path in stages.
They should subsume the nature of their mind,
Transcending all phenomena,
Into the space-like absence of all action.

This stanza demonstrates the actual ultimate result, the state that is free of action. Yogis who have realized the view of the Great Perfection, the quintessential Atiyoga, which is devoid of deliberate action and effort, know for certain that the teachings on the karmic law of cause and effect, which imply a practice based on effort, have been set forth in order to guide simple childish beings of lesser mental capacity to the path of the higher vehicles. All teachings that presuppose the law of cause and effect set forth a gradual path beginning with the lowest level. They are expounded simply as skillful means that cause beings to progress from the lower to the higher vehicles. Practitioners should be convinced that this is the path of beings of lesser fortune, ridding themselves of all misconceptions on that account. As we find in Ngari Paṇḍita,

As long as there's no ending to the operations of the mind,
The vehicles of teachings are inconceivable and endless.

For they are resting places,
Signposts on the pathway of the one and only journey,
And they bring forth ever higher fruits.

And Longchenpa has said,

> It is as the text tells us, "Things performed in play when one is young are wearisome when one is old." Likewise, the eight lower vehicles are designed for those of lesser mental scope. By contrast, for those of greater capacity there are the quintessential teachings of Ati, which speak of the exhaustion of phenomena in their natural state.

When yogis come to the conclusion that all the teachings on cause and effect, which imply action and effort, partake of the space-like fundamental nature that is beyond all deliberate action, they should subsume (assimilate) awareness, the nature of their mind, which transcends phenomena like action and effort, into the state of nonaction similar to space. Such is the character of the actual view of nonaction according to Atiyoga, which itself transcends all effort and any kind of practice conceived in terms of cause and effect. A person who practices in this way is a yogi of nonaction. As we find in *The All-Creating King*,

> In me the relative is, from the first, exhausted.
> It is exhausted from the outset.
> Thus there is no need to meditate upon the view.
> From the outset it is pure,
> And thus there is no need to keep samaya.
> From the outset all abides in the enlightened state;
> There is thus no need to train
> On the ten grounds and levels of vidyādharas.

Fifth, action is shown to be misleading.

30. Beings are misled by action—
Look at the deceptive seemings of samsara.
Beings are affected by their efforts;
Think of the turning wheel of suffering.
From sin and virtue comes a ceaseless
Stream of pain and happiness.
Through their actions, beings wander
In samsara high and low.
No occasion do they have to flee
The ocean of existence.

From beginningless time until the present moment, beings fail to realize that awareness is beyond deliberate action, bondage and freedom, and are consequently misled by the various exertions of word and deed, as well as by the mental activities of adopting, rejecting, and so on. "Look!" the root verse says. We roam constantly through the various, hallucinatory appearances, or seemings, of samsara. As *The Great Garuḍa* says,

Tangled in the trammels of your clever mind, ·
You will not go beyond the triple world.

All efforts, pure or impure, positive or negative, produce strong effects. For their result is to enter the turning wheel of sorrow in infernal destinies among the famished spirits, beasts, and so forth. One should think well upon the endless ripened effects of action—those that have been, are, and will be experienced. Through the belief in the intrinsic reality of virtue and nonvirtue (the impure causes), there occur the uninterrupted experiences of happiness and sorrow (the ripened effect of such causes). Through the performance of positive action, beings attain the mere happiness of the divine and human states, and when their karma is exhausted, they fall again into the lower destinies. The performance of negative action leads to birth in the lower states, and turning and turning therein, beings have no occasion to achieve freedom. In short, they are deceived by conditioned phenomena. Longchenpa says that owing to actions good or bad, beings wander respectively through the higher and lower regions of samsara, the end result of which, he says, is that they have no chance of escaping the ocean of existence. On this topic *The All-Creating King* says,

> If unmoving rest in evenness,
> The greatest of all cures, is not applied,
> Even causes for the higher realms will be defiled.
> Forever one will wander in samsara,
> Never finding stainless peace.

One should therefore discard all such effortful activities and capture the stronghold of the state of nonaction similar to space. This is the most important—indeed the supreme—key point.

Sixth, the absence of deliberate action is subsumed within the state of dharmakāya.

> 31. If you break the stream of virtue and nonvirtue
> And dwell within the dharmatā and never part
>   from it,
> You are a yogi of the ultimate great secret.
> Free of effort and of striving, you will reach
> The primal ground and take the royal seat
> Of ever-present dharmakāya.

As it was explained above, when one understands that every kind of striving to adopt virtue and reject evil is a darkness that hides the face of awareness (the dharmatā) and when one remains completely immersed in awareness, ineffable, luminous, empty, and utterly devoid of virtue and nonvirtue, the stream of positive and negative actions and, indeed, all striving therein is cut. One dwells in dharmatā, pure, space-like awareness, the mind of all the buddhas past, present, and to come—the great equality of all-pervading dharma-dhātu. One does not part—one is inseparable—from it. As it is said in *The Heap of Jewels Tantra,*

> The groundless, rootless dharmatā—
> How wonderful to settle in it without striving!

Fortunate practitioners who are able to accomplish the state of nonaction similar to space are yogis of the ultimate great secret. For all beings throughout the three levels of existence, they are an object of veneration. Having realized that phenomena are like space, beyond all conceptual construction, such yogis progress through the grounds and paths without effort or travail and come at last to the level of the supreme kingdom of dharmakāya Samanta-bhadra, the ever-present primordial lord. For it is in the royal palace of the effortless, ever-present dharmakāya that they attain the ever-lasting dominion of primordial purity free of action—the inner luminosity that is absorbed within but not obscured, the fundamental stratum that is the "ever youthful body enclosed within a vase." As *The All-Creating King* tells us,

> However things appear, in suchness they are one.
> Let no one meddle with this fact.
> In the kingly state of uncontrived equality,
> There dwells the dharmakāya, the state beyond conception.

Seventh, the preceding stanzas are brought to a conclusion.

32. In the very moment things appear,
They are beyond all misconception
And all language that expresses name and meaning.
All acts and all exertion based on cause and its result,
Adoption of the good, rejection of the bad—
All are nonexistent things
And nonexistent actions, just like space.

Whoever knows this has subsumed
All things within the state of nonexistence.

The foregoing passages have explained in detail the fact that phenomena have the character of space beyond all action. So it is that whatever appears in the expanse of the aware but empty dharmadhātu, the space-like freedom from all conceptual construction—be it the impure appearances of samsara (the aggregates, the elements, and sense fields) or the pure phenomena of nirvana (the ground, the path, and the result)—is, in the very moment of its appearance, beyond all possible misconceptions of existence or nonexistence, identity or distinction, emptiness or non-emptiness. It is beyond the language that expresses such things in terms of word and meaning. Activities and exertion with respect to the causal process of adopting what is positive and rejecting what is negative and so on have never existed. It is just as when the reflection of the moon appears in the water. From the very moment that it does so, there is never any [real] moon present there. So it is that when one is certain that in the very moment that phenomena appear, they are without existence within the expanse of awareness, and when one understands or rather realizes that such phenomena are simply a space-like state beyond all conceptual construction and action, one will have subsumed all the phenomena of samsara and nirvana within the state of nonexistence. As we find in *The All-Creating King*,

> The buddhas of the ancient past—
> Even they sought nothing other than their minds.
> Suchness they did not contrive;
> They did not cultivate conceptual concentration.

3. Section Four: A Clear Conviction Is Gained That Phenomena Are without Existence

When the certainty that all phenomena are without intrinsic being arises in one's mind, one comes to a clear conviction that they have no existence. This section consists of eight stanzas. First, one reaches the clear conviction that none of the ontological extremes can be upheld.

> 33. The clear conviction that phenomena are
>   nonexistent
> Is reached essentially as follows.
> Because phenomenal existence,
> All things in samsara and nirvana,
> Is without intrinsic being,
> It transcends the status of existence.
> Since it is unceasing in the way that it appears,
> It transcends the state of nonexistence.
> Not existent and not nonexistent,
> It transcends the state of being both.
> Not being both,
> It goes beyond the state of being neither.
> Being neither both nor neither,
> Its ultimate quintessence
> Is beyond all thought and word,
> Beyond all indication.

Even though all the phenomena of samsara and nirvana, arising within the expanse of awareness, appear unceasingly, clearly, and distinctly, they do not in fact exist in the slightest way separate from awareness. There are numerous ways of arriving at the conviction that this is so—numerous ways of determining it clearly and definitively. In the present text, however, all these methods are condensed into one essential point, which is as follows.

When the nature of all the phenomena of samsara and nirvana, which have arisen within awareness, is established with reasoning based on the nature of things, it is understood that however such phenomena appear, they do not have—in the very moment that they are perceived—the slightest fragment of intrinsic being. This is why phenomena—distorted through the belief in the phenomenal self—are said to transcend existence, meaning that they are without intrinsic being.

It might be thought that if such appearances are without intrinsic being, they must be [utterly nonexistent] like the rabbit's horns. But this is not so. Since the appearing mode of phenomena is ceaselessly and vividly present in the expanse of awareness (in the same way that reflections arise in a mirror), these same phenomena are said to transcend nonexistence as well.

It might be thought that if they are not existent and not nonexistent, they are perhaps simultaneously existent and nonexistent. But since it has been demonstrated separately that phenomena are neither existent, on the one hand, nor nonexistent, on the other, it stands to reason that they transcend the state of being both [existent and nonexistent].

If phenomenal appearances cannot be established as being both existent and nonexistent at once, one may perhaps wonder whether they can be established as being neither existent nor nonexistent. But since it has been shown that they cannot be established as being both existent and nonexistent at once, it follows that they are also beyond the contrary position of being neither existent nor nonexistent. For example, if one cannot say that the mountain is over there, there is no sense in saying that it is over here.

Accordingly, when one realizes that phenomena are beyond the four extremes—existence, nonexistence, both, and neither—one has no words to describe their fundamental nature, their ultimate quintessence, namely, awareness free of conceptual construction. No expression is able to designate this nature. It is beyond all ontological extremes—beyond word, thought, and expression. With this realization, one truly becomes the king of supreme mind beyond the mind. As it is said in *Awareness Self-Arisen*,

> They are not simply nonexistent,
> And they're not existent either.
> Transcending nonexistence and existence,
> They do not come into the minds of realized yogis.

Second, because phenomena, in truth, transcend apprehension and fixation, a clear conviction is reached that those who apprehend their [nonexistent] characteristics are proper objects of compassion.

> 34. The nature of phenomena is primordially pure,
> But childish beings, ignorant of this,
> Adopt some things, and others they reject.
> Clinging to their various views, they're permanently
>   fettered.
> Clinging to the features they perceive, how pained
>   they are!
> Clinging to a self in what is nonexistent, how they
>   are deluded!
> Clinging to the aspects of the aspectless, how they
>   tire themselves!
> Drifting in samsara constantly, how pitiful they are!

As has been said previously, suchness, the fundamental nature of phenomena, is primordially pure, beyond the reach of action, of taking and rejecting. But beings who do not recognize this and have a strong inclination to adopt and reject things on the basis of their own dualistic perceptions are ignorant of their fundamental nature. Because of their inferior karmic fortune, they engage in the paths of the eight lower vehicles. These foolish, childish beings cling to the self, that is, inherent existence, and to the characteristics of things, and thus they are attached to the views of different doctrines and tenet systems. Their eyes are blind to the truth of suchness, and they are constantly hampered by their deluded clinging to the reality of phenomena.

Enthralled by their perception of existence in what is not existent, they fixate and grasp at things as being endowed with characteristics. How afflicted and deluded they are! Although the endless appearances of phenomena are groundless and rootless, beings are ignorant of this fact. They are consequently enslaved by [their powerful tendency] to apprehend a self in what has no existence. How deluded and confused they are! Although the dharmatā, the primordially pure fundamental nature of things, cannot be analyzed into various aspects, beings are ignorant of this, and clinging to systems of categorization, they analyze and fixate on all-pervading awareness. How exhausted they must be! Beings wander through samsara constantly, as though turning on a waterwheel. Alas, how pitiful they are!

Third, a clear conviction is reached that [awareness] is beyond the causal structure of virtue and nonvirtue.

> 35. The sun of ultimate reality, awareness, self-arisen,
> Is covered by white clouds of virtue
> And black clouds of sin.
> It is overwhelmed by lightning bolts:
> Passionate endeavor in adopting and rejecting.
> Beings thus are drenched in pouring rains,
> The false appearances of happiness and sorrow.
> These bring samsara's seeds to ripeness
> As the crop of six migrations.
> Beings are tormented, and how pitiful they are!

In summertime, rain clouds form in the sky and block the light of the sun. Nevertheless, it is thanks to the rainy season that various plants start to sprout in the fields, eventually producing their crop. In similar fashion, the two karmic obscurations of white and black actions are produced by deluded beings who strive with their body, speech, and mind and contrive "white" actions, which appear to bring benefit, and negative or "black" actions, which seem to do harm. Inasmuch as these black and white actions both hinder the actualization of self-arisen primordial wisdom—namely, awareness—they are not in any way different. This is what is meant when it is said that both sin and virtue obscure in equal measure.

Sunlike self-arisen awareness—namely, ultimate primordial wisdom—dwells naturally within the minds of the entire infinity of beings. Yet it is veiled by the white clouds of positive actions and the black clouds of negative actions (the causes). The lightning flashes of passionate endeavor in adopting and rejecting happiness and sorrow (the results of such causes) constantly overwhelm the sun of awareness. And as beings engage with increasing avidity in both wholesome and unwholesome deeds, the various hallucinatory experiences of happiness and suffering fall on them like an endless rain. Seeds are thus planted in the regions of samsara, and these ripen into a limitless crop, the joys and sorrows of the six worlds of deluded beings, who wander aimlessly through the immense field of samsaric torment. Just consider this! Alas for poor beings, constantly afflicted by the three kinds of suffering in the lower and higher destinies through their deluded adoption and rejection, through their virtue and misdeeds! They fail to recognize the very face of awareness, which is beyond such good and evil, beyond both cause and effect. See how they are deluded and how pitiful they are! The pivotal key point is therefore to actualize awareness beyond good and evil, beyond the principle of karmic cause and fruit—the radiance or expression of the great state of nonaction—and to be clearly convinced of it.

Fourth, one is admonished to come to a clear conviction concerning the law of cause and effect.

> 36. Just as ropes and golden chains bind equally,
> Virtuous and unvirtuous states
> Bind equally the ultimate, definitive quintessence.
> Clouds, black and white, enshroud the sky in equal
>   measure.
> Likewise, virtue and nonvirtue equally obscure
>   awareness.
> It is crucial thus to understand
> That yogis who have realized suchness
> See beyond the causal law of virtue and of sin.

In truth, open, unimpeded awareness in its present immediacy, free of all conceptual elaboration, is not something that can be either helped by virtue or marred by nonvirtue. Consequently, it is unsullied and cannot be indicated by any means. Primordial wisdom—which gives rise to profound certainty regarding the secret key point of the realization of the ultimate nature of phenomena—is like the very essence or heart of the sun. This wisdom should not be fettered by any kind of action, effort, or mental fixation. For if it is, it will be fettered equally by both sin and virtue, because the latter is equally binding and obscuring. To tie up a stallion with a golden chain or an ordinary rope comes to the same thing: the horse is tethered either way. Likewise, awareness is fettered as much by positive, virtuous states of mind as by negative, unvirtuous states. For both prevent it from manifesting. It is just the same as with the clouds, which, white or black, block the light of the sun equally. Both virtue and nonvirtue, generated on the basis of grasping and exertion, equally conceal self-cognizing primordial wisdom. This is why the most important pith instruction states that yogis who realize suchness, the fundamental nature—self-cognizing primordial wisdom just as it is—must preserve the natural state of awareness that lies beyond the causal processes of good and evil. The two examples given here refer to the fact that all chains are equally binding and all clouds are equally obscuring.

Fifth, a clear conviction is reached concerning the ultimate quintessence.

> 37. Self-arisen wisdom wells up from within.
> The dark night of causality is scattered.
> The massing clouds of good and evil melt away.
> The sun of ultimate luminosity
> Shines in the sky of dharmadhātu—
> You gain a clear and final certainty.
> You come to this conviction
> Without need of the ten elements.
> All the causal vehicles are surpassed thereby.

As soon as self-arisen primordial wisdom—which dwells in the ground of the dharmakāya and is like the sun—manifests from within, it dissipates all activity and striving based on the belief in the causal law, which is by contrast like the dark of night. Phenomena classified in terms of evil and virtue, causes and effects, or adoption and rejection—all of which are like obscuring clouds—simply disappear and are no more. As a result, the sun of ultimate self-arisen luminosity appears in the vast expanse of the dharma-dhātu, which is like the sky free of the three impurities.[50] This is the dharmatā. When this is realized, one acquires a clear and final certainty. A definite conclusion about the key point of nonexistence, previously explained, is effortlessly attained without striving in the practice of the ten elements of tantra. This brings into focus the extraordinary feature of the present path. The vehicle of Ati-yoga, which transcends the causal law and is beyond all action and striving, is the resultant vehicle superior to the eight lower vehicles, which appeal to causes and results. As it is said in *The All-Creating King*,

> Adepts of the causal and resultant vehicles
> Strive in me with the ten elements of tantra,
> Wishing thus to see me and my nature.
> It is like stepping out into thin air
> And falling down to earth.

And,

> My nature is like space,
> The example that applies to everything.
> In pure space, there's no striving
> And there's nothing to be sought.
> Space transcends all action, effort, and exertion.

Sixth, a clear conviction is reached that all cognitive acts are the pure self-experience of awareness.

38. You reach a clear conviction
That awareness—self-cognizing, open, unimpeded,
Free of all appearance,
Beyond all concentrated meditation on an object,
Devoid of all conceptual construction—
Is the state wherein phenomena are all exhausted.
They are all exhausted in awareness.
Awareness, too, as a phenomenon,
Itself comes to exhaustion.
"Exhaustion," "non-exhaustion"—
Yogis understand them both to be unreal.
They are convinced beyond all doubt
That things transcend existence, nonexistence,
Definition, and expression.
Without a point of reference, thinking "It is this,"
Yogis are enveloped in an all-pervading vastness.
For them phenomena are all exhausted,
The ordinary mind is passed beyond.
And for such yogis what a joy this is,
A joy that is a seamless state of dharmatā!
In this, the yogis of the past, the future,
And the present time are merged
With the single ultimate expanse of wisdom mind.
The realization of such yogis equals
That of buddhas and vidyādharas.

When the level of the exhaustion of phenomena in a state beyond the ordinary mind is reached, the hallucinatory perceptions of conventional phenomena no longer occur. This is a state beyond any kind of meditation involving focused concentration on an object. A state is attained that is as free of meditative objects as it is of a meditating mind. It is the realization of an open, unimpeded state of self-cognizing awareness free of mental elaboration, the naked state wherein phenomena are exhausted. It is the fundamental stratum of the dharmakāya.

One reaches a clear conviction that in this expanse, all hallucinatory phenomenal appearances come without exception to the original, primitive state of exhaustion, that is, the great primordial purity. This is where phenomena reach their final state. They are exhausted in the dharmatā, their ultimate condition—a state in which even the word *phenomenon*, being exhausted, has no existence. Indeed, phenomenon (*dharma*) and the nature of phenomena (*dharmatā*) are not even nominally distinguished as being either exhausted or not exhausted. One comes to a clear conviction that all things are a state of great equality beyond conceptual elaboration.

Yogis are thus convinced from the depths of their being. They realize that phenomenal appearances are beyond existence and nonexistence, beyond definition and something to be defined, and beyond expression and a meaning to be expressed. For them, notions like "They are this; they are not that" dissolve into a state that is without reference, in which the utterly open and free condition of primordial purity is laid bare. They are enveloped in primordial purity, a state of awareness that knows no limit and falls to no extreme. They are immersed, as in one taste, within the all-pervading immensity of the dharmatā. They have reached the level of the exhaustion of phenomena in their final condition, the ultimate level in which there is no more training and no further progress. These yogis are in a state beyond the ordinary mind, a state that is free and relaxed, beyond limit and extreme. Thus they are at ease and, as Longchenpa says, "What a joy this is!" The great joy that dwells primordially in the ultimate expanse of dharmatā has been made manifest. It is said in the tantra *The Lion's Perfect Power,*

> The dharmakāya lies beyond the limits of existence and of
> nonexistence.
> This alone is buddhahood, exceeding every measurement.
> The dharmakāya is beyond the dualistic clinging to "it is"
> and "it is not."
> Beyond fixated thought, awareness self-cognizing is great
> bliss.

And in the tantra called *The Supreme Array of Studded Jewels*, we find,

> The supreme mandala is beyond all seeing and all thought.
> How blissful is the mind that understands this teaching of
> the Great Perfection!

When the state of the exhaustion of phenomena beyond the ordinary mind is made manifest—a state of bare, unimpeded awareness, free of all delimitation and extreme—a great joy wells up. And in this state of joy, the dharmatā realized by the great yogis of the past, present, and future merges inseparably with the great dharmadhātu experienced by all the buddhas of the three times in a single ultimate expanse. Because it is the expression of the one dharmatā, because it is the state of the one dharmatā, and because it is the all-encompassing dimension of the one dharmatā, the range of these yogis' experience seamlessly coincides with the utterly pure sphere of the experience of the vidyādharas and the buddhas.

Seventh, a clear conviction is reached to the effect that phenomena are beyond names. They are a state of great emptiness.

> 39. This same expanse, unchanging,
> Unconditioned, indivisible,
> Is the space of self-arisen primal wisdom
> That transcends all effort and all striving.
> It is the same expanse wherein phenomena
> Transcend mere names,
> All thought and all expression.
> In this dimension of Samantabhadra,
> Which is free of action,
> Everything that there appears
> Is nothing but Samantabhadra's vast expanse.
> And in Samantabhadra's ultimate expanse
> There are no appearances; there's no emptiness;
> There is neither good nor bad.

> When what does not exist is taken as existent,
> Identifying labels are affixed
> To what is but a false hallucination.
> But even as the labeling takes place,
> There's no hallucination and no absence of the same.
> A clear conviction thus is reached
> That phenomena transcend all names.
> Such is the fundamental nature
> Of the natural great perfection.

The ultimate enlightened mind is referred to as an indestructible vajra, because it is endowed with the latter's seven unchanging qualities. It is primordial wisdom, imperishable and indestructible. To describe it, as the root verse does, as "unchanging, unconditioned, and indivisible" implies that it is devoid of all movement and change. The fundamental nature, self-arisen primordial wisdom, is not something contrived through action. Therefore, when the root text says that this expanse is not produced through effort and striving and is beyond the reach of the mind, the sense is that it is not something that is brought about through effort and practice. When it is said that all phenomena in both samsara and nirvana are but names and nothing more, this means that they are beyond the eight conceptual extremes and therefore that they constitute an expanse that transcends thought and expression and is beyond all conceptual construction. Within the immense abyss of the wisdom mind of Samantabhadra, which is free of all action like the nine activities,[51] whatever appears—be it samsara or nirvana, good, bad, and so on— is none other than the vast expanse of Samantabhadra. As it is said,

> Within Samantabhadra's vast expanse
> There is nothing that's not perfect.
> All is equal, all beyond both good and bad.

In the expanse of Samantabhadra, therefore, there is no difference between appearance and emptiness, good and bad, and so on. All is but the one Samantabhadra. Other than this, not even the names of buddhas and beings, relative and ultimate, or awareness and ignorance are to be found. As it is said in *The Mirror of Samantabhadra's Mind*,

> Since there is no ultimate,
> There is not even any name for relative.
> Since there's no awareness,
> There is not even any name for ignorance.
> Since there are no buddhas,
> There is not even any name for beings.
> Since there are no teachings,
> There is not even any name for teacher.

Awareness, the precious enlightened mind, is without movement or change. It is beyond effort and striving, beyond thought, expression, and classification. However, because one takes for existent what is not existent, chains of deluded thoughts constantly proliferate. One is powerfully caught up in such hallucinations, and applying different names to self and other and all sense objects, one apprehends them all as distinct things. As a result, one is deluded with regard to each and every entity. Nevertheless, the truth is that in the very moment that the labeling of phenomena occurs, there is no difference between the states of hallucination and the absence of hallucination. They are of equal status. As it is said in *The Mirror of Samantabhadra's Mind*,

> Since there are no buddhas,
> There is not even any name for them.
> Since there is no clinging,
> There is not even any name for beings.
> Since there are no thoughts,
> There is no ignorance; there's no delusion.
> Since there's no fixation, no assumption,
> There is not even a discursive mind.

Therefore, the phenomena of samsara and nirvana are neither existent nor nonexistent, neither identical nor different, neither things nor nonthings, neither permanent nor discontinuous. They have no reality even on the nominal level. Thus one comes to a clear conviction that they are all a vast expanse of equality beyond all conceptual construction. This is the unmistaken fundamental nature, the natural great perfection. One reaches a clear certainty of mind that they are a great emptiness beyond all naming.

Eighth, the preceding stanzas are brought to a conclusion.

> 40. Thus you're clearly certain that all things
> Within phenomenal existence, samsara and nirvana,
> Are neither hallucinations nor are they not
> hallucinations,
> And that nirvana is not gained by shunning of samsara.
> You are certain that phenomena are neither born
> nor unborn.
> All the objects that you clung to—origin, cessation,
> Existence, nonexistence—all are now transcended.
> Convinced that things are neither pure nor impure,
> You see them as a space of evenness,
> As neither good, to be adopted,
> Nor as bad, to be rejected.
> You reach a clear conviction that all things
> Are within Samantabhadra's vast expanse.

In truth, awareness, the enlightened mind, is changeless and unmoving throughout the continuity of the three times. It is free of the characteristics of samsara and nirvana. It is the complete subsiding of all conceptual construction. Because the phenomena of samsara and nirvana arising within the expanse of awareness are all the display of this same awareness, they are subsumed within it—they are pervaded by it and have no existence apart from it. Seeing this, one acquires a clear certainty that hallucination and non-hallucination do not have even a nominal existence. So it is that what we call nirvana (the absence of delusion) is not something to be achieved through the rejection of something called samsara (the deluded state). Samsara and nirvana are beyond adoption and rejection. As it is said in *The Tantra without Letters*,

> Concerning the view of self-arisen primordial wisdom, there is no object of discernment. There never was such an object in the past and neither will there be such an object in the future. In the present, there is no appearance at all. There is no such thing as karma, there are no habitual tendencies, there is no ignorance, there is no mind, there is no mental consciousness, there is no wisdom, there is no samsara, there is no nirvana, and there is not even awareness itself.

And, in like manner, since phenomena (which are without origin and cessation, without the characteristics of going and coming) are beyond conceptual construction, one comes to a clear certainty that they cannot be characterized chronologically by statements such as "Things are being born in the present" or "They were not born in the past" or "They will be born in the future." Phenomena therefore transcend all objects of reference and clinging, such as origin and cessation, existence and nonexistence. They are the all-pervading, aware, and empty state of equality beyond mental elaboration. As Karma Lingpa has said,

> Things are unborn by their very nature.
> They do not stay, they do not cease,
> They neither come nor go.
> Free of reference, free of features, they exceed all thought
>   and word.

Thus one acquires a clear certainty that all phenomena arisen from the expanse of awareness—whether pure deities and buddha fields or the impure hallucinations of samsara—all subsist without distinction in the expanse of great nondual equality. They partake of an all-pervading evenness. They are neither good nor bad, neither to be adopted nor rejected. Everything in phenomenal existence, samsara and nirvana, is equal in the dharmakāya, the expanse of the wisdom mind of Samantabhadra. To be utterly convinced of this is the supreme key point.

A Concluding Statement of the Vajra Topic's Name

Here ends the word commentary on the first vajra topic of *The Precious Treasury of the Fundamental Nature*, which establishes that phenomena are in every way inexpressible.

2. THE SECOND VAJRA TOPIC: EVENNESS

This topic demonstrates that phenomena are unconfined and do not fall into any extreme. The teaching itself, which concludes with a statement of the vajra topic's name, has four sections: the key points are revealed, they are essentialized, they are subsumed, and a clear conviction is reached in their regard.

3. Section One: The Key Points Are Revealed

4. A Brief Explanation

> When the fundamental nature of phenomena—
> Their nonexistence—is correctly grasped,
> The nature of their evenness is understood.
> According to the precepts of the Atiyoga,
> Summit of all vehicles,
> Samantabhadra's vast and spacious mind,
> The greatest of the great,
> Is like the sky, beyond both center and
>   circumference.
> It has the character of unbroken great equality.

As these words imply, when the fundamental nature of things, in other words, their nonexistence, is properly grasped, the nature of their evenness—their uninterrupted equality—will be understood. According to the ultimate teachings—the view of Atiyoga, the very summit of the nine vehicles—the mind of dharmakāya Samantabhadra is the vast expanse of the dharmadhātu. It is like the sky, unconfined and beyond all extremes. It is free of center and circumference. Within the vast and spacious mind of Samantabhadra, the greatest of the great—that is, within the expanse of open, unimpeded, uninterrupted equality—the infinite appearances of phenomena are indivisible and of one taste. As it is said in *The Natural Subsiding of Characteristics*,

> The Atiyoga teachings are the peak
> Of all the other vehicles.
> Like Sumeru, they are the supreme summit,
> The greatest of the great.
> Samantabhadra's space-like mind.
> By their strength, these teachings overwhelm
> The eight preceding vehicles.

The Tantra of the Six Expanses also says,

> The nature of the mind cannot be spoken of;
> Words appear, but nothing do they say.
> It is beyond the reach of thought and of expression—
> This is what I, Samantabhadra, teach.

4. A Detailed Explanation

There now follows a detailed explanation presented in eight stanzas. First, the nature of evenness is revealed.

1. The fundamental nature, as it is,
Of things belonging to phenomenal existence

> And of the enlightened mind devoid of form
> Is never parted from the state
> Of freedom from conceptual construction.
> Here there is no center, no periphery, no thought—
> Its evenness subsists
> Within a vast, uninterrupted state.

The fundamental nature—just as it is—of phenomenal existence, whether of samsara and nirvana, or of the ultimate enlightened mind devoid of form, never stirs from the dharmatā, the state of equality, the evenness that is free of all conceptual construction. This evenness is devoid of center and circumference and cannot be encompassed by thought and word. Generally speaking, therefore, phenomena, in the very moment of their emergence, are unconfined and do not fall into any extreme. The *ground* is therefore evenness, equality itself. And likewise, now, in meditation, since there is no conceptual reference and fixation, the *path* too is evenness, equality itself. Finally, since there is neither the hope of attaining nor the fear of not attaining the result (the four kāyas, the five wisdoms, and so on) and since there is neither movement nor change, the *result* too is the state of equality itself. *The Six Consciousnesses Overwhelmed* has this to say:

> Samsara, nirvana, and all vehicles are overwhelmed.
> Freedom from intentioned action—this one thing
>   dominates them all.
> Nothing lies outside its scope—there's nowhere one
>   might go
> Beyond the one space of nonaction.

Therefore, the key point is that one should first understand that nothing has ever moved from the nature of evenness (the single state of unbroken equality free of conceptual construction) and that one should then rest within this state, remaining in it firmly.

Second, it is shown that the object to be apprehended and the apprehender are even, without distinction, similar to space.

> 2. All things that appear as objects of the senses,
> In the instant of appearing,
> Are free of substance, free of parts—
> A state of infinite and all-embracing evenness.
> Neither can the mind, awareness, self-cognizing,
> Be divided into instants, earlier and later.
> It is a space-like state
> Of infinite and all-embracing evenness.
> The past is gone, the future not yet born.
> The present moment does not stay.
> All is groundless in the enlightened mind,
> All is rootless, without substance,
> Beyond the reach of indication.
> By nature it's a state of utter evenness,
> The vast immensity of space.

Phenomena that appear in the outer world as objects of the senses are, in the very first moment of their being perceived, the forms of emptiness. They do not exist on the level of particles or as part-possessing entities. They are without substance and directional parts. Throughout the sequence of the three times, they are empty, a state of infinite, all-embracing, space-like evenness. It is said in *The All-Illuminating Sphere*,

> There are no objects.
> The apprehender and the object to be apprehended—
> Both are utter purity.
> Awareness, self-cognizing,
> Dwells in its own radiance.
> And space, by nature pure, is permeated
> With the utter space of dharmatā.

Phenomena are unconfined. They are a limitless and inconceivable state of evenness. Consequently, the object, the ordinary mind itself, and their common ground (awareness) are a state of evenness, equality.

Likewise, since awareness, the ultimate enlightened mind, cannot be divided into past and future, whatever arises is empty of the indivisible instants of consciousness; it too is a state of evenness. The unceasing display of manifold appearance also partakes of this same state. And the knowing mind is also a state of infinite, all-embracing, space-like evenness.

Past cognitions have ceased. In their state of nonexistence, they are an infinite all-embracing evenness, a state of equality. Future cognitions are not yet born. Therefore, they too are nonexistent and are also an infinite all-embracing evenness, a state of equality. Present cognitions are beyond the reach of word, thought, and expression. They have no dwelling place. Within the ultimate enlightened mind, they partake of infinite, all-embracing evenness, the state of equality. Both the objects and agents of knowledge are groundless and rootless; they have no substantial entity. They cannot be indicated by means of words and definitions. Every appearing object is an empty form; every cognizing subject is awareness—self-arisen and empty. Objects and subjects both arise within the expanse of one self-arisen wisdom. In this sense, they are not differentiated but are utterly even in their nature. Within that state, which is like the vast immensity of space, they partake of an infinite, all-embracing evenness, an infinite equality. As it is said in *The All-Illuminating Sphere,*

> Within the ultimate expanse of dharmatā,
> The sun of self-cognizing primal wisdom dawns.
> It reveals all things impartially.

Third, it is shown that in the state of evenness there is neither action nor effort.

3. In the ultimate quintessence free of all extremes,
Not falling to one side or to another,
No view is found and no empowerment,
No mandala, no mantra recitation.
There are no grounds, no paths, and no samaya;
There is no training and no progress on the path.
All are groundless. In the vast space [of awareness],
They are an endless, all-embracing state of evenness.
They all subsist in dharmatā, the enlightened mind.

Awareness—luminous and empty, free of center and circumference, seamless and even—is the fundamental nature. It is a state of great equality, free of all extremes. It falls neither to one side nor another and is beyond all conceptual definition. In this ultimate quintessence there is no view, no empowerment, no mandala, and no mantra recitation. There is neither path nor samaya; there is neither training nor progress. In the same way, there are no activities, there is no resultant wisdom, there is no dharmatā, and so on. No effortful striving in these ten elements of tantra is found within this state. The actualization of great equality devoid of all conceptual construction constitutes the actual view of the ultimate mode of being, the fundamental nature, of the Great Perfection.

As it is said in *The All-Creating King*,

In ultimate reality, the space-like nature of the mind,
There is no view to meditate and no samaya to observe.
There's no activity in which to strive,
No obscuration veiling primal wisdom.
There is no training on the grounds and paths,
No path to be traversed.

The ten elements of tantric practice are all groundless and rootless. Within the spacious expanse of all-pervading awareness, free of effort and striving, they are all an infinite, all-embracing state of evenness. And this uninterrupted evenness is the dharmatā beyond benefit and harm—the enlightened mind itself. All the phenomena of samsara and nirvana subsist and are equal in its vast expanse. This is the supreme key point of great and uninterrupted evenness.

Fourth, it is shown that spontaneously present appearances are, in their evenness, naturally pure.

> 4. Inasmuch as it is understood that all things,
> In whichever way that they appear,
> Are by their nature without origin,
> Without abiding or cessation,
> They are all spontaneously present.
> They are not existent and not nonexistent;
> They are beyond the reach of all conceptual fixation.
> They are completely pure, and in the dharmatā,
> The great perfection,
> They are an endless, all-embracing evenness.

All phenomena that appear as extramental objects are understood[52] as being—by their nature and from the very beginning—without origin. Just as water is wet, pervaded by humidity, all appearing things are unborn, pervaded by an absence of origin. It is just as when the form of the moon appears in a lake: the reflected moon is not something other than the water. And when a rainbow appears in the sky, it is not something other than the sky itself. In the same way, although phenomena all arise from the expanse of unborn awareness, it is understood that they remain within this same expanse. Not even an atom of them is found elsewhere. And the natural character of awareness is neither existent nor nonexistent, neither permanent nor discontinuous. It subsists within the state of the absence of origin and conceptual construction. And yet, all phenomena are spontaneously, distinctly, and unceasingly present within it.

In *The Instantaneous Severance of the Three Times* it is said,

All is gathered into one, the single ultimate expanse,
The single thing unborn, the dharmadhātu unoriginate.
Appearances that are born within the unborn ultimate
    expanse
Are without limit in indefinite variety.

Since the phenomena that appear as sense objects are neither existent nor nonexistent, they are—from the point of view of the cognitive subject, the mind—beyond conceptual fixation; they are inconceivable and inexpressible. So it is that phenomena have the nature of the one, utterly pure dharmatā. Appearing, they are empty; being empty, they appear. Their nature is the inseparability of appearance and emptiness. From the very beginning, they rest evenly and equally in the fundamental nature, the natural great perfection.

    Fifth, it is shown that the naturally luminous [dharmatā] is a great evenness.

> 5. Awareness, the enlightened mind,
> Ultimate and quintessential,
> Is not seen in the extremes;
> It is beyond distinctive features.
> Words and logic do not serve to prove it.
> It is beyond the reach of symbols.
> It has neither growth nor diminution.
> It is neither permanent nor discontinuous.
> It neither comes nor goes.
> Within the vast expanse of its spontaneous equality,
> All is utterly immaculate—
> An unbroken evenness
> Devoid of limitation and of falling to one side.

Awareness, great emptiness, the ultimate enlightened mind, which pervades samsara and nirvana, is the ultimate quintessence, the

naturally luminous dharmatā. It is devoid of substantiality; it is
without defining features and is beyond ontological extremes.
Being free of all extremes, it is not found therein and cannot be
an object of reference. One cannot fix on it, saying "It is this." It is
free of the distinctive features of an effortful meditative practice.
It is free of thought, free of expression, and free of all mental elaboration. For this reason, it is not something that can be proven
through clever scholarship, through evidence and arguments,
through the words and specificity of logical demonstration. Ever-
dwelling, lucent, and limpid awareness is beyond the indication of
symbol and example. It is beyond both object and agent of knowledge. It cannot be found in a view that is eternalist or nihilist, in a
meditation that may either develop or diminish, or in a result that
is considered either to come or to go. For all these things are completely empty and dwell primordially in an infinite, all-embracing
evenness, the state of equality that is like the vast abyss of space. All
appearances arise within awareness, the state of Samantabhadra.
They are the display of its unceasing radiance and are utterly pure
in the immense expanse of spontaneous equality. When this is
realized, both samsara and nirvana and all arising, dwelling, and
subsiding become undifferentiated within the expanse of great
emptiness, the dharmakāya Samantabhadra. The key point is to
relax in a great and uninterrupted evenness—the state of equality
free from all limitation and all falling to one side or another.

Sixth, it is shown that self-arisen primordial wisdom is the great
state of evenness.

> 6. There is neither hope nor fear
> Regarding the bestowal of wisdom.
> Thus, no matter what arises,
> All is but unbroken, endless, all-embracing
>   evenness.
> In seamless, self-arising, unimpeded openness,
> There is never any risk of being caught
> Within the cage of clinging.

It is impossible to alter or spoil primordial wisdom, which is all-pervading like space. One can therefore rest free from any hope and fear: the hope that the profound wisdom of the teachers of the three lineages of transmission might be transferred into one's mind, and fear that it might not be so transmitted. For primordial wisdom is self-arisen; it dwells in great evenness. Whatever arises within the expanse of awareness is an uninterrupted, infinite, all-embracing evenness. It is empty, open, and unimpeded: the state of equality. As it is said in *Meeting the Three Kāyas*,

> However one reflects, one reflects within one's nature.
> However one may think, one thinks within one's nature.
> The enlightened mind is, from the first,
> Devoid of all reflection and mentation.
> The mind of the Victorious Ones,
> Past, present, and to come,
> Is free from thinking and reflection.

Whatever arises in awareness arises and subsides seamlessly all by itself. This self-arising, which self-subsides in an open, unimpeded expanse that is free of reference, is described as the seamless evenness of arising and subsiding. It is like the ocean's waves that arise and sink back naturally, like the fish that leap out of the ocean but cannot leap utterly beyond it.

It is said in *The All-Illuminating Sphere*,

> In the sea of self-arisen primal wisdom,
> The movement of discursive thought
> Is like the movement of the golden fishes in the sea.

When it is understood that whatever arises is the creative power of awareness and when all that arises seamlessly subsides, there is never any risk of getting trapped in the cage of clinging and fixation. And the realization of uninterrupted evenness—that is, the state of equality where everything arises and subsides seamlessly—will come. It is therefore of the utmost importance that one remains relaxed in an unbroken evenness.

Seventh, it is shown that evenness means the state of the exhaustion of phenomena.

> 7. All phenomena sink back
> Into the state of evenness.
> Their nature is beyond the frontiers
> Of adoption and rejection.
> Just as the universe and its inhabitants
> Are empty in the vast immensity of space,
> Adoption and rejection, craving and aversion,
> All dissolve in the primordial expanse.
> Nowhere else do they depart.
> When thoughts that leave no trace behind
> Become the state of infinite and all-embracing evenness
> Within awareness seamless and unbroken,
> The frontier of one's clinging
> To both hope and fear is crossed.
> The tethering peg—the object to be apprehended
> And the apprehender—is torn out.
> The city of samsara's false appearances is emptied.

Just as clouds appear, remain, and finally fade back into the southern sky, all phenomena arise within the expanse of awareness; they dwell within awareness and at length sink back into it. If this is recognized, the mind and all mental factors of adopting and rejecting, attachment and aversion revert back to their source, the vast expanse of awareness. Delusion is cleared away in primordial purity. This is what the pith instructions say. Delusion vanishes into a state of evenness, which is empty in and of itself and is devoid of all distinction. It is said in *The Natural Subsiding of Characteristics*,

> Because their causes have sunk back
> Into the single sphere [of dharmakāya],

Hopes and fears concerning the result are cut
And there is just a state that's similar to space—
The sky-like spacious mind of the Victorious Ones.
And in the vast space of this one and only sphere,
There is nothing to eliminate and nothing to obtain.
All things subside within their very nature—
There is neither realization nor the absence of the same.

As this text describes, all things that manifest return to their source, the expanse of awareness. This is the same as saying that they subside into what is their own nature. Being by nature the great state of openness and freedom that is awareness, they transcend the boundaries of adoption and rejection. They vanish into the state of exhaustion, the state of evenness. All the phenomena of the world and its inhabitants manifest within the bosom of space. They do not exist, however, in any ultimate sense. From the very beginning, they subsist, empty, within that same expanse. In the same way, all the phenomena imputed by the mind, which manifest in terms of adoption and rejection, attachment and aversion, dissolve into the expanse of awareness, their primordial ground of manifestation. Whatever cognitive states arise, they vanish without a trace in the expanse of self-arisen awareness. To be sure, there is no other destination for them, no other place where they might go. So it is that all acts of cognition are traceless like the flight paths of birds. In the reaches of uninterrupted awareness devoid of all conceptual construction, they themselves are an infinite all-embracing evenness, the state of equality. They subside in awareness, which transcends all the limitations of hope and fear, in the state of wakeful, all-embracing evenness. It is then that the object to be apprehended and the apprehender are uprooted like a peg torn from the earth. Their entire structure fades away into empty space. Their nature of evenness free of reference is made manifest, and the city of the hallucinatory appearances of samsara is emptied. Then it is that one comes to reign in the kingdom of dharmakāya, free of all delusion.

Eighth, the preceding key points are brought to a conclusion.

> 8. All apparent extramental things,
> Together with all inner mental states,
> Are manifested as the play
> Of mind's creative power.
> Those who understand that everything
> Is from the outset emptiness and evenness
> Reveal the key point of phenomena:
> They are all even.

Phenomena do not extend beyond the reach of awareness and its creative power. All phenomena belonging, for example, to the six gatherings of consciousness—which appear in the aspect of outer, extramental things—arise through the creative power of awareness. And the inner [ordinary] mind itself arises from the mind's unborn nature. The way in which all these manifest belongs to the mind's power of display. It is essential to understand that phenomena are primordially empty and even. No matter how the phenomena of samsara and nirvana manifest, they are in truth none other than the creative power and display of the space-like expanse of awareness, the ultimate enlightened mind. Those who realize that all such things are beyond every delimitation and extreme—that they dwell in the evenness of their primordially empty nature, the dharmatā—reveal the key point of phenomenal existence, namely, that it is a state of evenness. And this single crucial point brings together hundreds of key points related to the appearance of phenomena (apprehensible objects and apprehending mind), revealing that they are the great freedom and openness of the primordial expanse of the ground.

In short, phenomena are the great state of evenness beyond the reach of conceptual construction. All outwardly manifesting things, which have arisen thanks to the creative power of awareness, appear because one assumes and clings to a supposed self or identity of what is but the radiance of awareness. All these things appear in the same way that a woman one has seen in the past might appear in one's dreams. And the mind and mental factors likewise all arise owing to the assumption that the unceasing manifestation of cognitive potency possesses a self.[53] Hallucinatory dualistic appearances manifest as the display and ornament of the self-experience of awareness—its creative power. Therefore, the knowledge that all is but a clear yet nonexistent appearance—an empty form in the manner of a magical illusion and a dream—reveals the most important key point of phenomena in terms of empty awareness: the state of great evenness.

3. Section Two: The Key Points of Evenness Are Essentialized

This consists of five stanzas. First, evenness is essentialized as the state of Samantabhadra, which is free of both the apprehender and the object to be apprehended.

> 9. All aspects of the nature of phenomena are
>   essentialized
> As your awareness, luminous and empty,
> Primordial wisdom, evenness.
> The latter is not bound—restricted—by an
>   apprehender.
> It transcends all objects to be apprehended.
> Within it there is nothing that might
> Act as target, nothing to refer to.
> Alert and wakeful, open, undistracted,
> It is the state of wisdom wherein mentation is
>   exhausted—
> The sky-like, endless, all-embracing state of
>   evenness,
> Transcending meditation and the absence of the same:
> The great space of Samantabhadra's wisdom.

All aspects of the ultimate nature of phenomena are essentialized as one's awareness, empty and luminous, the expanse of primordial wisdom, evenness, inconceivable and inexpressible. The dharmatā is not bound or restricted by an inner apprehender. For acts of cognition subside all by themselves. They are like the untraceable flight paths of birds and the knots tied on snakes that disentangle themselves. The dharmatā transcends whatever outer objects might be apprehended. For whatever appears is like a magical illusion. Like a dream, it has not the slightest inherent existence.

In brief, [awareness-dharmatā] transcends the sphere of apprehender and objects to be apprehended. It is empty and devoid of the slightest thing that could act as a target, the slightest thing that could be referred to. When one relaxes in the fundamental stratum of primordial purity, in the alert and wakeful, spacious state of equality, if one can remain undistracted, without following whatever thoughts may appear in one's mind, this is referred to as wisdom wherein mentation is exhausted. When one remains vividly in this pristine, naked, and untrammeled state, one actualizes space-like, infinite, all-embracing evenness—the state of equality. Here, not even the words *meditation* or *absence of meditation* are found. It is the great expanse of the wisdom of Samantabhadra, the all-pervading sovereign lord, essentialized as a vast and uninterrupted evenness.

Second, the free and relaxed state of the six consciousnesses is essentialized as evenness.

> 10. In this vast expanse of empty, luminous
>   awareness,
> The varied features of phenomena
> Unceasingly arise.
> Sense faculties perceive them in their freshness;
> Awareness, nature of phenomena, is clearly present.
> Appearance is untrammeled.
> However it arises,
> The mind is in a state of bliss.

The six gatherings of consciousness are all relaxed.
This expanse of self-arising primal wisdom,
Open, spacious, neither outside nor within,
Is the state of luminosity. It is present of itself within
The supreme natural state devoid of all contrivance.

When one rests in a state of meditative equipoise in the great, spacious expanse of awareness, luminous and empty, devoid of all features such as above and below, outer and inner, center and periphery—in other words, the limitless expanse that does not fall into any extreme—all the characteristics of different phenomena, arising through the creative power of awareness, appear and are perceived unceasingly and vividly, like a brocade cape unfurled. Whatever phenomena arise and however they appear, they subside all by themselves. Their arising and subsiding is seamless. When one settles in the state of empty, luminous awareness, limpid and free of all fixation—that is, when one settles in this state of utter evenness, spacious vastness, vivid clarity, and lucid emptiness—the objects of the five sense faculties appear clearly and uninterruptedly. And yet the observer is not caught up in them. It is as when a little child is carried into a temple [free and unconcerned by the sights and sounds that it perceives]. When the five sense doors are in a balanced state,[54] appearances are unrestrained and clear; the six consciousnesses are uninterrupted and relaxed. And in whichever way the objects of perception appear, they do not become occasions for clinging. Their nature is simply perceived, nakedly. Awareness—the ultimate nature of things—unstained by mental activity, is vividly present. This great state, in which everything is left just as it is, dwells neither in the extreme of appearance nor in that of emptiness. It is a state of great evenness and is called the "relaxation of the six consciousnesses."

As it is said in *The Tantra without Letters*,

This state of wisdom, ocean-like,
Where all is left just as it is,

Is neither an appearing thing
Nor that which makes such things appear.
It is not emptiness or something that exists as empty.
It is not luminous, but of great luminosity it is the
    field.
It is not a state of dullness,
And from agitation it is naturally free.
It has never moved,
It does not move,
And never will it move.

When one rests in this way, outer appearances are free and untrammeled, while inner mental states, however they may be, arise and subside all by themselves. They are, in their arising, the mere ornaments of awareness. In the expanse of great bliss, they appear and yet are empty and they are empty and yet appear, just like the reflections seen on a limpid stretch of water. If outer appearances are left to themselves, manifesting unrestrained and free, and if the six consciousnesses are left in a state of relaxation, then whatever manifests is a state of luminosity within the expanse of awareness, self-arisen primordial wisdom. It is open, spacious, neither outside nor within; it is a state beyond both center and periphery. It is present of itself in the vast expanse of great emptiness, the fundamental nature of things, the natural state free of all contrivance. This is how the state of equality is essentialized as the free and relaxed state of the six consciousnesses.

Third, the mind's natural flow is essentialized as great evenness.

> 11. When your consciousness is carefree,
> Like a person who has nothing more to do,
> And, not tense or loose,
> Your mind and body rest at ease,
> Awareness, endless, all-embracing evenness,
> Immaculate as space,

Rests in the dharmadhātu,
Never to be parted.

When yogis relax their three doors in their natural condition free
of all contrivance in a spacious, even state and when they leave their
minds without a care, they naturally let go of all activities, like
people who have no more work to do. They are like old people sitting in the sun, profoundly relaxed, their body, speech, and mind
at rest, their every task complete. It is thus that the objects of sense
and the mind itself both subside into nonduality. Empty, luminous
awareness—the state of great evenness of the dharmakāya—is realized. As we find in *Meeting the Three Kāyas*,

> Indeed the ground of everything
> Is the enlightened mind.
> Though the various features of phenomena
> Arise unceasingly,
> When nakedly perceived
> By faculties of sense,
> The dharmatā is evident
> In all appearances.
> The mind is carefree
> Like a person who has nothing more to do.

When there is nothing for the mind to do, when it is neither tense
nor loose, when the body and mind rest relaxed, carefree, and
easygoing, a state of immense spaciousness arises, similar—so it is
said—to the mind of the Victorious Ones. This is awareness. It has
the nature of an infinite, all-embracing evenness or equality similar
to the utterly immaculate sky free of the three impurities. This is
the self-cognizing primordial wisdom of the path, which dwells
inseparably in the fundamental nature of the ground, the dharmadhātu beyond all conceptual construction. The natural flow of the
mind is thus essentialized as great evenness.

Fourth, the sign of realization that derives from confidence in the state of wisdom is now described.

> 12. When dharmatā is realized, luminous and empty,
> Every bond subsides in its expanse.
> Awareness is revealed
> As evenness, unbroken, all-embracing.
> Unfettered by fixation, it transcends all thought.
> All is gathered in the single
> And completely even space of wisdom.
> The blissful mind is mingled with the bliss of peace—
> The state of the enlightened mind
> Where outside and within are of a single taste.
> The fundamental nature then is seen,
> The dharmatā where all comes to exhaustion.

When awareness, luminous and empty, the ultimate nature of things, is realized exactly as it is, hallucinatory appearances, perceived as when one's vision is impaired, dissolve into the expanse of unborn, empty awareness. It is as when mist and clouds dissolve into the sky. The true nature of the latter, devoid of all three impurities, becomes apparent. It is then that all the ties and traps of delusion subside where they stand and awareness is revealed as an uninterrupted, infinite, all-embracing evenness free of conceptual construction: the state of great equality. Since the objects that outwardly appear are no longer inspected, these same objects of apprehension are purified where they stand. And since the inner mind is untrammeled by fixation on whatever appears within it, this same mind (the apprehender) is intrinsically and primordially pure. Appearances and the mind blend indivisibly in a state that is beyond all choosing [in the sense of adopting or rejecting], beyond all thoughts. At that time, awareness, which dwells within the mind, mingles with the ground, the fundamental stratum of the dharmatā, the state of great bliss. And everything is gathered into a single, utterly even, and immense expanse of wisdom. For yogis who have attained the fundamental nature—the dharmatā in which phenomena are all exhausted—the realization in which they truly see the dharmatā arises from within. Their minds rest uncontrived just as they are, in the state of dharmatā, the great bliss of peace. Their blissful minds mingle inseparably, as the root verse says, with the bliss of peace. Outer appearing objects are purified in their own groundlessness, while the inner apprehending mind subsides in the dharmakāya. Both mind and appearances—equal from the very beginning—mingle in a single taste. And in the vast expanse of the ultimate enlightened mind, the everlasting kingdom of unchanging bliss is won. The fundamental nature, the dharmatā in which phenomena are all exhausted, is directly beheld.

Fifth, the preceding stanzas are brought to a conclusion.

> 13. In the instant when the object,
> Faculty of sense, and mind's intent all meet,
> In the evenness of mind,
> Appearances are vast and blissful.
> In this naturally luminous and limpid state,
> Unfettered by fixation and by clinging,
> The key point of phenomena
> Is essentialized as an unbroken evenness.

In the very moment when three factors: the outer objects of the six consciousnesses, the dominant condition of the six inner senses, and the immediately preceding condition of mental intent all coincide, appearances are brought onto the path. They are seen to be spacious and blissful in the state of great evenness, the nature of the mind. And in this state, which is naturally limpid and luminous and which, from the very beginning, is unfettered by fixating thoughts, primordial wisdom is found, pristine and lucid. It is free from the trap of something good called meditation, and it is free from being overwhelmed by something bad called ignorance. It is not entangled in view, meditation, and activity. Here, the self and its object, the so-called agent and object of knowledge, have no existence. Within this primordial, naturally occurring, absence of conceptual construction (which the ordinary mind can never experience)—that is, uninterrupted evenness—the supreme key point [of phenomena] is thus essentialized.

3. Section Three: Phenomena Are Subsumed into Evenness

This consists of six stanzas. First, evenness is primordially sealed by the vajra expanse.

> 14. In the space whence objects, mind, and clinging
> Have been cleared away,
> Awareness, free of memory and thoughts,
> Self-seeking, and aversion,
> Is subsumed within the pristine clarity of evenness.
> It is the vajra dance of unconfined, unbroken
>   dharmatā—
> Expanse of suchness, primal wisdom of equality—
> Marked from the outset with the seal
> Of the wisdom of Samantabhadra.

Whatever objects, whatever states of mind, and whatever states of clinging appear, they are naturally cleared away in the openness and freedom of the unconfined immensity of unborn awareness. In this sky-like expanse, hallucinatory phenomena, the mind and its objects—as with the recollection of places previously visited, all inquiring thoughts, self-seeking desire, and mind-disturbing anger—are absent from the very first. They subsist in the pristine clarity of awareness, the state of primordially present evenness. This is known as the ultimate truth, the invincible, utterly indestructible vajra principle. As it is said in *The Lion's Perfect Power,*

> Great voidness is the blazing vajra—indestructible.
> Intensely does the stainless vajra blaze in what is gross and
>   subtle.

So it is that awareness, which is subsumed within the ultimate truth—the unoriginate and indestructible vajra principle—does not arise newly. It is primordially present and spontaneously arisen. Therefore, if it is understood that whatever arises (appearances and mental states) is the creative power and display of the indestructible and ultimate vajra and if without any accepting or rejecting, one can let it dissolve in the unbroken, unconfined immensity [of awareness] free of all reference, this is known as the "vajra dance" of the ultimate nature of things. The fundamental nature thus actualized is referred to as the dharmatā, the expanse of suchness, the principle of the primordial wisdom of equality beyond all conceptual construction. For, from the very first, it is marked with the seal of the unchanging wisdom of dharmakāya Samantabhadra.

On the level of the practice, if yogis rest in meditative equipoise in the supreme primordial wisdom, where the minds of all the Victorious Ones of the three times are blended into one, they become inseparable from this same wisdom. This practice therefore has an immense benefit.

Second, the general principle of the enlightened mind is presented.

> 15. Just as various dreams are all subsumed in sleep
> And are the empty, false perceptions of the mind,
> Just so, the universe and beings—
> All within samsara and nirvana—
> Are subsumed within the mind.
> They appear within the mind's expanse;
> They have no real existence.

All the things that one dreams about—the various appearances, outer and inner, of the universe and beings—are apprehended in the same way as the things of waking life: as pleasant, unpleasant, or neutral. And one is deluded. All these dream visions are, however, subsumed within one's sleep. They are the creative power and display of sleep and nothing more—the untrue and empty perceptions of the mind. Similarly, on the assumption that the universe and beings, the phenomena of samsara and nirvana, possess a real identity, one appropriates them in terms of "I" and "mine." But whatever experiences one has, whether pleasant, unpleasant, or neutral, they all arise within the mind's expanse; they dwell within the mind and dissolve back into it. So it is that samsara and nirvana are subsumed within the mind alone. They appear as the creative power and display of the vast expanse of mind. They are simply the clearly apparent and yet nonexistent phenomena that manifest as the display of awareness. They do not have the slightest existence as specifically characterized entities. It is as we find in *The All-Creating King*,

> All that is contained within phenomenal existence,
> The universe and its inhabitants,
> All that is summed up
> As buddhas and as sentient life
> Is present in myself,
> The all-creating and enlightened mind.
> All is simply the enlightened mind.

Third, the principle of evenness itself is presented.

> 16. Just as in the bosom of the vast expanse,
> The universe and beings it contains,
> In all that great immensity,
> Are an unbroken evenness
> Beyond both center and periphery,
> So too within the reaches of awareness,
> All appearances of things and minds—
> Everything both outside and within—are even:
> All the mind's perceptions are subsumed in
>   emptiness.
> This demonstrates that all phenomena
> Are subsumed within the enlightened mind—

That evenness falls neither to one side nor to another,
For it is free of apprehender
And of objects to be apprehended.

All things that appear within the expanse of empty space—worlds and beings in all their vastness and multiplicity—do not extend beyond the expanse of space itself, which is devoid of center and periphery. It is but the creative power and display of uninterrupted evenness. It is subsumed within this same principle of evenness. Likewise, within the expanse of awareness, phenomena in all their inconceivable multiplicity (samsara and nirvana, the appearances of things, and mental states) are free of all characteristics—outer and inner, above and below, center and circumference—abiding from the very beginning in the state of great evenness. Phenomena, which are the subjective perceptions or experiences of the mind, are all subsumed within the actual expanse of primordially pure awareness, the primordial wisdom of great emptiness.

It is said in *The All-Creating King*,

> All appearing things, together with the mind,
> Are from the outset but a single ultimate reality.
> Do not think of them in terms of causal law.

So it is that awareness is evenness itself. This means that all phenomena are subsumed within it, the state of equality of the ultimate enlightened mind. It also means that evenness—the state of equality, devoid of characteristics and of falling to one side—is therefore free from an apprehender and objects to be apprehended. It is thus demonstrated that phenomena are subsumed in the vajra principle of all-pervading equality.

Fourth, it is shown that the principle of awareness is inconceivable and inexpressible.

17. The enlightened mind subsuming all phenomena
Is itself subsumed within great evenness,

> Devoid of all extremes and falling to one side.
> Like space's vast immensity,
> Containing both the universe and beings,
> It has no center, no periphery.
> It is beyond both thought and all expression.

It was shown above that all phenomena are subsumed in the principle of awareness, the enlightened mind, which is an uninterrupted evenness. But what, one may go on to ask, are the characteristics of this awareness? It is free of all extremes and does not fall to one side or another. It is free of characteristics. It is subsumed in the principle of open, unimpeded evenness and is blended in a single taste with the dharmadhātu, free of all conceptual construction. Where are the universe and beings subsumed? They are subsumed in the vast abyss of space. Likewise, awareness is subsumed in the principle of the wisdom expanse of Samantabhadra, the great space-like emptiness, which transcends word, thought, and expression. It is indivisibly blended with it in a single taste. It is said in *The All-Creating King*,

> All things have the character of space.
> The character of space is suchness.
> The triple kāya likewise has this character.

Fifth, it is shown that the principle of awareness is the source of everything.

> 18. Awareness is the great condition of equality,
> Free from all extremes.
> All things of phenomenal existence,
> Samsara and nirvana,
> Ceaselessly arise therein.
> But in the moment they appear,
> The mind and all phenomena
> Are indefinable as this or that.
> They are subsumed within the evenness of dharmatā.

In the space of awareness, the expanse of equality or evenness, free from all extremes—existence and nonexistence, both and neither, permanence and discontinuity, coming and going, identity and difference, entity and nonentity, and so on—all things within phenomenal existence, samsara and nirvana with all their individual characteristics, ceaselessly manifest. They arise within awareness, they appear within awareness, and they subside within awareness. They are all subsumed in awareness. Therefore, in the moment of their appearing within the expanse of awareness, both mind and phenomena are beyond the four or eight conceptual extremes; beyond arising, dwelling, and ceasing; beyond the thirty-two misconceptions; and so on. It is therefore impossible to indicate them with words and definitions, saying such things as "This is how they are." They are all subsumed within the evenness of dharmatā, awareness. It is said in *The All-Creating King*,

> The enlightened mind is one great, vast domain.
> The buddhas, beings, worlds, and their inhabitants
> All dwell within it. All is indivisible
> Within the utter purity of dharmatā.
> All is beyond ascription or denial.

Sixth, the description of the vajra principle of Samantabhadra is concluded.

> 19. The seal of the enlightened mind,
> Beyond which none can go,
> Is set primordially upon phenomena
> By the vast expanse, Samantabhadra.
> It is subsumed within the wisdom of the teacher,
> Lord of beings, lord of Dharma.
> This primordially awakened state
> Is sealed with the signet of the vajra essence.
> The final meaning of the mighty secret
> Lies beyond the scope of everyone

> Except for those of highest fortune.
> The principle of the vajra peak,
> Beyond all change and movement—
> The great space of awareness, self-cognizing,
> The state of luminosity—
> Is hard to realize, though it lies within yourself.
> Only through the kindness of the glorious master,
> Teacher, lord of Dharma, is it seen.
> Thus all phenomena are said to be
> Subsumed in an unbroken evenness.

All phenomena are subsumed within the principle of awareness, Samantabhadra. From the very beginning, nothing and no one can be outside this expanse. Since apart from awareness, the enlightened mind, there are no phenomena, this same awareness sets its seal on all things or, to put it another way, phenomena are subsumed within awareness.

It is said in *The All-Creating King*,

> Apart from mind, there are no other things.

Since the phenomena of samsara and nirvana never stir from the vast expanse of dharmatā Samantabhadra, all phenomena bear its seal primordially. It is said in *The Six Consciousnesses Overwhelmed*,

> In Samantabhadra's state, free from action,
> Samsara is Samantabhadra, nirvana is Samantabhadra.

In what way, one may ask, is it possible to actualize such a profound fundamental nature? Thanks to the blessing power of one's spiritual teacher, the sovereign of beings and lord of Dharma, the realization of the latter's mind is transferred into one's own mind and the wisdom of the vast immensity of the teacher's mind is introduced. In this very wisdom, the fundamental nature is subsumed.

The *Guhyagarbha* says,

The hidden meaning comes forth from within.
It dwells within the heart of the compassionate teacher.

This awareness, realized or actualized through the kindness of the teacher, is a state of evenness that transcends the extremes of existence and nonexistence. As *The All-Creating King* declares,

> Swift primordial wisdom,
> Free from any thought,
> Is like a precious jewel that manifests
> By virtue of the master.

It may seem that when, through the kindness of one's teacher, one realizes the fundamental nature of the ground, one does so newly for the first time. Yet the nature of the ground is awakened from the very beginning. It is the ultimate truth beyond birth and death, change and movement; it is sealed with the signet of the indestructible vajra essence of luminosity. The difference between realization and non-realization lies simply in the recognition or nonrecognition of it.

The realization of this "vajra peak" is the exclusive preserve of those of highest fortune, those who possess the karmic deposit accrued from the gathering of the two accumulations for many kalpas in the past and from their previous aspirations. It does not lie within the reach of ordinary folk, people of lesser fortune. As it is said in *The All-Creating King*,

> Yogis who have karmic fortune
> Accrued from countless kalpas in the past
> And who have faith in me,
> The all-creating and enlightened mind . . .

Such words show the necessity of the appropriate karmic fortune. Aside from those of the highest mental capacity, this final meaning of the great secret does not lie within the reach of beings. It is the ultimate truth beyond birth and death, movement and change, defeat and destruction. It is the principle of the invincible vajra peak.

And although the self-arisen awareness, the great expanse of the wisdom essence of luminosity, dwells inseparably and from the very beginning within them—like the heat of fire and the wetness of water—beings are powerless to recognize it. They are like a poor man who does not know that his very hearthstone is made of gold. And yet, even in the midst of the uninterrupted proliferation of hallucinatory appearances, self-arisen awareness can in fact be seen thanks to the kindness of the glorious sovereign, one's own teacher, the lord of Dharma, who points it out clearly through the transference of his blessing power.

So it is that all the things of phenomenal existence never stir from the expanse of equality, the uninterrupted evenness of all-pervading awareness, free of conceptual elaboration. Phenomena are therefore said to be subsumed within its vast expanse.

3. Section Four: A Clear Conviction Is Gained That All Phenomena Are an Uninterrupted Evenness

This section consists of two stanzas. First, a clear conviction is reached that the nonexistence of outer and inner phenomena corresponds to their evenness.

> 20. A clear conviction then is gained:
> The ultimate quintessence of phenomena
> Is evenness.
> All outer things are empty and unborn.
> They do not stay; they do not come or go.
> They are beyond all indication and expression.
> All inner states arising seamlessly subside.
> There is no finding them—
> Like paths of birds that fly across the sky.

Clear conviction with regard to evenness refers to the fundamental nature, the ultimate quintessence, of phenomena. Outer phenomena, which appear within awareness—that is, the appearing objects of the six sense consciousnesses—are primordially unborn. Within the expanse of emptiness, they clearly appear and yet are nonexistent. They are like reflections in a mirror or rainbows in the sky: they arise and yet do not exist in truth. They do not stay. They neither come from nor go anywhere. They are thus beyond all indication and expression. It must be decisively resolved—that is, a clear conviction must be reached—that they are beyond conceptual elaboration and are similar to space. Inner phenomena, namely, the apprehending cognitions related to the six consciousnesses, seamlessly arise and subside all by themselves. They are like the paths of birds that fly across the sky. There is no finding them. They are groundless and rootless.

So it is that whatever appearances of the ground arise within the expanse of the unborn ground awareness, they are primordially beyond thought and expression. It is said in *The Tantra of the Blazing Relics*,

Although the ground's appearances have no intrinsic being,
They seem to be phenomena that may be
Talked about, conceived, expressed.
And yet they dwell from the beginning
In the equality of the three times.

Second, a clear conviction is reached that empty awareness is beyond the causal law.

21. Just like phenomena and mental states,
So too awareness self-arisen
Has no existence even as a simple name.
It is beyond all indication and expression,
All conceptual elaboration.

Since like space it does not act,
It is a state of emptiness.
Free of action, free of all exertion,
It transcends both good and bad, all virtue and all sin.
It is beyond the causal law;
Ten elements of tantra have no place in it.
It is a vast, completely even space
Beyond all indication and expression.
Within awareness, virtue and nonvirtue
Are primordially empty; they have never been.
A clear conviction thus is reached
That this nature, inconceivable and inexpressible,
Is the great perfection
Beyond the reach of ordinary mind.

In the same way that appearing objects and the apprehending mind have no existence, the same is true of self-arisen awareness. When [one tries to] ascertain it closely, it has no existence, not even as a name. This is why the mind cannot picture it and why it is beyond the reach of verbal expression. It is free of all conceptual elaboration. Since, like space, it is a state in which all phenomena come to exhaustion beyond the ordinary mind, it does not act in any way; it does not stray from the state of emptiness. It is beyond action and effort; it transcends both good and bad, both virtue and nonvirtue. It is beyond the causal process, which is why it cannot be accomplished through effort and practice in the manner of the ten elements of tantra. Self-arisen awareness is a vast spacious expanse; it is uncontrived, a state of utter evenness. Within this expanse, which is beyond all indication and expression, all virtue and nonvirtue are primordially empty. It is a state beyond conceptual elaboration, which has never existed as anything, except in the sense of being like space. Empty awareness, which lies beyond the causal process and is beyond all conception and expression, is itself the nature of emptiness. It is the nondual fundamental stratum of the way of being that is beyond all dualistic perception and beyond all striving and clinging of the ordinary mind. It is the fundamental nature, the great perfection. It is of crucial importance to take a firm stand and to have a clear conviction that it is so.

A Concluding Statement of the Vajra Topic's Name

Here ends the word commentary on the second vajra topic of *The Precious Treasury of the Fundamental Nature*, which establishes that all phenomena are an unbroken state of evenness.

2. THE THIRD VAJRA TOPIC: SPONTANEOUS PRESENCE

This topic demonstrates that phenomena are spontaneously present primordially. The teaching itself, which concludes with a statement of the vajra topic's name, has four sections: the key points are revealed, they are essentialized, they are subsumed, and a clear conviction is reached in their regard.

3. *Section One: The Key Points Are Revealed*

This consists of eleven stanzas. First, it is shown that spontaneous presence is like a jewel.

> 1. And now the nature of spontaneous presence is revealed.
> It abides, not made by anyone, from the beginning.
> Like an all-providing jewel, the enlightened mind
> Is ground and source of all things in samsara and nirvana.

Now that evenness has been established, the principle of the primordial spontaneous presence of awareness, the enlightened mind, the wellspring of all things, is now revealed. For though awareness does not exist as anything at all, its creative power is able to manifest as anything whatsoever.

Since awareness, the enlightened mind, has not been created by any agent through causes and conditions, it does not exist as a thing. And yet, since its creative power may manifest as anything at all, it is, from the beginning, spontaneously present as the all-doer, or all-creator. As *The All-Creating King* tells us,

> Enlightened mind, of all things the essential core,
> Is by nature, from the first, spontaneously present.
> No need is there to look for it
> By means of the ten elements.

A wish-fulfilling jewel is a ground or source able to provide all that one might need or desire. It is the same with awareness, the ultimate enlightened mind. Although it does not exist as anything at all—for it is empty—its creative power can manifest as anything. It dwells from the very first as the ground of all qualities. It is therefore the basis whence everything in phenomenal existence, both samsara and nirvana, arises. It is said in *Meeting the Three Kāyas*,

> In the expanse of spontaneous presence
> Is found the ground whence everything arises.
> The wheels of the adornments
> Of enlightened body, speech, and mind
> And all enlightened qualities and deeds
> Come forth from it in their entirety.
> The dharmadhātu is therefore a precious gem
> Fulfilling every wish.
> There is no need to strive,
> For everything is there, spontaneously present.

Second, it is shown that the appearances of the ground constitute great spontaneous presence.

2. The things appearing in phenomenal existence
Are all manifest in space.
Likewise, both samsara and nirvana
Ceaselessly appear in the enlightened mind.
Just as various dreams occur while beings sleep,
The six migrations and the three worlds
Manifest within the mind.
All things, in the very instant of arising,
Subsist within awareness.
They are the great appearances of the ground,
Empty yet spontaneously present.

Just as phenomenal existence, the universe and its living contents, arises ceaselessly and distinctly in the bosom of space, all appearances, whether of samsara or nirvana, arise within the enlightened mind. For it is just as with the various experiences one has when one dreams about the world and its inhabitants. They arise as the creative power of the state of sleep. In the same way, the appearances of the six classes of beings and the three worlds arise spontaneously within the state of the ultimate enlightened mind as the display of its creative power. Beings, however, do not recognize their true nature because their minds are darkened by ignorance, with the result that they apprehend them in terms of "I" and "mine." So it is that these appearances are in fact hallucinations. Nevertheless, in the very moment that these appearances arise as the mind's display, they do not stir from the state of awareness. They are the empty, spontaneously present appearances of the ground, the state of equality beyond all conceptual elaboration. They are ineffable, inconceivable, and inexpressible.

Third, it is shown that spontaneous presence is groundless.

3. The ground and the appearances arising there
Are not identical and yet are not distinct.
The ground's appearances are from the first
Spontaneously present—

> Arising through the portal of awareness.
> Nirvana and samsara, the display of its creative
>   power,
> Appear distinctly: pure or else impure.
> But in the very moment of appearing,
> They are neither good nor bad:
> They are a single ultimate expanse.

The ground awareness, the empty, luminous enlightened mind, is naturally and unceasingly endowed with the spontaneous presence of the three kāyas. Within the dimension of the ground awareness, the appearances of the ground arise unceasingly and spontaneously. The phenomena of samsara and nirvana, arising through the portal of spontaneous presence, appear to be either good or bad. And yet, arising from the one expanse of precious[55] spontaneous presence, they are neither good nor bad, neither identical nor different. As the creative power of primordial wisdom, they are, from the very first, spontaneously present—arising through the portal of awareness, great primordial wisdom. In the text *The Instantaneous Severance of the Three Times*, it is said,

> In one thing all is gathered—the one and only ultimate
>   expanse.
> In one thing all things are unborn—the unborn
>   dharmadhātu.
> The display that's born in the unborn expanse
> Is unconfined and can appear as anything.

The manifested display of the ground awareness, great spontaneous presence, may have the aspect of samsara (which is said to be bad) or of nirvana (which is said to be good). But although these two aspects appear distinctly as pure and impure, the fact is that in the very moment of their appearance, they are but the single expanse of precious spontaneous presence in which there is not even a hair of good or bad. It is said in *The All-Creating King*,

Buddhas, kāyas, wisdoms, perfect qualities,
All beings with their bodies and habitual proclivities,
All that is gathered in phenomenal existence—
The universe together with the beings it contains—
Are from the outset the enlightened mind.

Fourth, it is shown that the three kāyas are great spontaneous presence.

> 4. When five lights shine unhindered
> From a crystal sphere,
> These same lights are perceived
> According to their different colors.
> Neither good nor bad,
> They are but the display
> Of the single crystal sphere.
> The ground, awareness, self-cognizing,
> Is like this crystal sphere.
> Its emptiness is dharmakāya,
> Its radiant luminosity is the sambhogakāya,
> And its unobstructed ground for the unfolding
> Is nirmāṇakāya.
> The three kāyas in the ground's expanse
> Are all spontaneously present.

When the five-colored rays of light appear distinctly and unobstructedly from a crystal sphere, they are perceived according to their different hues: white, yellow, red, green, and blue. None of them is either good or bad. The crystal and the colors within it are nothing but the crystal itself. Neither good nor bad, they are just the display of the single crystal sphere. As Longchenpa says in his autocommentary,

> Awareness—empty, crystal-like—is the dharmakāya.
> The luminosity of awareness, which is like the five

lights inside the crystal, is the sambhogakāya. The unobstructed way in which awareness can manifest, which is similar to the ability of the crystal to radiate light outwardly (without actually doing so), is the nirmāṇakāya.

Therefore, since the three kāyas of the ground are of a single nature, they are in truth one, without any qualitative distinction in terms of good or bad. Self-cognizing awareness, the ground, with its twin aspects of inner luminosity and outwardly radiating luminosity, is empty, lucent, and unobstructed, like a sphere of crystal. The nature of awareness, which, like space, has no existence as any thing whatsoever, is the dharmakāya. This awareness, which does not exist as any thing, nevertheless possesses a luminous radiance in the form of five-colored lights. This is the sambhogakāya. Finally, just as there is in the crystal the unobstructed capacity for the five lights to be projected outward, likewise the luminous radiance, self-cognizing primordial wisdom, is the unobstructed ground of manifestation. And this is the nirmāṇakāya. It is thus that the three kāyas of the ground share a single nature. The basis for their imputation is self-cognizing primordial wisdom itself. It is important to understand this key point.

The three kāyas are spontaneously present in the ground, which is the expanse of awareness beyond all conceptual elaboration. The two rūpakāyas, both of which arise within awareness, appear differently for pure and impure beings to be trained,[56] and yet in truth, they do not stir from the dharmakāya. It is said in *The All-Creating King*,

> I, the all-creator, am the triple kāya.
> My nature is the dharmakāya—
> I transcend the mind's elaboration
> And abide in nonconceptual equality.
> I am also the sambhogakāya, fulfilling every wish—
> My character [is luminous],
> Whence the display of birth unfolds.

And I am the nirmāṇakāya, the knowing power
That helps all beings in accordance with their needs.

Fifth, it is shown that everything is the spontaneously present enlightened mind.

> 5. When appearances arise within the ground—
> The three pure kāyas, the buddhas' self-experience,
> As well as the impure phenomena
> Of both the universe and beings—
> All are by their nature
> Empty, luminous, and manifold.
> All are the display of dharmakāya,
> Of sambhogakāya, and nirmāṇakāya.
> The displayed appearances of the ground (the triple
>   kāya)
> Are all spontaneously present—
> Awareness that experiences itself.
> Do not seek for them elsewhere.
> When this analysis is understood correctly,
> All phenomena in both samsara and nirvana
> Will be realized as the pure field of the triple kāya,
> Spontaneously present in the enlightened mind.

So it is as we have explained above, the three kāyas are spontaneously present and complete in the ground awareness itself. When the appearances of the ground, which are also spontaneously present, manifest outwardly from within this same awareness, whatever appearances occur, whether pure or impure, do not go beyond the nature of the three kāyas. In terms of the three pure kāyas, the self-experience of the buddhas, a pure display occurs: the dharmakāya buddhas, the sambhogakāya buddhas of the five families, and the variously manifesting nirmāṇakāya. But then there is also the [manifestation of the] impure samsaric body, speech, and mind, and these have also arisen as [the display of] the three kāyas. They are all empty, the single ultimate expanse of spontaneous presence. Indeed, whatever impure appearances of the universe and beings may manifest, they are all marked by a threefold character—they are empty, luminous, and manifold. They are the display of the dharmakāya, sambhogakāya, and nirmāṇakāya. They are the displayed appearances of the ground, the triple kāya.

In brief, within the nature of the spontaneous presence of the ground, the three kāyas merge into one. The appearances of the universe and beings arising from that state manifest as the display of those same three kāyas. They are the appearances of the ground. When one takes these two elements [the ground and the appearances of the ground] to be one, one inevitably understands that the nature of spontaneous presence is called the *triple kāya*, or *trikāya*. The three pure kāyas of buddhahood and the impure body, speech, and mind of the samsaric state are neither good nor bad; they are all the ornament and display of the ultimate expanse of spontaneous presence. As we find in *The Six Consciousnesses Overwhelmed*,

> The nature of the mind, spontaneously present, is the
>   expanse of changeless space.
> Its various display is the expanse of manifestation of its
>   cognitive power.
> There is nothing that is not the ornament of the immense
>   expanse.
> Hindrances and defects are not found elsewhere.

Therefore, all the pure and impure appearances of the universe and beings have the nature of the spontaneously present trikāya, and what is referred to as the three kāyas of the spontaneously present self-experience of awareness should not be sought elsewhere. If one grasps this analysis correctly, one will understand that samsara and nirvana are the buddha field of the trikāya. Furthermore, since the ultimate enlightened mind is spontaneously present as the ground of manifestation of all phenomena in samsara and nirvana, it must be understood that even the trikāya buddha field of samsara and nirvana manifests, remains, and subsides within the state of the enlightened mind.

Sixth, it is shown that everything is the enlightened mind.

> 6. The kāyas and the wisdoms
> Of the buddhas of the triple time,
> The body, speech, and mind
> Of beings of the triple realm,
> And karma and defilement—
> Everything belonging to phenomenal existence—
> Are not other than enlightened mind.

The scripture says that all Victorious Ones are one within the space of primal wisdom. The body, speech, and mind of all the buddhas of the three times—their wisdom and qualities of knowledge, love, and power, the twenty-one categories of undefiled knowledge, such as the ten strengths, the four fearlessnesses, and the eighteen distinctive qualities,[57] together with (to state the matter briefly) the thirty-seven factors leading to enlightenment[58] related to the ground, path, and result—are all the enlightened mind. It is also said that the twenty-five elements—namely, the fivefold enlightened body, the fivefold enlightened speech, the fivefold enlightened mind, the fivefold qualities, and fivefold activities (in other words, the pure appearances of the kāyas and wisdoms)—are all the enlightened mind. Moreover, the body, speech, and mind, which beings in the six realms and the three words identify as their own— together with all their activities good and bad, the whiteness of their virtue and the blackness of their sin, all their defiled thoughts of desire and aversion, and all their habitual tendencies (in short, all the things of phenomenal existence that appear in the experience of beings)—are in fact none other than the enlightened mind.

Consider, for example, a statue made of precious gold, which is an object of admiration, or ornaments like golden bracelets that are considered beautiful, and compare them with a bedpan made of gold, which would be regarded as unclean. They are all one and the same in being made of gold. And inasmuch as they are gold, there is no qualitative difference between them in terms of good or bad. In just the same way, the pure kāyas and wisdoms of the buddhas and the impure body, speech, and mind of ordinary beings, their actions, their virtue and nonvirtue, their obscurations and habitual tendencies—however they may be labeled—are in truth none other than the ultimate enlightened mind: awareness, self-arisen primordial wisdom.

Seventh, it is shown that spontaneous presence is an all-supplying treasury.

> 7. Within spontaneous presence's expanse
> Is found the ground whence everything arises.
> All that has appeared as form—
> The outer world and its inhabitants—
> Lists to neither one side nor another.
> All arises as the wheel of ornaments
> Of the enlightened body.
> Sounds and languages,
> Excellent, indifferent, or inferior,
> List to neither one side nor another.
> All arises as the wheel of ornaments
> Of the enlightened speech.
> Ordinary mind and primal wisdom,
> Realization and the lack of it,
> List to neither one side nor another.
> All arises as the wheel of ornaments
> Of the enlightened mind.
> Likewise, enlightened qualities and deeds
> List to neither one side nor another.
> Thus the dharmadhātu is a precious jewel
> Fulfilling every wish.
> There is no need to strive,
> For everything arises naturally.

This is why it has been called
Primordial wisdom, self-arisen and spontaneously
   present.

The notion of spontaneous presence is applied here to awareness, the enlightened mind. The reason for this is that although awareness, the enlightened mind, does not *exist* as anything at all, it is spontaneously present as the ground of a creative power that is able to *arise* as anything at all. This is the reason why awareness is spoken of in terms of spontaneous presence. It is, from the very first, spontaneously present as the source of the manifold arising of creative power. Since pure and impure appearances arise within the expanse of spontaneously present awareness, this same awareness is their support and ground. One therefore speaks of the spontaneous presence that is awareness.

Therefore, the ground awareness, great spontaneous presence, is a kind of treasure house, the basis or source for the arising of all appearances both pure and impure. Through the creative power of the precious spontaneous presence, the appearances of the ground arise in six ways: as cognitive power, as light, as primordial wisdom, as deities, nondually, and in a manner that does not fall into any of the ontological extremes. They also arise as the door of pure primordial wisdom and as the door of impure samsara. And the ground for the arising of these six ways and two doors—altogether, the eight doors of spontaneous presence—is awareness, precious spontaneous presence itself.[59]

Therefore, all outer objects and living beings, everything that appears as form and is the field of the visual faculty, arise—without falling into one side or another in terms of good or bad, adoption and rejection—as the inexhaustible wheel of ornaments of the enlightened body, which itself has the nature of awareness, the precious spontaneous presence.

In the same way, the field of the auditive faculty, sound and language, pleasant, unpleasant, excellent, inferior, or indifferent—in other words, everything that resounds—does so without falling to one side or another in terms of good, bad, or neutral. It arises as the inexhaustible wheel of ornaments of enlightened speech, which has the nature of awareness, the great spontaneous presence.

Likewise, all perceptions of the mind and the manifestations of primordial wisdom—which are the field of the mental faculty, such as realization or absence of realization, as well as all hallucinatory appearances, such as happiness, sorrow, and indifference—arise without falling into one side or another. They are the inexhaustible wheel of ornaments of the enlightened mind, which has the nature of awareness, the precious spontaneous presence of primordial wisdom.

To grasp this properly and to rest meditatively in this understanding is a supreme key point. The same applies to enlightened qualities and activities. In short, all the pure appearances of body, speech, mind, qualities, and activities of buddhahood and all the impure appearances of the body, speech, mind, and activities of deluded beings appear through the creative power of awareness, precious spontaneous presence, without falling to one side or another in terms of good or bad. And just as all one's needs and wishes are fulfilled when one prays in the presence of a wish-fulfilling jewel, in like manner all excellence naturally derives from the spontaneous presence that is awareness, precious dharmadhātu, without there being any need to strive for it. This is why awareness is referred to as "spontaneously present, self-arisen primordial wisdom."

Eighth, it is shown that spontaneous presence is beyond all effort and practice.

> 8. The ground, spontaneously present,
> Of the various array of things
> Is the enlightened mind,
> Ever and spontaneously present.
> Therefore, there's no need
> To look for the three kāyas,
> For you have them naturally within yourself.

In the causal law concerning good and ill,
There is no need for you to strive.
Resting in the natural state,
You will be called a yogi free of action,
Free of effort in adopting or rejecting.
The vast space of spontaneous presence
Is yours from the beginning.
Therefore, make no effort now in dharmatā!

The spontaneously present ground of the whole variety of appearances (the objects of the six impure consciousnesses) and of the manifestations of pure primordial wisdom is the enlightened mind. This ultimate enlightened mind, namely, the actual, uncontrived primordial wisdom, is always, from the very beginning, spontaneously present as the ground for the manifestation of phenomena, whether of samsara or nirvana. Consequently, all the phenomena of the resultant stage (the three kāyas, the five kāyas, the five wisdoms, and so on) are—within the expanse of awareness, the precious spontaneous presence—one's own natural birthright. There is no need to search for these enlightened qualities, for they are primordially complete within oneself. This is why the root text says that there is no need to strive to adopt the whiteness of virtue and to reject the blackness of evil in order to accomplish within one's mind the three kāyas and the other qualities of the result. As *The All-Creating King* tells us,

I am the all-creator and am so from the first.
I do not say that I must now be rendered so.
My retinue would be afflicted with the malady of effort,
And primal wisdom, self-arisen, would then be denied.
All such defects would ensue.

Those who dwell in the great spontaneous presence, in the natural state of awareness that is beyond all striving in the causal process of virtue and sin, are called "true yogis free of action." Such yogis, free of effort and action in adopting and rejecting, lay hold of the primordial fortress in the expanse of awareness, spontaneous presence. They are the ones who actualize primordial dharmatā. There they take their stand upon this fundamental stratum and remain within it. To think that one must make an effort now in the present moment in order to achieve this goal is an obstacle to this path. Therefore, Longchenpa strongly advises us not to contrive, or to alter, anything.

Ninth, it is shown that spontaneous presence is beyond all action.

> 9. Even the enlightenment
> Of all Victorious Ones, past, present, and to come,
> Is spontaneously present
> As the great bliss of the natural state.
> Therefore, do not have recourse
> To teachings on the causal law,
> Designed for those of lesser fortune,
> But watch the nature that, like space,
> Transcends intended action.

If one rests in the state of awareness, the ultimate enlightened mind, precious spontaneous presence, this is the same as dwelling in the dharmadhātu, the mind of all the buddhas of the three times. As *The All-Creating King* says,

> The enlightened buddhas of the ancient past
> Likewise searched for nothing other than their minds.
> Suchness was not something they contrived.

And,

> The same is true for those abiding in this present age
> And those who in the future will appear.

For through the evenness devoid of thought
Their own accomplishment is gained.

The Illusory Net of Manifestations also says,

This is what the buddhas of the past have taught.
The buddhas of the future too will set it forth.
The perfect buddhas of the present
Also teach it time and time again.

The minds of all the buddhas of the three times, the dharmadhātu, the ultimate enlightened mind, are—in the spacious natural state, the expanse of self-cognizing primordial wisdom—like water mixed with water. It is a nondual union, spontaneously present within the state of great bliss. The preservation of this state, the ultimate nature of things, is like a wish-fulfilling jewel. By contrast, the teachings on the causal law and on the principle of adopting and rejecting— when compared with the profound doctrine—are like instructions for the tutoring of childish beings of lower fortune. For however much one may strive in the implementation of such teachings, it is like polishing some ordinary material and praying in front of it. The stone will not turn into a miraculous gem that can grant all that one might wish. If one fails to rely on teachings that transcend the karmic law of cause and effect, one will fail to gain enlightenment no matter how much one may implement teachings that require effortful action in accordance with the causal process. These teachings are intended for childish beings, and therefore one should not have recourse to them. As we find in *The All-Creating King*,

A man who wishes to obtain a wishing-gem
May burnish all he likes a piece of wood.
It will never turn into a jewel.

And,

> Even if these teachings were directly shown
> To those of little fortune,
> Who lack the proper karmic disposition,
> They would fail to understand them.
> For they are poisoned by their striving
> In the principle of causes and their fruits.

And,

> Thus the Great Perfection, which transcends causality,
> Is not the sphere of those of lesser fortune,
> Who should instead engage in teachings
> Based upon the causal law.

So it is that people of high fortune, who are capable of being guided by teachings that transcend exertion based upon the causal law, do not have recourse to teachings destined for those of lesser fortune. Longchenpa gives them this advice: avoiding the trap of striving in the karmic process of cause and effect, they should watch—in a manner that is devoid of any object of watching—the space-like nature that lies beyond all deliberate exertion.

Tenth, it is shown that since spontaneous presence is primordial, there is no need to accomplish it now.

> 10. Suchness as it is
> Has now no need to be accomplished.
> Within spontaneous presence,
> Primordial and uncontrived,
> Abandon hope and fear within your mind
> Concerning the transmission and reception
> [Of the teacher's blessing power.
> Just recognize the ultimate expanse
> That is spontaneously present
> And thus need not be sought.

Other than arriving at a sure certainty that the precious spontaneous presence—suchness just as it is, unceasing self-cognizing
awareness, empty and luminous—is now completely in one's possession, there is now no need to accomplish the result, the dharmakāya, as though it came from somewhere else. It is just as when the
sun rises, there is no need to look elsewhere for its beams. One
should take a firm stand on the awareness that one possesses quite
naturally from the very beginning—the enlightened mind, the
great, uncontrived spontaneous presence. One should be completely confident that this is so. Right now, in this very moment,
one should completely cut through all hope and fear about whether
or not the empowering blessing [of the teacher] will be received
or whether his wisdom will be transmitted. It is thus that Longchenpa encourages us simply to recognize and have an unhesitating
confidence in the dharmadhātu, which is spontaneously present
and requires no action or effortful seeking.

Eleventh, in conclusion, it is shown that spontaneous presence
beyond hope and fear is the essence of the three kāyas.

> 11. Just as each and every thing
> Is the display of dharmakāya,
> Sambhogakāya, and nirmāṇakāya
> (The triad uncontrived
> Of nature, character, and knowing power),
> So too samsara and nirvana are themselves the triple kāya,
> The expanse of the enlightened mind,
> Spontaneously present as a great and uncontrived
>   equality.
> Samsara, thus, is not to be abandoned,
> Nirvana likewise not to be achieved.
> Ascription and denial in their regard subside.
> Samsara and nirvana
> Dwell within the ultimate quintessence.
> This reveals the key point:

Phenomena subsist within the enlightened mind,
Spontaneously present from the first.

All phenomena within the whole of samsara and nirvana appear as the display of the dharmakāya, the sambhogakāya, and the nirmāṇakāya, which are themselves the expression of the uncontrived triad of nature, character, and cognitive power. The empty nature is the dharmakāya, its luminous character is the sambhogakāya, and its unceasing cognitive power arising in all its variety is the nirmāṇakāya. If it is correctly understood that phenomena are the spontaneous radiance of the three kāyas, it will be seen that everything in phenomenal existence, the whole of samsara and nirvana, does not extend beyond the trikāya, the expanse of awareness, the enlightened mind. On the contrary, it is, from the very first, spontaneously present as the great state of uncontrived equality. Within this expanse of awareness—the great spontaneous presence of the enlightened mind—samsara and nirvana transcend any notion of impurity or purity, of being something to be feared and something to be hoped for. They are both spontaneously present as the three kāyas, the great primordial wisdom of all-embracing equality. This is the ultimate key point.

So it is that what we call samsara is not to be eliminated as something evil, endowed with inherently existing characteristics. On the contrary, it is empty, groundless, and rootless. Likewise, what we call nirvana does not exist as something excellent to be sought for and accomplished. It is a non-referential state of unimpeded openness.

All phenomena belonging to samsara and nirvana are nothing but an open state of equality beyond conceptual elaboration. They are beyond the misconceptions of deluded beings. They are beyond such things as ascription, which imputes existence to what does not exist, and beyond denial, which imputes nonexistence to what in fact exists. All concepts of existence and nonexistence utterly subside. The phenomena of samsara and nirvana abide in their ultimate quintessence, which is their fundamental nature. Thus the key point of the phenomena of both samsara and nirvana is revealed. Without the need for any effort on our part to make them so, they abide already, spontaneously present from the very first within the ultimate enlightened mind.

3. Section Two: The Key Points of Spontaneous Presence Are Essentialized

This consists of five stanzas. First is the way in which the mind becomes the teacher.

> 12. All things are now essentialized
> As spontaneous presence.
> The five great elements,
> The appearing world and its inhabitants,
> Arise as teachers, all spontaneously present,
> In a state that, from the first,
> Is free of all discursive thought.
> When there is no thought of self and other,
> They are themselves intrinsically pure.
> They are essentialized as your own mind,
> Free of all activity and effort.
> Do not block appearances,
> But leave the six sense consciousnesses
> In a state of relaxation.

Awareness—namely, self-arisen primordial wisdom—is primordially pure, empty, and luminous, like a sphere of crystal. Within it are the five lights of its luminous character—the inner luminosity of spontaneous presence—which constitute the so-called great elements. These are the inner elements, the quintessence of the five elements. When these lights radiate outward, they do so in the same way that the inner lights of a crystal appear outwardly. And when in the very beginning, they are apprehended as being possessed of self, they become the five corrupted elements, which are mistakenly taken to be the universe and the beings it contains. And these are the outer, or lesser, elements.

Everything in phenomenal existence is essentialized as awareness, great spontaneous presence. This happens in the following way. When beings are deluded with regard to the appearances of spontaneously present inner luminosity, it is then that the array of hallucinatory samsaric appearance occurs—the world with its mountains, rocks, houses, and so on. Therefore, in our present situation, the time of hallucinatory appearances, when the five great [inner] elements and the five lights arising from them as an outwardly radiating luminosity are apprehended as being possessed of self—as being inherently existent—they are reduced to the five [ordinary] elements, which are a corrupted residue perceived as the phenomena of the universe and its inhabitants. But if [in the very moment that such phenomena are perceived], one is able right from the start to refrain from thinking of them in terms of self and other and if one relaxes in the great equality of awareness, these same phenomena—when one has no thoughts about them—will become spacious and easy to manage. They will seem tenuous in their lack of real existence. They will be perceived, but because one does not have thoughts about them, one will not fixate on their hallucinatory appearance. Phenomena will arise and subside quite naturally. And as they subside into the state of equality, the five elements appear as the spontaneously present teachers who introduce one to the five features of nonconceptual equality. As it is said in *The All-Creating King*,

> Within the utterly enlightened mind,
> The five great elements of the nature of the mind
> Arise as the five teachers of the enlightened mind.

And,

> Five teachers of the enlightened mind
> Thus reveal the nature of phenomena.

The teachers—namely, the five outer elements—demonstrate the five features of nonconceptual equality. Accordingly, as one refrains from considering the five elements and so on in terms of self and other, they themselves [are seen to be] intrinsically pure. Therefore, the key point of whatever appears is that it is necessarily essentialized as one's own mind, which is itself unborn and free of all activity and effort. It is a state of openness that is free of all conceptual elaboration.

When the teachers—the five elements, which are the self-experience of awareness and the outward manifestation of inner luminosity—appear to oneself, the five teachers of the enlightened mind, namely, the five elements that in their own nature are pure, demonstrate that all things are the sphere and display of suchness, the ultimate nature of phenomena. All appearances manifest as spontaneously present teachers. As it is said in *The All-Creating King,*

> The primal wisdom of the enlightened mind
> Naturally arises in the form of teachers.
> They do not teach in words and syllables,
> But they reveal awareness, self-cognizing.

As it is said, when one does not block appearances, all six gatherings of consciousness arise as teachers, who are themselves the self-experience of awareness. Whatever arises naturally subsides—and so, Longchenpa tells us, we should just relax and let it be. To know how to introduce this view, sealing [it with confidence], and to know how to essentialize all phenomena within it is a key point.

Second, it is shown that the sense consciousnesses unsullied by conceptuality are essentialized as being empty.

13. Awareness, spontaneous presence,
Luminously radiant,
Is the fundamental source of all.
The key point is to leave

> The five sense doors unmodified
> And to be without the to-and-fro of thoughts.
> Recognize the dharmakāya state,
> Spontaneously present, aware and empty.
> Be certain of it; leave it free
> Of all conceptual movement.

The outer and inner phenomena of the world and its inhabitants arise distinctly and vividly. When this happens, awareness, spontaneous presence, the source of all these things, must not be allowed to lose itself in the perceptions of the five sense consciousnesses. It must instead remain radiantly luminous, vast, spacious, and utterly empty, naked, and free. It should not stray into the objects of perception, mixing itself with them, but should instead be like a drop of mercury that has fallen in the dust. At that time, the five sense powers are left unmodified and in a state of equilibrium.[60] Their objects manifest unceasingly. And yet within a state that is free from movement, from the to-and-fro of thoughts, awareness remains free—a seamless, vast expanse. This is a key point.

This state of empty awareness, the dharmakāya, the condition of precious spontaneous presence, should be recognized as the present, uncontrived, and ultimate mode of being of the fundamental stratum of the mind. Thus one comes to a decisive conviction that all appearances, pure and impure, which arise through the creative power of spontaneous presence, are none other than awareness—empty and free of conceptual movement, the primordial wisdom of equality. And to rest meditatively in this empty, luminous state of awareness, which transcends all reference, thought, and conceptual construction—a naked, uninterrupted state of knowing—is a most important key point.

Third, everything is essentialized as a natural meditative absorption.

> 14. In the vast and pure expanse
> Of uninhibited awareness, self-cognizing,

All appearances—objects, mental states—
Are an unbroken state of evenness.
They are all essentialized
As a seamless and spontaneous presence,
A natural meditative absorption.
At all times like the current of a mighty stream,
Primordial wisdom,
Not cultivated through one's meditation
But spontaneously present, is unceasing.
The essential core of all phenomena
Is the expanse, primordial, self-arisen,
That in its full measure corresponds
To Samantabhadra's actual wisdom mind.

All phenomena of both samsara and nirvana occur within the vast expanse of self-cognizing awareness. When awareness is left in a free and open state, one rests at ease in the recognition of the nature of these same phenomena without blocking them. Free of any reference point, awareness rests uninhibited and pure in a state of equality in which phenomena naturally arise and subside. It is consequently said that these same phenomena are essentialized as the state of all-encompassing openness. As *The Six Expanses* declares,

> Within the nature of the mind, beyond adopting and
>   rejecting,
> All appearances without distinction naturally subside.
> This is the "state of all-pervading openness"
> And is what I, Samantabhadra, teach.

Whatever appears—whether objects of apprehension or appre-hending mental states—within the great and all-pervading openness of the vast expanse of uninhibited and self-cognizing awareness, the crucial point is to recognize that these appearances are simply awareness and to relax naturally in this recognition. In this state of uninhibited, even, nonconceptual, and uninterrupted equality, all such things arise and naturally subside.

In the same way, when one rests at ease in the uncontrived and naturally open state, one is in a meditative absorption that is primordially present. This is essentialized as the expanse of vast, uninterrupted, spontaneous presence—pristine, empty, and luminous. At all times, this meditative absorption is unceasing like the current of a great river. Even though one makes no effort to cultivate it, primordial wisdom, self-arisen and spontaneous, is constant like a stream of pure water.

In short, the essential core of all phenomena, whether of samsara or nirvana, is inseparable from the self-arisen primordial expanse, which is, in its full measure, the ultimate wisdom mind, the fundamental nature, of Samantabhadra. The crucial point is to rest naturally in it—the great, natural meditative absorption of the primordial wisdom of great bliss.

Fourth, spontaneous presence is essentialized as the state where everything is left just as it is.

> 15. The root of all phenomena
> Is the enlightened mind,
> Which is like space—
> The all-applicable analogy.
> All things are contained in the abyss of space,
> And all is pure by nature
> Without striving or exertion.
> Likewise, in the state beyond intended action,
> Beyond the reach of ordinary mind,
> Where all things that appear
> Are left just as they are—
> It's here that is essentialized
> The key point of phenomena,
> Spontaneously present
> Both outside and within.

The root of all phenomena is the ultimate enlightened mind. It is compared with space, which is the universally applicable example. In what sense is this comparison made? Space is beyond distinctions such as outside and within, up and down, center and circumference. It is without movement and change, and within it the cardinal points and the intermediate directions have no meaning. In the same way, the enlightened mind is beyond such distinctions as outside or inside and so on. Indeed, all the many vast and wonderful configurations found within the universe and its inhabitants are all contained in the abyss of space. And in terms of their fundamental way of being, they are all effortlessly and by nature pure, while remaining individual and distinct. In like manner, whatever phenomena, pure or impure, of nirvana or samsara appear, they are all contained in the expanse of the enlightened mind. They never stir from their ultimate nature, which is beyond the range of the ordinary mind and is the all-pervading expanse of awareness beyond any kind of action and effort. When left uncontrived and just as it is, whatever appears in this natural state of spontaneously present equality is empty, luminous, and unconfined. The outer and inner appearances of samsara and nirvana, spontaneously present and self-arisen, are essentialized in this crucial point of leaving everything as it is. To settle freely and without contrivance in this ultimate nature of phenomena—which is none other than their fundamental nature—is a supreme key point. It is said in *The Word-Transcending Tantra*,

> As for all impure hallucinations,
> The key point is to leave the sense doors uncontrived,
> To leave them free, without manipulation.
> Do not stray from this. This is the pith
>   instruction.

Fifth, spontaneous presence is essentialized as the absence of all deliberate action and effort.

> 16. In suchness there's no origin, no ending,
> No going and no coming (and the rest).
> Therein the wisdom mind
> Of the Victorious Ones is gathered—
> The pure unwavering concentration
> Of spontaneous presence.
> In this state, transcending action,
> Phenomena are all essentialized.

Of the phenomena of samsara and nirvana, not one has ever been born. They are a state of equality beyond all conceptual elaboration, and it is consequently certain that in the present time also, they are unoriginate. But though unborn, they appear clearly and distinctly like rainbows in the sky. The root verse consequently describes them as unceasing. Arising at the very outset from the expanse of awareness, phenomena do not come from somewhere else. And since in their ending, they naturally subside in the expanse of awareness, they do not go elsewhere. The same applies to the rest of the eight extremes.

In short, phenomena beyond these eight conceptual extremes never stir from the fundamental stratum of the ground. Within this same expanse, the wisdom mind of the Victorious Ones of the three times is wholly gathered, mingling with it indivisibly like water mixed with water. When one abides in this state of suchness, the actualization of this state is called the "pure unwavering concentration of spontaneous presence," that is, awareness. The body is left as it is, unmoving like a mountain. The faculty of speech is left in silence like an echo that has ceased to resound. The mind is left without thoughts, like an immense space, a wide-open clarity of spontaneous presence. There, in the state of evenness, the absence of all action, phenomena are all essentialized. As it is said in *The All-Creating King*,

> The enlightened mind, the nature of phenomena
> Beyond acceptance and rejection, is similar to space.

It cannot be contrived, therefore, through thoughts and
    deeds.
It cannot be fixated on as "this" or "that,"
And thus one cannot meditate on it.
Space-like, utterly at peace,
It is completely free of all impurity.

The Tantra of the Six Expanses also says,

In the nature of the mind, exempt from every mental
    stirring,
The experience of deep insight without thought
Is wisdom free of coming and of going.
It is what I, Samantabhadra, teach.

3. Section Three: Phenomena Are Subsumed into Spontaneous Presence

This consists of three stanzas. First, all things are subsumed in the
purity of spontaneous presence.

17. **All things are subsumed within spontaneous**
    presence.
All phenomenal existence, spontaneously present,
Is the self-experience of awareness.
Samsara and nirvana,
Spontaneously present, are awareness's display.
Also, the enlightened mind is, from the very first,
Spontaneously present.
All phenomena are nothing other
Than spontaneous presence.

All phenomena are subsumed in awareness, that is, great spontaneous presence. This is so in the following way. Just as dream visions
are spontaneously present as the experience of sleep, the things that

make up the universe and beings are all spontaneously present as the self-experience of the ultimate enlightened mind. In the same way that the five lights projecting from a crystal are the display of that crystal's creative power, the phenomena of samsara and nirvana spontaneously arise as the display of the creative power of awareness. And awareness, namely, the enlightened mind, is spontaneously present as primordial, pristine pure awakening, the nature that is open and free from the very first. This being so, all phenomena in both samsara and nirvana are none other than awareness, the great spontaneous presence. Apart from this, there are no phenomena. It is said in *The Instantaneous Severance of the Three Times*,

> The ground of both samsara and nirvana is the enlightened mind.
> The ground of the enlightened mind is spontaneously present.
> That which is spontaneously present is itself without determination.
> Objects are unborn, that is, spontaneously present.

And,

> The nature of samsara and nirvana is the enlightened mind.
> The nature of enlightened mind is endless and beginningless.
> The ground, which is beginningless and endless,
> Is spontaneously present.
> That which has no end and no beginning
> Is without determination.

Second, spontaneous presence is subsumed within the absence of effort and practice.

18. Spontaneously present
Is the nature of the mind.

And thus the ground or root,
The essence [of phenomena],
Is gathered in the enlightened mind.
No need is there to seek it out
By means of the ten elements.
It is spontaneously present;
There is no need to strive for it
By means of view and meditative concentration.
There is no need to gain it by extraneous means,
As in the systems of causality.
There is no need to be preoccupied
With hope and fears regarding it.
For right now in the present time,
Spontaneous presence is primordial
    dharmakāya.

The nature of the mind—the simple, bare absence of conceptual elaboration, the equality of samsara and nirvana—is spontaneously present. Therefore, the ground or root from which all phenomena of samsara and nirvana arise and the essence on which they depend are gathered within the ultimate enlightened mind. And as the text says, this is spontaneously present. It is not something to be sought for or pursued by means of the ten elements of tantra— view, action, samaya, empowerment, mandala, and so forth. There is no need to strive for it [through the practice of] view, meditation, concentration, and so on. All is present naturally. As *The All-Creating King* declares,

> *Kyé!* The teacher of all teachers,
> The all-creating king,
> Bestows this teaching on his retinue,
> Whose minds are uncontrived. He says,
> "O you the yogis who have understood
> That all without exception is unborn,
> Do not strive in the ten elements of tantra!"

Furthermore, it is unnecessary for this to be accomplished through the agency of some extraneous cause, as in the lower vehicles, where causes and their effects are considered different and separate. The natural state of awareness, which is beyond all causation and striving, is spontaneously present. When one is decisively convinced of this, one has no need to worry about this natural state, hoping to find it or fearing that one will miss it. As it is said in *The All-Creating King*,

> The view and action of the Great Perfection
> Is not like practice based on causes and results.
> The view and action of the enlightened mind
> Are space-like in their nature.

Owing to the fundamental nature of spontaneous presence—namely, the enlightened mind, the state of great equality free of all conceptual elaboration—we are, in this very moment, face to face with the dharmakāya Samantabhadra, the primordial lord.

Third, a concluding statement demonstrating that spontaneous presence is unchanging.

> 19. The nature of the mind is an immense expanse
> Of space beyond all change.
> From this expanse of the three kāyas,
> Samsara and nirvana spontaneously arise,
> Although they never stir from it.
> Indefinitely various is its display:
> A treasure of illusory appearances
> Of cognitive power
> Arising solely as spontaneous presence:
> Samantabhadra.
> He is thus the master of samsara and nirvana—
> For they have never strayed elsewhere
> From this, the ultimate expanse.
> Samantabhadra thus is everything;

Nothing is there that could not be so.
All is the expanse, spontaneously present,
Of the vajra essence.
All things are primordially subsumed
Within spontaneous presence.

The unchanging expanse of the nature of the mind is naturally endowed with the three kāyas. The unchanging space-like expanse of the mind's nature, being empty, is the dharmakāya. Its luminous character is the sambhogakāya. Its unobstructed cognitive power is the nirmāṇakāya. All the phenomena of both samsara and nirvana seem to arise spontaneously from within the vast expanse of the three kāyas, and yet from the very beginning, they have never stirred from this same expanse, awareness itself. And it is certain that they will never do so at any time in the future.

Within the expanse of the undivided trikāya, which is awareness, spontaneous presence, the multifarious display of its creative power unfolds like a rainbow appearing in the heavens. Indeed, the entire rich variety of the illusory manifestations of cognitive power, arising from the treasury of precious spontaneous presence or awareness is, in itself, the sole spontaneous presence of Samantabhadra manifesting outwardly. For this reason, all appearances, pure or impure, partake of the one nature of Samantabhadra. And it is certain that there is nothing that could be anything else. As we find in *The Six Consciousnesses Overwhelmed*,

Within Samantabhadra, the state beyond all action,
Samsara is Samantabhadra, nirvana is Samantabhadra.
And yet within Samantabhadra's space,
Samsara or nirvana there has never been.
Appearance is Samantabhadra, and emptiness Samantabhadra.
And yet within Samantabhadra's space,
Appearances and emptiness have never been.

And,

> Birth and death are both Samantabhadra.
> Happiness and pain are both Samantabhadra.
> And yet within Samantabhadra's space,
> No birth or death has ever been,
> No happiness or pain.
> Self and other are Samantabhadra,
> Permanence and ending are Samantabhadra.
> And yet within Samantabhadra's space,
> No I or other, permanence or ending
> Has there ever been.

So it is that awareness, Samantabhadra, has the mastery of all the appearances of samsara and nirvana—which have arisen from its expanse as the display of its creative power. They never stir from the vast expanse of spontaneous presence, from awareness, Samantabhadra. Therefore, the root text says that they have never strayed elsewhere. Indeed, no phenomena could arise from anything other than the creative power of Samantabhadra. There is nothing that could do so. Therefore, everything in phenomenal existence has never, from the very first, stirred from awareness, that is, Samantabhadra, the spontaneously present space of the vajra essence. So it is that all the phenomena of samsara and nirvana are primordially subsumed within awareness, precious spontaneous presence. As it is said in *The Six Consciousnesses Overwhelmed*,

> The greatest of the great, Samantabhadra, dharmadhātu,
> Is like a king maintaining all in his dominion.
> He rules samsara and nirvana, which never stir from him.
> All things are thus Samantabhadra.
> This is so, though it may seem not so.
> Beyond the differences of good and bad,
> All is one within Samantabhadra.

It is thus that the principle of spontaneous presence is demonstrated.

3. Section Four: A Clear Conviction Is Gained That All Phenomena Are Spontaneous Presence

This section consists of eight stanzas. First, a clear conviction is gained that all phenomena partake of spontaneous presence, which is inconceivable and inexpressible.

> 20. A clear conviction thus is reached
> About their nature of spontaneous presence.
> Within spontaneous presence,
> Which transcends all boundaries,
> Outside and within,
> All things are but the self-experience of awareness.
> They neither go nor come;
> They lie beyond affirming and negating.
> All things are an all-encompassing expanse
> Devoid of all directions, up and down.
> Completely indeterminate, completely unconfined,
> Inconceivable and inexpressible,
> They cannot be identified.

What does it mean to say that one should definitively resolve or come to a clear conviction [about phenomena]? All appearances are awareness, and this is referred to as their nature of spontaneous presence. It is the enlightened mind, which is free of all conceptual elaboration, a wide-open clarity as vast as space itself. How is this so? Within the expanse of awareness, the enlightened mind—in other words, the precious spontaneous presence transcending all directions, zenith and nadir, outside and within, center and periphery—within this single, all-encompassing expanse, all the phenomena of samsara and nirvana, the self-experience of awareness, arise vividly and uninterruptedly just like a rainbow spread across the sky. In fact, however, these same phenomena have never stirred from the expanse of awareness, the great spontaneous presence. They are beyond all affirmation and negation, all movement and change, all coming and going. They have never wavered from the single space-like expanse of great, all-encompassing equality, beyond direction, up or down. As it is said in *Meeting the Three Kāyas*,

> In the dharmadhātu, things appear
> Both outside and within.
> And yet within the space beyond all action,
> No outside or within has ever been.
> Beyond both in and out, the nature of phenomena
> Is an open and untrammeled space.
> This state is indivisible
> And in it all activity is found.

This means that all phenomena are by their nature awareness. They are inconceivable, inexpressible, nondual, utterly indeterminate, and unconfined. They are a state of equality that falls neither to one side nor to another, a state beyond all conceptual elaboration. It is for this reason that they cannot be identified by words and expressions. They cannot be indicated by signs or analogies, and so on. Their nature is beyond both thought and expression. As *The All-Illuminating Sphere* declares,

> Unobstructed nature equals nonexistence.
> Since there is no watching it, it's neither seen nor found.

Second, a clear conviction is reached that spontaneous presence is the ultimate quintessence.

21. Because phenomena are,
By nature, pure from the beginning,
Because, by character, they are spontaneously
    present,
They are free of all extremes:

> Existence, nonexistence, permanence, discontinuity.
> This is the nature of nondual, enlightened mind.

The nature of phenomenal existence, samsara and nirvana, is primordially pure. Its character is luminosity. As *The Six Expanses* tells us,

> By nature, they are pure primordially;
> By character, they are spontaneously present.

As this citation declares, phenomena are without existence. By virtue of their nature of primordial purity, they are empty. But they are not nonexistent, for they have the character of being spontaneously present. Thus they are respectively free of the extremes of existence and of permanence; of nonexistence and of discontinuity. Freed in this way from the extreme positions of the four permutations regarding their mode of apprehension, phenomena are self-arisen and spontaneously present. And this is the ultimate way of being of awareness, which is primordially pure and beyond affirmation and negation, beyond movement and change. This is the ultimate nature of nondual, enlightened mind. As it is said in *The Lion's Perfect Power*,

> Buddhahood, beyond the four extremes,
> Is awareness, self-cognizing.
> Beyond existence, beyond nonexistence,
> Beyond both permanence and discontinuity,
> It is dharmakāya.

Third, a more detailed demonstration of the previous point.

> 22. By nature, primal purity
> Does not exist as anything at all.
> Its character is similar to space
> And pure from the beginning.

> In itself, spontaneous presence
> Has not been made by anyone.
> Its arising is unceasing,
> And anything may manifest.
> It is the source of both samsara and nirvana.
> It had no beginning in the past,
> And in the future it will have no end.

Awareness, the very nature of primordial purity, lies in no onto-logical extreme, such as existence or nonexistence. It is a state of equality, free from conceptual elaboration; it is inconceivable and inexpressible. As *The Six Expanses* tells us,

> Free of all conceptual elaboration,
> The primordially pure nature of phenomena
> Is the stainless countenance of the essential ground.
> Beyond both words and syllables,
> No description will determine it.

And,

> There are no buddhas and there are no beings.
> There are no phenomena;
> There is no perception of the same.
> There is nothing, there is nothing,
> There is nothing whatsoever.

As this text proclaims, the very nature of awareness has no exis-tence as anything at all. Just like the sky when it is free of the three impurities, the nature of awareness has a purity that is primordial. This is the primal wisdom of equality, which is nondual and spon-taneously present as the ground from which both samsara and nir-vana manifest. No one has created it; it is open and unobstructed like space. Nevertheless, even though awareness, this spontaneous presence, is the natural ground for the arising of both samsara and nirvana, the nature of awareness in itself is neither samsara nor nirvana. The latter are the display of awareness's creative power, which arises unceasingly as the pure or impure appearances that may be perceived. *The Tantra of Auspicious Beauty* says,

> Within me there is no delusion. Delusion occurs because of creative power. Self-cognizing awareness arises unceasingly within the unchanging ground. But because cognitive potency is undetermined, ignorance, the lack of awareness, occurs. It is like the clouds in the sky that have no real existence, for they arise adventitiously. Similarly, the ground has no ignorance; it is only when cognitive potency arises in the ground that ignorance occurs.[61] This is what is known as the fundamental nature of the spontaneously present ground.

Although the ground, the precious, spontaneous presence, which no one has created, is beyond conceptual elaboration, its [luminous] character manifests uninterruptedly. Every kind of appearance unceasingly occurs through the creative power of cognitive potency. The ground is thus endowed with the eight ways of arising, and this is referred to as the fundamental nature of the precious dimension. These ways of arising are said to be the source of samsara and nirvana. For that which manifests through the impure door is samsara and that which manifests through the pure door is nirvana. In brief, whatever appearances of samsara or nirvana occur and however they manifest in the past or the future, they do so without ever stirring from the state of awareness, which is beginningless and endless. As it is said in *The Six Consciousnesses Overwhelmed*,

> From the expanse of the trikāya
> Samsara and nirvana manifest,
> And yet they never stir from this expanse.

Fourth, a clear conviction is reached regarding the spontaneous presence of all that arises.

> 23. Indeterminate, unborn, spontaneous presence
> Is the ultimate ground. The way that things arise,
> Beginningless and endless,
> Cannot be arrested.
> The way things are—without intrinsic being—
> Cannot be identified.
> The way that things subside—without inherent
>   character—
> Cannot be interrupted.
> Clear conviction thus is reached
> That subsequently also
> All things dwell within the ground
> From which they have arisen.
> This is called the "dissolution in the dharmakāya,
> Exhaustion in the ultimate expanse."

Phenomena appear in various ways through the creative power of unborn awareness, spontaneous presence, like the planets and stars that appear reflected vividly on the surface of a stretch of water. In truth, however, they have never moved from the expanse of the ultimate ground: awareness, spontaneous presence, unborn and self-cognizing. First, phenomena manifest unceasingly within spontaneous presence, the expanse of awareness, which is unconfined and does not fall into any extreme. Subsequently, these same phenomena subsist within this same awareness. And finally, they subside in the same expanse of awareness, the enlightened mind. They cannot be found elsewhere. The beginningless and endless arising of all phenomena cannot be arrested. Phenomena arise and subside all by themselves.

In similar fashion, without ever moving from the great, spontaneous presence, the expanse of awareness, phenomena (being inseparable from this same awareness) subsist in a state of unobstructed openness. They have no existence as something different from awareness. The ultimate way of being of awareness and of all phenomena cannot be identified as this or that. It is an unimpeded openness beyond all reference.

Likewise, although phenomena arise unceasingly within the expanse of empty awareness, spontaneous presence, they do not in fact possess the slightest inherent character. Phenomena arise and subside all by themselves. In just the same way that waves emerge from the sea without being different from the sea itself, various appearances, manifesting within the expanse of awareness, subside uninterruptedly in the great process of self-arising and self-subsiding.

No matter how phenomena appear to arise, dwell, and subside, they never move from the expanse of spontaneously present, primordial wisdom, the ultimate expanse of the ground. They are said to retain their nature in the immutable fortress, in other words, the spontaneous presence, which is awareness. This is also referred to as convergence in the one sole sphere of the dharmakāya free of edges and corners. In his text *The Instantaneous Severance of the Three Times*, Garab Dorje declares,

> An unconfined and limitless extension
> Is the fortress of the ground,
> Of which the cardinal and intermediate directions,
> Up and down, are one smooth continuity.
> The buddhas therefore speak about
> A fortress hanging in the air
> Where all these values come together.
> All-accommodating, not leaning to one side or another,
> The view is like a fortress,
> The citadel of awareness—
> The citadel of the enlightened mind.
> The place is the expanse of unborn dharmadhātu.

The name is primal wisdom, self-arisen, all-surpassing.
The weapon is the razor's edge
Of spontaneous, indeterminate arising.

A clear conviction and certainty is reached that all the appearances of spontaneous presence—that is, all things that are manifest—also dwell subsequently in the ground from which they had previously arisen. Thus one speaks of their dissolving into the dharmakāya, the expanse where [phenomena] are exhausted.

When whatever appearances of spontaneous presence arise, if one is mindful that these hallucinatory phenomena, without any difference between them, are the self-experience of awareness, then when finally the seal of one's body breaks, it will be found also at that later time that these appearances dwell within the ground—the dharmatā, which is like the mother from which they first arose. One comes to a decisive certainty about this. And when one recognizes the spontaneously present appearances of the ground as the self-experience of awareness, this is like the meeting of a mother with her child.

Moreover, if the hallucinatory appearances of the mind's self-experience are destroyed by the razor-like instructions on how to recognize their nature, the subsiding of these same appearances in the expanse of the one sole all-embracing sphere of the dharma-kāya, the beginningless ground, is referred to as dissolution in the dharmakāya, the expanse of the ground of exhaustion.

Fifth, a clear conviction is reached regarding the dissolution of phenomena.

> 24. Like clouds that melt into the sky from whence
>   they came
> And like the crystal's lights withdrawn into the crystal,
> Samsara and nirvana
> (The ground's appearances
> Arisen from the ground)
> Keep to the primordial, pure nature

In the ultimate ground.
A clear conviction is acquired
That all phenomena are gathered
In the expanse of the fundamental stratum
Of spontaneous presence.
All mental movement naturally dissolves
In the expanse devoid of cognitive activity.

Clouds, white or black, appearing in the sky eventually vanish, dissolving into the abyss of space from which they first arose. When the sun's rays strike upon a crystal, its five-colored lights vividly appear. When the sun's rays cease, the lights are withdrawn again into the crystal. It is the same with the various pure and impure appearances of samsara and nirvana, the appearances of the ground, which arise from the expanse of precious spontaneous presence (the ground awareness) and are not separate or different from this same ground. If thanks to the view, one is decisively certain of this and if one maintains this view in meditation, avoiding the perilous path (of duality) with regard to one's behavior, one will actualize and manifest the genuine fundamental nature beyond hope and fear. Yogis who achieve this continue to live in bodily forms and are constrained by them. But when the seal of their bodies is broken, the hallucinatory appearance of an apprehender and things to be apprehended dissolves into its true condition. For five days[62] the yogis perceive only the appearances of nirvana: buddha fields, deities, and the primordial wisdoms. And when they recognize these as the self-experience of awareness, all the appearances of outwardly radiating luminosity (the deities and the visions of primordial wisdom) dissolve into the inner ultimate expanse. Like clouds melting into the sky and like the lights that are gathered back into a crystal, all the appearances of the ground—that is, the appearances of spontaneous presence—subside in the subtle primordial wisdom of inner luminosity, the ultimate ground. They keep to their own nature within the expanse of primordial purity, the dharmakāya.

Now although the rūpakāya is spontaneously present as the radiance of awareness, the dharmakāya, it is not perceptible while the yogi is still in the physical body. As soon as the seal of the body breaks, all phenomenal appearance is gathered into the ultimate expanse, the fundamental stratum of precious spontaneous presence. This is referred to as the phenomenal appearance that captures the stronghold of primordial freedom in the expanse of dharmatā. When this is realized, one comes to a final, decisive experience of phenomena. Hundreds of thousands of webs of conceptual construction effortlessly and quite naturally dissolve into the dharmatā, which is free of cognitive activity and is the expanse of the exhaustion of phenomena. And thus the ultimate nature of the primordial wisdom of the path is actualized. This is described as capturing the everlasting realm of the openness and freedom of the ground.

Sixth, two kinds of clear conviction regarding the nonexistence [of phenomena] are demonstrated.

> 25. When all the things that now appear—
> All objects of the six sense consciousnesses—
> Dissolve into the fundamental stratum, dharmakāya,
> You will be utterly convinced
> That both the outer and the inner blend together
> In the vast expanse: spontaneous presence.
> You will be utterly convinced
> That both samsara and nirvana,
> Self-experience of awareness,
> Are the enlightened mind devoid of form,
> The state of manifest awakening.
> Likewise, if you leave appearances and mental
>   movement
> In their natural state, the space of luminosity,
> Not making differences between them,
> Keeping to a natural flow without conceptual
>   elaboration,

You will be utterly convinced
That they are empty, luminous radiance
Of awareness, present and immediate.
This is called the "firm abiding in the precious
     sphere."

For yogis of the highest capacity, who gain freedom in this present life, the way in which all appearances of objects subside in their nature—free and open where they stand—without being relinquished, is as follows. The phenomena detected by the six sense consciousnesses appear through the unwholesome tendencies to which beings have grown accustomed from beginningless time. These yogis are completely certain of the unreality of such phenomena and they seize the citadel of the secret dimension of inner luminosity, the fundamental stratum of awareness unspoiled by mental movement, fabrication and manipulation. Whatever arises subsides, dissolving into the dharmakāya. It is thus that the appearances of outwardly radiating luminosity dissolve into the inner expanse, with the result that the outer and the inner blend together. This brings about the clear conviction that these appearances are the spontaneous radiance of awareness within the ultimate expanse endowed with six special features.[63] These yogis gain a clear conviction that samsara and nirvana, the self-experience of awareness, are the ultimate enlightened mind devoid of form, the sphere of subtle primordial wisdom of inner luminosity—which, though absorbed within, is not obscured. It is here, within this dimension, that these yogis attain their actual awakening in this very life.

Alternatively, the state of freedom is gained at the moment of death through the clear conviction of awareness. This happens in the following way. All the appearances and mental processes that arise at the time of death should be left in their natural state without contrivance or manipulation. The object of meditation, the outer ultimate expanse of luminosity, the expanse devoid of conceptual elaboration—awareness that is the ultimate nature—is like a mother. The agent of meditation, the inner ultimate expanse of luminous dharmatā—awareness that is cognitive potency—is like a child. [At the moment of death] they come together—like a mother meeting with her child. The two expanses blend together into one. And as one rests therein, one is no longer hindered by a body that is the result of habitual tendencies, and no distinction is made between the two expanses. One remains in a natural flow, free of all conceptual elaboration. This, when it occurs, is referred to as meditative equipoise in the empty and luminous radiance [of awareness]. This means that, at the moment of death, one gains a clear conviction that awareness in its present immediacy is the indivisible union of awareness and the ultimate expanse. This refers to an extremely profound pith instruction called the firm abode within the dimension of precious spontaneous presence.

Briefly, this pith instruction is as follows. The outer ultimate expanse (namely, the mind of the Victorious Ones of the three times, the great dharmadhātu) and the inner ultimate expanse (namely, self-cognizing awareness in its present immediacy) are linked together through the door of the eyes, through a state of awareness that is lucid and alert. When the seal of the body is torn asunder, these outer, inner, and intermediate expanses mingle together indivisibly as one. It is said in *The All-Illuminating Sphere*,

> The space within one's room
> And the pure space of one's awareness, self-cognizing,
> Are—through the unobstructed opening of the door—
> Both clear and unobscured.

When all-encompassing awareness is projected via one's eyes into space and the ultimate expanse (the mother) and awareness (the child) mingle together, freedom occurs. This way of gaining freedom is according to the tradition of the pith instructions and is extremely secret and profound. It is called firm abode within the dimension of precious spontaneous presence. It is said in *The All-Illuminating Sphere*,

Awareness closed within the shell of habits
And awareness dwelling in the space outside—
These two are linked together
Through the door of primal wisdom.
When the body that arises from habitual tendencies
No longer hinders you,
These two are one inseparable vast openness.

And,

When you attain a realization of such great meaning,
You are like a lion that, with one great leap,
Encompasses the earth in its entirety.
Supreme and open, unimpeded wisdom
Breaks through into the precious sphere.
There is no start, no ending of the bardo state,
For you are dwelling in the great primordial wisdom.

The way that freedom occurs can be described as follows. The ground awareness, empty, luminous, and unborn (the mother luminosity of spontaneous presence) and the primordial wisdom, clear, unborn, empty, and self-arisen, on which one meditates on the path (that is, the self-arisen child luminosity) are able to blend together inseparably owing to the fact that they are both clear and luminous. And therefore, at the moment when the seal of the material body breaks, the mother and child luminosities mingle together, and there is freedom.

Seventh, a pith instruction on the importance of having a clear conviction.

26. If now you lack a clear conviction
In the fundamental stratum of the ultimate expanse,
It is not later that you'll find
Your freedom in the primal ground.
If freedom in the ground expanse you fail to gain,

> Your rigid meditation will not lead to liberation
> But to high celestial states.
> So now it is of great importance
> To embrace with clear conviction
> The kind of concentration
> Where you're naturally at rest
> Within the pristine inner ultimate expanse.

If at the present time, one does not have a clear conviction—gained by maintaining a natural meditative absorption—in the empty, luminous awareness of the inner ultimate expanse, the fundamental stratum of primordial purity, the mind will continue in its ordinary courses. And though it may be stabilized through the practice of calm abiding, it will not gain freedom subsequently in the expanse of the primordial ground. Moreover, if one fails to achieve freedom in the expanse of the mother luminosity of the ground, then no matter how much one trains in calm abiding devoid of thoughts or in a tightly contrived meditation hidebound with attitudes of adopting and rejecting, of affirming and negating, one will achieve no more than birth in the celestial abodes of the higher realms. One will never accomplish liberation in the place of everlasting freedom. As it is said in *The Oral Lineage*,

> You know how to meditate but not to gain your freedom.
> How then do you differ from a god sunk in samadhi?

And,

> Without sharp clarity of deep insight,
> Even certain animals can stay in calm
>   abiding.

This is why right now in the present, it is important to be convinced and certain of the kind of concentration where one naturally rests in the inner pristine expanse, empty, luminous, and unobstructed.

If now, while one is training on the path, one meditates in a way that emphasizes the luminosity of the inner expanse, it will happen that when one's body is cast aside, this luminosity will blend indivisibly with the precious spontaneous presence, the dharmakāya, and the two rūpakāyas will strive for the sake of beings, permanently, all-pervasively, and spontaneously.

At the moment of one's death, the last breath is exhaled with the sound "Ha." One cannot breathe in again with the sound "Hu." Awareness separates from the inner wind. And since the ordinary mind of habitual tendencies is no longer present, there arises the space-like state of the unborn dharmakāya, and directly in that very instant, buddhahood is attained. The young of the garuḍa, king of birds, become fully developed in their strength while still in the egg. Therefore, when they hatch, they can immediately take to the air in flight. This ability is possessed by no other bird; only the garuḍa has it. In the same way, yogis develop the strength of their realization while still inside the shell of their bodies. And as soon as this breaks open, they become inseparable from the space-like dimension of the dharmakāya, the ultimate expanse of the ground. Freedom is accomplished at once. This extraordinary quality is unique to Atiyoga. None of the other eight vehicles has it.

Moreover, even while they are still in the egg, the garuḍa's young have power over the *nāgas*. In the same way, although yogis dwell for the moment in their physical forms, they nevertheless surpass the eight lower vehicles by the strength of their realization of the ultimate nature of phenomena. As we find in *The Natural Subsiding of Characteristics*,

> The great garuḍa, for example, king of birds,
> While still within the egg, holds nāgas in his power.
> While in the egg, his wings develop fully,
> And as soon as he is hatched, he soars above the earth.
> Now, how could this be easily achieved by other birds?
> Only the garuḍa has this power—
> He takes at once to the skies in easy flight.

And,

> Without realization and without
> The lack of realization,
> There is freedom.
> Without this life and without future lives
> There is equality.
> Without interruption all subsists
> Within the equal state.
> Those who think that freedom is attained
> Through the nine vehicles—
> Who think it is attained through training,
> Through elimination and through transformation—
> All such people are at ease in Mahāyāna.

And,

> In this body of habitual tendencies,
> The power of the [vajra] essence is complete.
> Once the body is relinquished,
> There is neither birth, nor death, nor intermediate state.
> The one and sole awareness
> Is inseparable from everything.

And,

> This is not possible within the lower vehicles.
> This crucial point of the result
> Is possible, it's said, exclusively in Ati.

Eighth, the present section is brought to conclusion.

27. You will come to clear conviction
That all things are awareness,
Spontaneous presence.

You will come to clear conviction
That spontaneous presence
Is the fundamental stratum
Of primordial purity.
You will come to clear conviction
That primordial purity is free
From reference, thought, expression.
This is the clear, definitive conviction
Of spontaneous presence.

Because all phenomena of both samsara and nirvana arise from the expanse of great spontaneous presence or awareness and because they inevitably and finally subside into it, one will come to a clear conviction that they *are* awareness, spontaneous presence. One will come to a clear conviction that spontaneous presence, awareness, *is* the great dharmakāya, primordial purity, the fundamental stratum of the inner ultimate expanse. One will come to a clear conviction that primordial purity, the great dharmakāya, *is* the simple absence of cognitive activity, the freedom from reference, thought, and expression. The decisive certainty of the ultimate state and practice of the dharmatā corresponds to the clear, definitive conviction of spontaneous presence, awareness.

A Concluding Statement of the Vajra Topic's Name

Here ends the word commentary on the third vajra topic of *The Precious Treasury of the Fundamental Nature*, which establishes that from the first, phenomena are spontaneously present.

2. THE FOURTH VAJRA TOPIC: SINGLE NATURE

This topic demonstrates that phenomena are the single self-arisen primordial wisdom. The teaching itself, which concludes with a statement of the vajra topic's name, has four sections: the key points are revealed, they are essentialized, they are subsumed, and a clear conviction is gained in their regard.

3. Section One: The Key Points Are Revealed

This consists of ten stanzas. First, it is demonstrated that the root of all phenomena is the one awareness.

> 1. And now the one sole nature [of phenomena] is
>   shown.
> The one awareness is the ground of all phenomena.
> However many they may seem,
> They do not waver from their one sole nature.
> So it is said. Their one and only root
> Is primal wisdom self-arisen.
> In certain situations, from a single gem,
> Fire and water, different and distinct, may both
>   emerge.
> And yet their root is one, the pure and precious lapis
>   lazuli.
> Likewise, even though from one awareness,
>   self-cognizing,
> Nirvana and samsara both arise,
> Their root is one, the ultimate enlightened mind.
> The difference that divides them is illusory,
> Deriving from the recognition or nonrecognition of
>   awareness.

Longchenpa now shows how all phenomena, pure and impure, of samsara and nirvana, are established as being by nature the one sole primordial wisdom, self-arisen and self-cognizing. The ultimate enlightened mind, the one awareness, is the great ground of everything without exception, in samsara and nirvana. Therefore, even though at the moment, the infinite appearances of samsara and nirvana arise as a multiplicity, the fact is that they have never, do not, and will never move from the expanse of the one sole self-arisen awareness, the ultimate enlightened mind. This assertion demonstrates that their one and only root is self-arisen primordial wisdom. When a jewel of lapis lazuli is touched by the light of the sun, fire is produced. When it is touched by the light of the moon, water is produced. Fire and water, different and distinct, may both appear depending on specific conditions. Nevertheless, their root is the same, the pure gem of lapis lazuli. In similar fashion, all appearances are nothing but the one self-cognizing awareness, the ultimate enlightened mind. And yet, when they are not recognized to be so, they appear as samsara and there is a straying into an uninterrupted chain of hallucinatory appearances that are themselves the source of endless suffering. When they are recognized, however, they appear as nirvana and freedom occurs in the expanse of the one sole perfect sphere of self-cognizing awareness. Therefore, although the one self-cognizing awareness arises in the perception of beings as either samsara or nirvana, depending on the purity or impurity of these same perceptions, the fact is that the root or source from which all such appearances proceed is nothing other than the ultimate enlightened mind, the one sole sphere of awareness. The [apparently objective] characteristics of samsara and nirvana have no reality whatsoever. As it is said in *The All-Creating King*,

> All things are one within their root,
> The enlightened mind.
> In this enlightened mind,
> The essential core from which they spring,
> Buddhas, beings, the world and all it holds—
> Phenomenal existence in its entirety—
> Do not exist as separate things and yet are numberless.

If one therefore recognizes the nature of awareness, the enlightened mind, one is a buddha. If one fails to recognize it, one strays into the condition of an ordinary being. This difference between recognizing and failing to recognize is simply a matter of the mode of appearance, similar to the appearance of a horse or an ox in a magical illusion. It is said in *The Tantra of Samantabhadra*,

> The ground of all is uncompounded.
> Beyond expression, it is vast—
> An all-encompassing expanse.
> If one recognizes, one is buddha.
> If one does not recognize, one is deluded.

Second, it is demonstrated that everything is a single ultimate expanse, the one self-arisen primordial wisdom.

> 2. Phenomenal existence, samsara and nirvana,
> All things appearing in awareness,
> In the moment of their being perceived,
> Have but the nature of emptiness alone.
> They are like magical illusions, dreams,
> Like moons reflected in the water.
> Wholly empty and primordially empty,
> Beyond conceptual elaboration,
> They dwell within awareness,
> Space-like, insubstantial,
> The ground of their appearance.
> Since all is, in the one expanse,
> Primordially pure,
> There is no dualism, no "two."
> All is gathered in a single sphere,
> The dharmakāya without edges, without corners. *Émaho!*

All the phenomena of samsara and nirvana appear within awareness, and but for their appearance in awareness, they do not at all exist in any other way. In the very moment of their being perceived, they are just appearances: clear yet nonexistent. They are inseparable from the one expanse of emptiness, the nature of phenomena. Just as dream visions have the nature of the one state of sleep, just as the transformations of a magical display are the one appearance of empty forms, and just as the reflection of the moon has the one nature of water, phenomena dwell within the one expanse of awareness, their ground of manifestation, which is by nature insubstantial and pure like space. They are primordially empty, wholly empty, and beyond the elaborations of the conceptual mind.

Therefore, all the phenomenal appearances of samsara and nirvana are primordially pure within the one expanse of awareness, the dharmadhātu. This means that empty awareness and the empty phenomena appearing within its expanse—two emptinesses—mingle in a seamless state of equality. One cannot say that phenomena and awareness are two [separate entities]. Their root is gathered in a single taste within the expanse of nondual dharmakāya, the one sole sphere without edges or corners. In short, it must be understood that they are one ultimate expanse; they are one vast space. They have one taste and one root. It is said in *The All-Creating King*,

> The root of all phenomena
> Is the enlightened, all-creating mind.
> However things arise, they share my nature;
> However they occur, they are but my display.

Therefore, all phenomena are a single ultimate expanse of clear yet nonexistent appearance. They are a single vast space, free of all conceptual elaboration, within the nature of awareness. Awareness and the emptiness of phenomena are of a single root and are of one taste in the ultimate expanse of the nondual dharmakāya, the one sole sphere without edges or corners. And how marvelous this is! It is a truly amazing thing!

Third, the purity and equality [of phenomena] are shown to be self-arisen primordial wisdom.

3. That which appears as the five elements—
That very thing is the enlightened mind.
It does not stir from the one state: unborn equality.
The appearances of animate existence
Are but the empty forms of six migrations.
The appearances of the ground do not depart
From the condition of awareness.
Happiness and woe may both appear,
And yet they are the single essence,
The enlightened mind.
They do not waver from the one and only
Primal wisdom self-arisen.
So it is that you should understand
Phenomena are but a single ultimate expanse,
The state of emptiness.
They are the unborn, the enlightened mind.

Within the expanse of primordial wisdom, empty, luminous, and self-cognizing—which is similar to space and yet endowed with supreme qualities—the universe and all its multifarious appearances arise as the five elements. They arise in the enlightened mind, they remain in the enlightened mind, and at the last, they subside in the enlightened mind. None of these appearances ever moves from the enlightened mind, which is their root. They are inseparably of one taste with the unborn dharmadhātu, the state of equality: emptiness endowed with supreme qualities. They never stir from this condition.

Similarly, the whole of animate existence, the many living beings that appear within the expanse of self-cognizing awareness—great primordial emptiness—arise in that same expanse; they appear within it and subside in it. Therefore, the beings in the six migrations are in themselves empty forms. They are the appearances of the awareness of the ground expanse, that is, great primordial emptiness. From the very first, they have never moved from the state of primordial wisdom, empty yet aware. It is said in *The Word-Transcending Tantra*,

> Indeed, of all conditioned beings,
> There is not one that is not buddha.
> Because their nature is concordant
> With primordial wisdom, self-arisen,
> From the outset they have never wandered in
> samsara.
> Each and every being thus is buddha.

It is in this way that all things that appear in great emptiness, the vast expanse of the mother—all good and evil, all happiness and sorrow—arise within their ground, the essence, the enlightened mind. They abide within it, and into it they finally subside. They never move from primordial wisdom, self-arisen and pure from the beginning. All are indivisible from awareness and are of one taste with it.

We should therefore understand that the whole of phenomenal existence, samsara and nirvana, is spontaneously present within the one ultimate expanse. We should understand that it is the enlightened mind, space-like and unborn, abiding within the immensity of great emptiness, or awareness. This is the key point that introduces the purity and equality [of phenomena] as being one with primordial wisdom.

Fourth, the abode of awareness is shown to be the vast expanse.

> 4. Within this ultimate dimension,
> The vast expanse of awareness, self-cognizing,
> There dwells the one sole wisdom
> Of Victorious Ones, past, present, and to come.
> Do not think of it as manifold,
> For it transcends all thought of having parts.
> It is the palace of the essence

Of unwavering enlightenment,
Where nothing but primordial wisdom, self-arisen, dwells.

In the vast abyss of self-cognizing awareness, the ultimate expanse
that is pure like space, the one sole wisdom of the dharmadhātu
dwells. It is the wisdom mind of the victorious, blissfully proceeding buddhas of the three times. This wisdom dwells there, blended
indivisibly in a single taste with self-cognizing awareness, like
water mixed with water. To think of the wisdom minds of the buddhas of the three times as being separate and individual is a gross
error. For this wisdom cannot be thought of as a multiplicity, being
utterly beyond the concept of parts. As it is said, the Victorious
Ones are one within the expanse of primordial wisdom. And *The
All-Creating King* further states,

> Undivided is my nature,
> Free from all conceptual elaboration.
> I call it the abode of dharmadhātu,
> Where there's nothing other than enlightenment.

Therefore, the nature of awareness—primordial wisdom that from
the very first is pure and empty—cannot be divided from the mind
of the Victorious Ones of the three times. It is the dharmadhātu,
free of all conceptual elaboration. It subsists indivisibly from the
one sole sphere of their wisdom mind. It dwells in the nature of
unwavering dharmakāya, free of all mental movement. This place
is the palace of the primordial wisdom of the essence of self-arisen
enlightenment. It is there that self-arisen primordial wisdom
dwells inseparably—meaning that there is no difference between
the dweller and the dwelling place. It is nowhere else. As *The All-
Creating King* declares,

> Since in my nature, all-encompassing,
> There is no obscuration,
> It is a luminous expanse,

The palace measureless of primal wisdom,
Where nothing but this primal wisdom dwells.

Fifth, the three kāyas are shown to be the ultimate expanse from which samsara and nirvana both arise.

5. It is the wish-fulfilling, jewel-like,
Treasury of all phenomena,
The buddha field of the three kāyas,
Spontaneously present.

The mind of all the buddhas, past, present, and to come, the great dharmadhātu that is inseparable from primordial wisdom, self-cognizing awareness, is like a precious wish-granting jewel. It is the secret and profound treasure house of all phenomena.

All the hallucinatory appearances of the six migrations of samsara and all the pure appearances of nirvana—in short, the ocean-like infinitude of the phenomena of both samsara and nirvana—are in truth inseparable from each other. They are simply the ornament and display of the creative power of the three spontaneously present kāyas, the buddha field of purity and equality that is the buddhas' self-experience. This refers not only to the phenomena of the infinity of pure fields, for in truth, the body, speech, and mind of all the beings of the three realms do not extend beyond the three kāyas. As *The Word-Transcending Tantra* says,

Indeed, since none who live in the three worlds
Transcend their body, speech, and mind,
There is no need to seek elsewhere for the three kāyas.
For even if one searches, there's no way to find them.

Moreover, the pure buddha fields of the five families, the six impure migrations and all the three worlds are none other than the body, speech, and mind of Samantabhadra, and the whole array of his buddha field. As it is said in *The All-Creating King,*

I am the very essence whence all things arise.
And thus the five great elements,
The six migrations, the three worlds
Are nothing but my body, speech, and mind.
They are my nature, my array.

Sixth, it is demonstrated that the root of everything is one.

6. The one sole great expanse
Was made by none.
All things without exception
That emerge from it
Are the single fundamental ground
From which they came.
For to its cause does the result return.
This ground is the immensity
Of luminous and empty dharmatā.
It exceeds all limits, all directions;
It is everywhere—like pure, unsullied space.

What is the root whence all phenomena, impure and pure, of samsara and nirvana, emerge? They manifest from awareness alone, from the enlightened mind. Where does awareness come from, the one sole sphere of the great expanse? And who has created it? Not engendered through causes and conditions, nor produced by any agent, the nature of awareness is an all-encompassing openness that is free of all conceptual elaboration and is similar to space. Just like the reflections of the moon and stars seen on the surface of the water, or like rainbows appearing in the sky, all phenomena, both pure and impure, unfold within awareness, the precious ultimate enlightened mind. All phenomena of samsara and nirvana without exception, emerging from the ultimate enlightened mind that is their cause, appear as its result: the ocean-like infinitude of phenomena. These endless appearances first arise within the expanse of awareness. They then subsist in this expanse and into this same expanse they finally subside, returning thus to the ground from which they first emerged. That ground, whence all things come, is the one sole awareness, empty and luminous.

This awareness, the single ground for the manifestation of the infinite phenomenal field, is the dharmatā, empty and luminous, transcending all extension and measure. It is indeed a great immensity exceeding every limit and direction (above and below, center and circumference). It is everywhere like immaculate space. Having neither delimitation nor compartments, it is inconceivable.

Seventh, the one sole awareness is shown to be the dharmadhātu.

> 7. The maker of all things, samsara and nirvana,
> Is one and self-arisen.
> Yet this root, awareness, none has made.
> Beyond all action and exertion, it abides like space.
> The example and the thing exemplified concur—
> It is a single vast expanse
> Where all ascriptions and denials are stilled.

When it is said that all phenomena are made by self-arisen awareness, the one dharmatā that encompasses both samsara and nirvana, the meaning is this. When there is a failure to recognize awareness, which is beyond all delimitations and extremes, and is empty, luminous, and space-like, when the self-experience of awareness is taken to be something separate from it, impure samsara is produced. The universe and its inhabitants appear. And with the continuous succession of birth and death, beings wander onward, straying from one state of delusion to another. But when this same awareness is recognized, nirvana occurs, and the five kāyas and wisdoms and so on are made manifest. One is liberated at once and the primordial realm is captured. Therefore, self-arisen awareness alone is the creator of samsara and nirvana. By contrast, the nature of awareness, the universal root, is itself uncompounded, unconditioned, and made by none. Like space, it is inconceivable dharmatā beyond action and exertion.

One gains an understanding of this through the example (space), the thing exemplified (unborn awareness), and the evidential sign (the unobstructed arising of appearances within the enlightened mind). As it is said in *The All-Creating King*,

> I, the teacher, all-creator, am the enlightened mind.
> This same enlightened mind is the all-creating king.
> The buddhas of the three times
> Are all made by the enlightened mind.
> The beings of the three worlds
> Are all made by the enlightened mind.

And,

> At the time of cause, it makes the five great elements.
> At the time of fruit, it makes the beings of the triple world.
> At the time of an example, it makes space the all-applicable
> analogy.
> At the time of the exemplified, it makes all things unborn.
> At the time of evidential sign, enlightened mind makes all.

And,

> It harmonizes cause and fruit,
> The example, the exemplified, the evidential sign.

The example is thus in harmony with the thing exemplified. In a single vast expanse, where numerous misconceptions—ascriptions and denials of existence, the apprehension of the characteristics of entities, hopes and fears, adoption and rejection, affirmation and negation—naturally subside, one gains freedom in the space of the equality of awareness, the one enlightened mind.

Eighth, it is shown that awareness is beyond conception and expression.

8. Within the ultimate quintessence
Transcending being and nonbeing,
Whatever things appear displayed unceasingly,
Their nature is an inconceivable and inexpressible
    expanse
Beyond conventions of both speech and language.

Awareness, the enlightened mind, is beyond the extremes of existence and nonexistence. It is the ultimate quintessence, inconceivable and inexpressible. The phenomena of samsara and nirvana, in
all the clarity and distinctiveness of their multifarious display, arise
unceasingly within its vast and all-encompassing expanse. They are
like the bright reflections of the stars and planets appearing on the
surface of a lake. This awareness and the phenomenal display that
arises within it cannot be differentiated and separated from each
other. Their nature is an empty, inconceivable, and inexpressible
expanse, the fundamental stratum of primordial purity beyond
the four and eight extremes, the thirty-two misconceptions, and
so on. It transcends conventional speech and language and is like
the indescribable, all-encompassing openness of space.

   Ninth, it is shown that phenomena do not stir from the one sole
awareness.

9. In the enlightened mind,
The quintessence whence all things have sprung,
There's no duality and yet uncountable variety.
Buddhas, beings, phenomenal existence,
The world and its inhabitants are clearly present.
Yet they do not stir from suchness, dharmatā alone.

The ground or quintessence, whence all appearances arise, is
awareness, the enlightened mind. The nature of this one awareness cannot be divided dualistically (in the manner of appearance
and emptiness, and so on). And this is certain, for awareness is

the one sole sphere beyond all expression and conceptual elaboration. Nevertheless, although it does not exist as anything, it can manifest as anything. And if one were to attempt to quantify such manifestations, they would be beyond counting. As it is said in *The All-Creating King*,

> Within the enlightened mind,
> The quintessence whence all things arise,
> Appearances have no individual existence
> And yet are numberless.
> Buddhas, the three kāyas,
> Beings with their bodies and their speech
> Are all the enlightened mind,
> Primordially free of apprehender
> And of objects to be apprehended.

Although the nature of awareness does not exist as anything whatsoever, it is able to give rise to every kind of manifestation. Therefore, buddhas, sentient beings, and so on—the phenomenal universe of samsara and nirvana, the world and all it holds— manifest clearly and distinctly. And yet, however they may appear, they are primordially empty by their nature. They never stir in the slightest way from suchness, their fundamental nature, that is, awareness, the enlightened mind, the expanse of the one dharmatā beyond conceptual elaboration.

Tenth, in conclusion, everything is shown to be included in the one awareness.

> 10. All things are connected to this one and only
>   thing
> In which they're perfectly included.
> This is the supreme quality of the enlightened mind.
> From the very instant that a thing appears in it,
> The misconception that it differs from it
> Is to be eliminated.

It should be understood that outer things
Are but the empty radiance
Of the nondual nature of the mind,
While things within the mind
Are just awareness bare and open,
Neither one nor many.
The realization that their nature
Is the single, ultimate expanse
Reveals a key point of awareness.

All phenomena are linked to the one awareness. They are perfectly included in its expanse. When the rays of the sun strike upon a crystal, one's understanding that the five-colored lights are linked with the crystal and are perfectly included within it will counteract the thought that they are something unconnected and separate from it. Similarly, if one understands that the phenomenal appearances that arise within the expanse of awareness are indivisibly linked with it and are fully included therein, one will be able to overturn of the attitude of thinking that phenomena are different from awareness. And the fact that everything is linked to this one awareness and is perfectly included within it is the supreme quality of the ultimate enlightened mind, awareness, self-arisen primordial wisdom, great perfection. So it is that in the very moment that phenomenal appearances arise within the expanse of awareness, one should eliminate the misconception that they are different and separate from awareness. One should be quite certain that in the same way that the crystal's lights are inseparable from the crystal itself, the appearances of the ground are likewise inseparable from the ground.

The [apparently] extramental phenomena that have arisen through the creative power of awareness—empty, luminous, and free from all delimitations and extremes—are simply the radiance of the great state of emptiness that pervades both samsara and nirvana, the radiance of the nature of the mind, wherein there is no apprehender and nothing to be apprehended, no subject, no object, no identity, no difference. Thanks to the understanding that they do not possess the slightest degree of existence in themselves, one realizes that appearing objects have no reality. In the same way, inner mental phenomena—all the cognitions of the apprehending mind—are understood to have no existence even on the level of partless instants of consciousness. And stripped naked in a state of bare and open awareness, which is like a sphere of pure crystal, the apprehending cognitions are neither one nor many in the great primordial purity that is in fact their groundless ultimate nature. It is thus that the ultimate nature, the fundamental state of the equality of object and mind, is actualized.

When it is realized that outer and inner phenomena are the single ultimate expanse of the self-experience, the display, of the nondual enlightened mind, the key point of all phenomena is at that moment revealed as the one self-arisen awareness in which all things are contained. This concludes the present section.

3. Section Two: The Key Points of the Single Nature Are Essentialized

All phenomena are essentialized as the one self-arisen primordial wisdom. This section consists of five stanzas. First, appearances and consciousness are essentialized as primordial wisdom.

> 11. In one taste all things are essentialized.
> All appearing objects are illusions;
> They are the state of emptiness.
> However they appear,
> Rest without contrivance in the one awareness.
> No matter what appears,
> The one sole empty luminosity arises.

All phenomena—external appearances and inner cognitions—are essentialized as the single taste of awareness, the enlightened mind, and a description now follows of how this is so. The unceasing phenomenal array, appearing as objects to be apprehended that have arisen within the expanse of awareness, is like a magical illusion or a dream. Everything that appears is an illusory, empty form. And the arising of such appearances is unceasing. However they may appear—in a limpid state free from stain, as in a mirror—one should be decisively convinced, without any contrivance or manipulation, that these appearances are nothing but awareness, the indivisibility of appearance and emptiness. And one should rest in that state. When one remains in the natural flow of awareness, regardless of whatever objects of the six consciousnesses present themselves, the one sole sphere of luminosity arises. From the standpoint of its emptiness aspect, it is beyond all conceptual elaboration. From the standpoint of its unceasing clarity, it is vivid and alert. One should be completely sure that this is the natural state of the dharmatā, the mind of all Victorious Ones, the dharmadhātu, primordial wisdom, the final destination of all things. And in a state of utter conviction, one should rest without distraction in meditative equipoise. *Phet!*

Second, the arising and subsiding of thoughts is essentialized as self-arisen primordial wisdom.

> 12. Thoughts, the mind's appearances,
> Fade naturally away.
> Whatever movement comes
> Within the state of emptiness,
> Just rest within the natural flow, relaxed.
> Through the movement and proliferation of your thoughts,
> The wisdom of the dharmatā will clearly appear.

Whatever mental appearances may occur of the eighty-four thousand kinds of mental states—the five or three defiling poisons, for example—they are like waves, which arise upon the ocean but never stir from it. They appear as the display and ornament of the ocean's creative power. They are like the rainbow-colored clouds that appear in the sky but never leave it. They are not just the display of the sky's creative power but are also ornaments wherewith the sky itself is made beautiful. Likewise, whatever mental states may occur, if one remains in the state of self-cognizing awareness, they will naturally disappear. Knowing that all movements of the mind occurring in the state of great emptiness are but the display of self-arisen primordial wisdom, one should simply rest, relaxed and free, within their natural flow. It is through the movement and proliferation of thoughts that the wisdom of the dharmatā, unceasing awareness, luminous and empty, is clearly manifest. Movement, stillness, and awareness blend into one, and great primordial wisdom—awareness left as it is[64]—is actualized. As it is said in *The All-Creating King,*

> Mental movement, memories, and thoughts
> Stir never from their unborn state.
> Thus, if you understand
> That any thought occurring is the meditation,
> Then, even without meditating,
> When everything you leave as it arises,
> You are not distracted.

And it is also said in *The Six Expanses,*

> In the nature of the mind that's free of mental focusing,
> All movement of the mind is pure appearance.
> Clinging naturally subsides and this is called *samadhi.*
> This is what I, Samantabhadra, teach.

Third, movement and stillness are essentialized as nonduality.

13. When you see that objects of the senses
And the mind are seamlessly the same,
When, free of focus and of reference,
You rest within the state of traceless natural purity,

Within its very radiance there manifests
The primal wisdom of deep insight.

As one rests in a state in which appearing objects [are understood to be] empty, there arises the one sole, empty, and luminous awareness. When this is maintained, and one remains relaxed in the natural flow of whatever mental experiences arise, their ultimate nature becomes evident. If these two states are properly maintained, the extramental object of apprehension and the inner apprehending mind will merge without differentiation into a seamless equality, free from conceptual elaboration. A state will manifest that is utterly empty, open, and lucidly clear. Preserving this experience and focusing one's mind on it without moving one's eyes, one rests in a naturally pure, traceless state that is free of target or reference. In doing so, one will actualize the fundamental nature or awareness, and one will discover within oneself the great dharmakāya, free from conceptual activity. It is said in *The Lion's Perfect Power*,

> When one watches as an object
> Dharmatā, aware and luminous,
> Awareness, free of all diversity,
> Is seen within. When one watches
> All the false appearances
> Of the many objects of the senses,
> The great dharmakāya free of cognitive activity
> Is inwardly discovered.

When the mind is left in this way, without taking or rejecting anything, awareness, free of all delimitations and extremes, is found within. This is said to be a great and all-embracing realization. As we find in *The Six Expanses*,

> In the nature of the mind devoid of taking and rejecting,
> The experience of all thoughts subsiding

Is called the "great and all-embracing realization."
This is what I, Samantabhadra, teach.

As this text says, when one rests without specific target or reference in a naturally pure and traceless state, then within its very radiance, one discovers the primordial wisdom of deep insight. One should be completely certain that this is without any mistake, the wisdom of the dharmakāya Samantabhadra. One should maintain continually the vision of its face. This is a matter of the highest importance.

Fourth, the foregoing stanzas are brought to a conclusion.

14. Essentializing into one quintessence
These three key points—
That realization and non-realization
Are both primordially equal,
That mind and object indivisible
Are the equality of dharmakāya,
That faults and obscurations are inseparable
From the equality of dharmatā—
You continually keep to ultimate reality.
Without rejecting or adopting, you will find
The ultimate quintessence.
Not coming and not going, you abide
Within the realization of the dharmatā.
All is gathered in this state
Wherein both change and movement are
    transcended.

What does it mean to say that the three preceding key points are "essentialized into one quintessence"? These three points are: first, appearances are left just as they are; second, awareness is left as it is; and third, movement and stillness are indivisible.

Taking these three points in order, the first shows that because all appearing objects are unreal, appearances are left as they are. The second point shows that because all mental states, all cognitions, naturally dissolve, awareness is left as it is. Finally, because there is no gap between sense objects and the mind, one speaks of the indivisibility of mental movement and stillness. It is thus that these three key points are essentialized into a single quintessence, which is awareness.

When, by leaving awareness as it is, one settles relaxed in the natural flow of whatever arises in the mind, there will manifest, on the basis of its apparent movement and proliferation, a state of wisdom in the form of a concentration on the dharmatā. Since the state of realization and the state of the absence of realization are primordially equal, one will discover a kind of wisdom that is free from all coming and going.

When, by leaving appearances as they are, one settles without fabrication in a state in which all appearances are empty and unreal, one will realize that the indivisibility of object and mind is the great dharmakāya. When this happens, one will discover a state of equality that is free from all rejecting and adopting. When one settles in the state of pure, traceless awareness that is free of focus or reference, it is then that stillness and movement become indivisible, and in the clearly present wisdom of deep insight, stillness, movement, and awareness will blend together. One will discover the ultimate mode of equality in the state of dharmatā—a state from which error and obscuration are in fact inseparable. This is referred to as keeping continually to the state of ultimate reality.

In short, the essentialization of these three key points demonstrated here means that the six gatherings of consciousness should be left free and relaxed within the vast expanse of awareness. It means nothing else. It is said in *The Six Expanses*,

> In the nature of the mind
> Where there is neither sinking nor excitement,
> Meditation that is a sublime state of evenness

Is the so-called relaxation
Of the six gatherings of consciousness.
This is what I, Samantabhadra, teach.

This is to say that when the six gatherings of sense consciousnesses
are left free and relaxed, it is by essentializing these three key points
as awareness devoid of all mental elaboration—without considering one to be more important than the other—that one will keep
to the ultimate condition of the exhaustion of phenomena in the
state beyond the ordinary mind. All appearances are simply a
vast, all-encompassing expanse of equality, which is from the very
beginning, beyond all adopting and rejecting. This constitutes the
discovery, or actualization, of the ultimate quintessence or truth.

When the equality of the three times is understood as being
the bare absence of conceptual elaboration within the nature of
awareness and when dharmatā or suchness is manifestly realized in
the absence of all conceptual characteristics—such as coming and
going—one dwells, at that very moment, within the vast expanse
of awareness, the level of the result, free of movement and change.
All the appearances of samsara and nirvana are gathered in the one
space of awareness, the ultimate truth.

Fifth, in conclusion, all is gathered into the one place of freedom.

15. Space-like is the vast immensity,
The mind of the Victorious Ones.
Beyond elimination and attainment,
It is the great expanse, the one sole sphere.
Freedom in itself, it is beyond the states
Of realization and non-realization.
The place of the exhaustion of phenomena is reached
In all-embracing evenness beyond the ordinary
    mind.
Above the summit of the victory banner, never to be
    lowered,
The sun and moon illuminate a myriad worlds.

What is the final place of freedom, the ultimate mode of being, the ever-youthful vase body? When all the appearances of the self-experience of awareness dissolve into the ultimate expanse of primordial emptiness, there manifests a vast and all-encompassing expanse—the space-like immensity mentioned in the root text—devoid of both direction and limit. It is referred to as vast because it refers to the dharmatā free of concepts and characteristics. It is space-like because it is illustrated by the example of the immensity of unlimited space. This ultimate mode of being is the mind of all the Victorious Ones of the three times, the final expanse of supreme primordial wisdom. It is totally devoid of conceptual characteristics concerning, for example, the obscurations that are to be eliminated and the result that is to be attained. Free of all the corners and edges of ordinary thoughts, it is described as a sphere. Awareness, supreme primordial wisdom, free of the defining characteristics of samsara and nirvana, is the one sole expanse of the final place of freedom, the ever-youthful body enclosed within a vase. As we find in *The Natural Subsiding of Characteristics*,

> Without distinction or exclusion, there is freedom
> In the vast expanse of spontaneous presence.
> Without a meeting or a parting, there is freedom
> In the vast expanse of the one sphere.
> Anything may happen, there is freedom
> In the indeterminate expanse.

Since this freedom occurs within the fundamental stratum of seamless, open awareness, it is a great freedom in which there is not even the name of realization or the absence of realization. Since this state is free from the beginning, it is a primordial freedom. Since it is completely free, it is an utter freedom. When one watches nakedly one's own nature, this same naked awareness, divested of all deluded thoughts of the three times, is called the great, naked seeing of spontaneous freedom. As it is said in *The Word-Transcending Tantra*,

> To its very core there's freedom—
> All exertion falls away.
> Primordial is its freedom—
> No need is there to free it once again.
> Naked is its freedom—
> Within the very place you see it, it is free.
> Total is its freedom—
> Its nature is immaculate.

When one awakens to the naked, primordial freedom of unimpeded, open awareness, phenomenal appearances come to the state of their exhaustion. They subside in the state of equality, in the all-embracing evenness of the state of the exhaustion of phenomena, which transcends the ordinary mind. When objects and the conditions for such objects reach their exhaustion, they subside all by themselves. The subsiding is natural. And since there is no question of four alternatives in terms of existence, nonexistence, both, and neither, one speaks of a great subsiding of extremes. It is said in *The Pearl Garland*,

> It is natural subsiding—objects and conditions fall away;
> It is naked subsiding—appearances are stainless;
> It is a subsiding of extremes—there are no four
>   alternatives.
> It is a subsiding into one—it is empty of plurality.

When open, unimpeded awareness is actualized, one attains the state of the exhaustion of phenomena within their ultimate condition. This is the profound realization of the great equality of the dharmatā. Illuminating a myriad world systems, the primordial wisdom of the level of the result is like the sun and moon that arise above the summit of the victory banner that, hoisted aloft, will never be lowered. The darkness in which both samsara and nirvana are bound is scattered, and freedom occurs.

3. Section Three: All Phenomena Are Subsumed Within the One Awareness

This consists of four stanzas. First, all is subsumed into a single ultimate expanse, self-arisen primordial wisdom.

> 16. All things are subsumed
> Within awareness, one and self-cognizing.
> All things of phenomenal existence,
> All samsara and nirvana,
> Infinitely, endlessly appear
> Arising from the ultimate expanse.
> Therefore, the expanse whence they emerge
> Subsumes them.

All phenomena, whether of samsara or nirvana, are subsumed in the expanse of the one self-cognizing awareness. The endless, infinite appearances of phenomenal existence, samsara and nirvana, emerge from space-like dharmatā, which is the expanse of the one awareness. This means that all phenomena are subsumed within the expanse of awareness, the dharmadhātu—the place whence they arise, the ground in which they appear. They never move from this space of awareness. They are of one taste with it, indivisibly blended.

Second, no matter how phenomena appear, they are all subsumed in awareness.

> 17. Even now, when various things appear,
> They do not from awareness stray elsewhere.
> Appearances are thus subsumed
> Within the vast expanse, awareness self-arisen.

All the phenomena of samsara and nirvana are subsumed within the expanse of self-cognizing awareness alone. Therefore, although in their infinite and limitless array, phenomena appear even now within the expanse of self-arisen awareness—ceaselessly, clearly, and distinctly like the stars and planets in the sky—they never move from the state of awareness and go elsewhere. These appearances are but the creative power and display of the one awareness. Appearance and awareness are not two things. So it is that all phenomena are subsumed within the primordial expanse of self-arisen awareness. It is as *The All-Creating King* says,

> As for what I am,
> I am enlightened mind.
> As for where I stay,
> I stay within the space of dharmatā.
> As for how I'm luminous,
> I shine within awareness' expanse.

Third, all things are finally subsumed in the one awareness.

18. Seamlessly arising and subsiding,
They dissolve into the ultimate expanse.
Appearances are not other than
The enlightened mind.
All things are subsumed within
The one primordial dharmatā,
The ground of their exhaustion.

Just as, at length, the clouds in the sky dissolve into the abyss of space, just as the five-colored lights are reabsorbed into the crystal from which they were projected, and just as the waves sink back into the sea—all things in phenomenal existence, which manifest from the expanse of awareness, seamlessly arising and subsiding, finally dissolve and vanish into the expanse of the dharmakāya, empty yet aware. Because they are not other than the expanse of the ultimate enlightened mind, the space of self-arisen awareness, they never separate from that expanse. As the display of the creative power of the dharmatā (awareness), all phenomenal appearances, which are indivisible from that same awareness, are exhausted in this same expanse of dharmatā. They are subsumed within the one, primordial dharmatā, the ground of their exhaustion, the state of supreme equality that is beyond all conceptual elaboration. As it is said in *The Natural Subsiding of Characteristics*,

> The mind that is deluded,
> Which grasps at something different from the ground,
> Subsides into the one—
> Sinks back into the space of dharmatā.
> The obstacle to its enlightenment—
> Its clinging to the pathways of samara—
> This too subsides into the self-arisen one,
> Into the space of primal wisdom.

Fourth, in conclusion, phenomena are subsumed into primordial wisdom.

> **19. Subsumed into the one and sole awareness,**
> **Phenomena have never left awareness,**
> **Essence of enlightenment,**
> **Beyond all change and movement.**
> **They are subsumed within the ultimate**
> **quintessence;**
> **They dwell in the expanse, unchanging,**
> **uncompounded.**

Since all phenomena of samsara and nirvana are fully contained within the one sole expanse of awareness, they are subsumed within that same awareness. *The All-Creating King* says,

> Just as all phenomena,
> The universe and all that lives in it,
> Possess no other dwelling than the vast abyss of space,

> Likewise in the vast expanse of the enlightened mind,
> Buddhas, beings, universes, and their denizens abide.

So it is that all phenomena contained within phenomenal existence—samsara and nirvana—never stray from the expanse of the one awareness. They do not move from it and they never will. They are subsumed within the essence of ultimate luminosity—awareness, the essence of enlightenment—beyond all movement and change throughout the three times. They are gathered within the great space of Samantabhadrī. There is nothing therefore that could be different from awareness, the enlightened mind. It is as *The Lion's Perfect Power* says,

> Within the vast expanse, Samantabhadrī's womb,
> Phenomenal existence lies in its entirety:
> Samsara and nirvana, the five elements.

All phenomena are thus completely contained within the unchanging, unconditioned vajra expanse of indestructible, invincible awareness, the ultimate truth.

3. Section Four: A Clear Conviction Is Gained That All Phenomena Are Self-Arisen Primordial Wisdom

This consists of four stanzas. First, a clear conviction is reached that all phenomena are the ultimate quintessence, beginningless and endless.

> 20. A clear conviction is attained
> That all phenomena are the one, sole,
> Self-arisen primal wisdom,
> The ultimate expanse,
> Beginningless and endless.
> All is there contained.
> All movement of the mind subsides,

And all abides within the dharmatā,
The ultimate quintessence.

A clear conviction or decision must be reached concerning the final status of phenomenal existence, samsara and nirvana. But what is this final status? It must be clearly resolved that all appearances are awareness, the enlightened mind alone. For it is in the expanse of self-arisen primordial wisdom that phenomena arise, subsist, and subside—all by themselves. All phenomena are contained within the ultimate expanse. This great primordial purity, beginningless and endless, is open and devoid of all conceptual construction. There, the myriadfold webs of mental activity subside or vanish, like a rainbow-colored cloud that melts away in the firmament. All phenomena dwell in their ultimate quintessence, the equality that is devoid of mental elaboration, the dharmatā, suchness, wherein appearance and emptiness are indivisible. To come to a clear conviction that this is so is a sublime key point.

Second, a clear conviction is reached that the object of apprehension and the apprehending subject are self-arisen, non-referential awareness.

21. Outer objects, therefore, and the inner mind,
Phenomena of both samsara and nirvana—
When gross are analyzed into the subtle,
No notion of a part remains.
Thus you are clearly convinced
That they are but the vast expanse,
Empty from the outset, similar to space.

All phenomena of samsara and nirvana, all outer appearances (the external vessel of the universe) and its inner contents (the beings that live there), are included in the categories of object of apprehension and apprehending mind. Gross, extended phenomena, mountain ranges and so on, are established as agglomerations of subtle, indivisible particles. But when these partless particles are subjected to analytical reasoning that focuses on their directionality and so on, they are shown to be empty. And the mind's apprehension of, and clinging to, appearing phenomena fade away.

In similar fashion, the apprehending mind is also by nature empty. One finds that, first, there is nowhere whence it came; second, there is nowhere where it dwells; and, finally, there is nowhere where it goes. When one understands that former mental states, having ceased, have no existence, when one understands that future thoughts not yet arisen have no existence either, and when one understands that present states of mind have no existence even on the level of indivisible moments of consciousness, one knows with certainty that the supposedly subtle objects of apprehension are completely unreal—that they are empty. They vanish naturally without leaving any trace. In short, when gross objects of apprehension and the states of mind that apprehend them are analyzed into their subtle components, part-possessing objects are not found. They are beyond the reach of conceptual understanding. One must come to a clear conviction or decision that they are primordial emptiness, that is, primordial purity beyond conceptual elaboration—the expanse of equality similar to empty space.

Third, a clear conviction is reached that awareness is beyond indication and expression.

> 22. Enlightened mind, when analyzed,
> Is found to be devoid of substance.
> It has no source, no dwelling place;
> It does not come or go.
> It eludes all indication and expression.
> You reach a clear conviction
> That it is the space of wisdom
> That transcends the ordinary mind.
> It's not an entity with features,
> Definable as this or that.
> Not known through words,
> It cannot be described.

When one examines the dharmatā—awareness, the enlightened mind—it too is found to be without substance. A bare absence of mental elaboration, it is completely devoid of origin. It is beyond the law of cause and effect and effortful striving. It has no dwelling place. It is like the pure and open sky. It does not come: it is ineffable, inconceivable, and inexpressible. It does not go: it is devoid of birth, death, decay, and decline. It eludes all indication: it transcends all conceptual characteristics and is thus ineffable, inconceivable, and inexpressible. A clear conviction is reached that awareness, transcending as it does the dualistic mind, is the expanse of Samantabhadra's wisdom. And this primordial wisdom, which is beyond all possible indication and expression, is indescribable. One cannot reveal it saying, "It is like this." It is not an entity endowed with features to be defined as this or that. It is substanceless like space. It cannot be known through language; it cannot be expressed in words. A clear conviction is reached that awareness is beyond indication and expression.

Fourth, a clear conviction is reached that the exhaustion of phenomena is the supreme state beyond all designation.

23. You reach a clear conviction
That all things in phenomenal existence
Belonging to samsara and nirvana
Are the vast expanse,
Devoid of mental movement and of naming.
You reach a clear conviction
That all things are the vast expanse,
Awareness, empty and unborn,
Primordial wisdom self-cognizing.
You reach a clear conviction
That all things arising from enlightened mind
Are but the vast expanse
Beyond both knowing and not knowing.
You reach a clear conviction that all phenomena,
Primordially empty and completely empty,

> Constitute the vast expanse,
> Unmoving and unchanging in the triple time.

The vast expanse, beyond all mental elaboration—even that of words and names—is the ground from which all phenomena arise. And when they finally subside, they do so in the selfsame expanse of awareness, empty and unborn, free of all conceptual construction and designation. One comes to a clear conviction that this is true of the phenomena of both samsara and nirvana. In the final analysis, therefore, every phenomenon first of all arises within the expanse of precious spontaneous presence and in the end subsides into it. When this is recognized through the power of awareness, freedom is gained in the expanse that is beyond the distinction of awareness and lack of awareness. As we find in *The Great Victory Banner Never to Be Lowered*,

> By means of its own power,
> Beyond both knowing and unknowing,
> Peerless primal wisdom knows
> Great bliss spontaneously present.
> Phenomena arise from nowhere else.

Phenomena subside indivisibly in the final place of freedom, the great expanse of awareness, empty and unborn. And yet for self-cognizing primordial wisdom, conventional phenomena still appear endowed with their individual names. Nevertheless, one comes—in a nondual manner—to a clear conviction that these same phenomena are self-cognizing primordial wisdom. By way of an illustration, one may make a difference between the space enclosed within a vase and the space contained in a house. But when the vase is smashed with a hammer, the space inside it blends inseparably with the space outside. Similarly, when speaking of the emptiness of individual things, one is, as it were, creating compartments in all-pervading awareness. Nevertheless, within the great expanse of awareness—unborn and empty, the final place of freedom, the mother expanse of great emptiness—there is no difference between self-cognizing awareness and the things that arise within it. As the victorious Longchenpa has declared,[65]

> All is a single ultimate expanse—
> Primordial wisdom self-arisen.
> Everything without exception
> Is pure and of a single taste.
> Thus it is established
> That all is one, not two.
> This is what is set forth in this precious commentary,
> Explaining the fourth topic.

The profound, fundamental nature of phenomena, the final truth, is the one sole sphere of the dharmakāya. Within this expanse, that which is undeluded (referred to as self-cognizing primordial wisdom) is not separate and distinct from that which is deluded (the mental states of ignorance). Just as it is impossible to find ordinary earth and stones on an island of gold, it is likewise said,

> In the space of All-Good Samantabhadra,
> There is not a single thing that is not good.
> There's neither "good" nor "bad"—
> All things are equal.

As these words indicate, one comes to a clear conviction that all phenomena arising from the ultimate enlightened mind are the vast expanse of equality, the dharmadhātu beyond the range of conceptual elaboration—in which there is neither awareness nor lack of awareness.

Awareness, the ultimate enlightened mind, is the fundamental nature of phenomena. It is the expanse of open and unimpeded primordial wisdom, free of all movement and change, whether in the past, present, or future. One comes to a clear conviction that this expanse of primordially empty dharmatā (the nature of the ground, pure from the beginning) and the phenomena that are established on the path as being primordially and utterly empty are indivisible within the expanse of great primordial emptiness.

A Concluding Statement of the Vajra Topic's Name

Here ends the word commentary on the fourth vajra topic of *The Precious Treasury of the Fundamental Nature*, which establishes all phenomena as the one self-cognizing primordial wisdom.

3. An Instruction concerning Those Who Are Able to Grasp This Teaching

The third part of Longchenpa's text consists of instructions concerning those who can grasp and uphold this teaching. It is divided into five sections: those to whom the teaching is given, the master who bestows it, the manner in which it is bestowed, the teaching itself, and the way it is implemented and the benefits that accrue therefrom.

1. The Recipients of This Teaching

The first section discusses two kinds of people: those from whom this teaching should be withheld and those to whom it should be given.

As a preface to this discussion, there is a general presentation of the teaching's potential recipients. This is followed by a more specific description of the character of these recipients: first, those to whom the teachings should be denied and second, those on whom it should be bestowed.

3. A General Presentation

> 1. This essence of the vehicle most profound
> Should be revealed exclusively
> To those who clearly have
> Both supreme fortune and intelligence.

> It should be withheld
> From those who bigotedly cling
> To lesser vehicles and to the causal principle,
> From those who are of lesser fortune and
> intelligence.

Regarding this quintessential nectar of the most profound and secret vehicle, it is as the saying goes,

> From the churning of the milk of holy Dharma
> There comes a buttery quintessence.

Generally speaking, the path of the Great Perfection comprises three classes: the mind class, the space class, and the pith instruction class. The present teaching belongs to the secret pith instruction class, and this in turn consists of four cycles of teaching: outer, inner, secret, and unsurpassed. The present text belongs to the last of these four, the Secret Heart Essence.[66] And since the latter is the quintessence—the essential blood—of the heart of a hundred thousand mother ḍākinīs, it is called the Heart Essence of the Mother Ḍākinīs.[67]

Those to whom this teaching may be imparted should have accumulated vast reserves of merit and wisdom, gathered in the course of many kalpas of time. They should belong to the family of the Mahāyāna and should be of the highest intelligence and fortune, endowed with extremely sharp faculties. They should have a firm, unshakable faith in this path, and they should be graced with sincere conviction and trust in it. Added to this, they should exhibit an endeavor that is neither slack nor tense and should be naturally imbued with love and compassion. It is to fortunate beings such as these that this teaching should be given.

By contrast, it should not be given to those who belong to the lower vehicles, who cling in a bigoted manner to their own tenets, and who entertain wrong views regarding the Mahāyāna. *The Heap of Jewels Tantra* has this to say:

Do not utter a single word of this in the presence of *śrāvakas*, *pratyekabuddhas*, and the like. For they are narrow-minded. They will be alarmed to hear such teachings. They will faint with fear. They feel no devotion for the Secret Mantra. They will repudiate it, and the fully ripened effect of such a rejection will be the experience of the Great Hell. Far from your actually instructing them and their listening to you, you must not even speak of such teachings in the wind that blows in their direction.

Furthermore, in the Wisdom Chapter of *The Way of the Bodhisattva*, there is a section that deals with the objections made by ordinary people and by the śrāvaka and Mind Only schools. At the beginning of the refutation of the śrāvakas, two questions are dealt with. It is first established that the Mahāyāna scriptures are the teaching of the Buddha, and then it is shown that the Mahāyāna path is the antidote [to subtle cognitive obscurations]. Since the śrāvakas do not accept the Mahāyāna as the teaching of the Buddha, when they state their own position, they refer to the Buddha's advice to Kātyāyana—which Nāgārjuna mentions in his *Root Stanzas on the Middle Way*,[68]

> In his *Counsel to Kātyāyana*,
> The Lord, through understanding
> Both existent and nonexistent things,
> Has rejected both the views: "this is" and "this is not."

When commenting on this teaching to Kātyāyana, the śrāvakas say that gross extended objects have no real existence. They do not, however, deny the existence of the partless particles. The śrāvakas also say that,

> Form resembles bursting bubbles.
> Feeling is like foam upon the water.

Perception may be likened to a mirage.
Conditioning factors are like magical illusions.
So the Kinsman of the Sun has said.

Accordingly, the śrāvakas assert the nonexistence of the phenomenal self only in the sense of gross extended objects. They do not assert fourfold or eightfold emptiness or the eighteen kinds of emptiness and so on, as propounded in the Mahāyāna scriptures. Indeed, they reject such teachings, which they disparage as being the dreadful view of nihilism. And even when the proofs of the authenticity of the Mahāyāna teachings are put forward, their response is to say that proof is lacking and that such teachings are not the buddha-word.

In the past, two Indian monks endowed with twelvefold training in virtue approached Atiśa and requested teachings. At first, Atiśa gave them instructions belonging only to the Hīnayāna and the monks were very happy. When, however, Atiśa went on to speak to them about fourfold emptiness and other teachings of the Mahāyāna, they stopped their ears with their hands and asked him not to say such things. So it is that the Mahāyāna is beyond the range of those who regard the view of Hīnayāna as supreme. Moreover, those with biased attachment to the teachings on karmic law who view everything in terms of the principle of cause and effect—beings, in other words, of narrow mind and lesser fortune—should not receive the profound and extraordinary teachings of the Mahāyāna. For if such space-like teachings are bestowed upon those who lack the proper disposition, they will misconceive and object to them, and as a result they will have to experience the sorrows of the lower realms. This is why the present teaching must be kept extremely secret and hidden from those of lesser fortune. It is said in *The All-Creating King*,

If I, the Great One, were to teach these things
To those who hold the causal vehicle,

Then just as with the teaching on the mundane causal
    law

... and so on. Moreover, the same text says,

> This teaching I, the all-creator, will not give
> To the adherents of the causal vehicle.
> For if I were to set it forth,
> They would retort that actions, good and bad,
> Produce their karmic fruits.
> Thus me, the Perfect One, they would disparage.
> And therefore, me, the Perfect One,
> They would not meet for many ages.

How could the reason for such concealment be that this profound
secret teaching is in some sense faulty? On the contrary, the crucial
reason for keeping it extremely hidden is to prevent those of lesser
fortune from having erroneous views in its regard.

3. A Specific Description of Those from Whom This Teaching Should Be Withheld

> 2. From those who criticize their teacher,
> Who show aggression to their vajra kindred,
> Who betray the secret, speaking of it openly,
> Faithless and tightfisted, of an evil disposition,
> Who are engrossed in temporal things—
> From all these keep this teaching secret.

A teacher's kindness is twofold if he grants empowerment and
explains the tantra. It is threefold if, in addition, he bestows the
profound teachings of the pith instructions. Far from mentioning
all these three together, if one has received only one of them, one
should never—even at the cost of one's life—mentally turn from

one's teacher, or speak of him or her with words of criticism. In Master Śūra's *Confession of the Fourteen Downfalls of Mantra*, it is said,

> The accomplishment of Vajradhara
> Is said to follow from the master.
> Therefore, first of all the downfalls
> Is to have contempt and scorn for him.

And in the tantra *Awareness Self-Arisen*, it is said,

> Not to show respect and reverence
> To the teacher, your own master,
> Ignoring all the kindnesses he shows . . .

And,

> An unexamined follower
> Is the master's enemy.
> Do not explain the teachings of the Great
>   Perfection
> To those who will not practice them.

And again, *The All-Creating King* declares,

> I now speak of the evil kind,
> Of those who are unworthy vessels.
> They delight in fame and worldly things,
> Are arrogant, and to the holy beings
> Show no reverence.
> And losing heart, they fail to persevere.

Moreover, if one criticizes a teacher, even one who has explained just a single verse of the profound doctrine of the Secret Mantra and if one fails to regard him or her as one's teacher, the fault is extremely grave. As it is said,

> Through the failure to consider as one's teacher
> One who taught the meaning of single verse,
> One will be, for a hundred lives, a dog
> And afterward be born in a bad family.

It is also a heavy fault to nourish anger against one's spiritual friends. Those who have received the profound empowerments of the Secret Mantra together—especially the ripening empowerments and instructions of the Great Perfection—are like twins. If they have animosity toward each other, the fault is very serious. Master Śūra has said,

> Anger felt toward the vajra kindred
> And talk about their misdemeanors
> Are the third [transgression].

Moreover, one should not betray, by failing to observe correctly, the various levels of the secret samaya pledges that were explained by the teacher when he or she introduced one to the profound and secret teachings. The profound teachings that are to be experienced through extremely secret methods are never to be proclaimed or transmitted to people whose samaya is impure or who lack the requisite fortune—without the permission of one's teacher. It is said in the tantra titled *The Union of the Sun and Moon*,

> The Secret Mantra has no fault,
> And it is kept most secret for the sake of beings.
> For the secret kept ensures attainment—
> Thus one speaks of "Secret Mantra."

And Master Śūra says,

The seventh downfall is to speak of secret things
To those who are unready.

And this is corroborated by *Awareness Self-Arisen*, beginning with
the words,

To practice Secret Mantra incorrectly . . .

So as these texts say, one should never speak of the profound
instructions to those who do not observe the samaya pledges of
the profound empowerments or to those who are unsuitable recipients of the profound pith instructions. For however much one may
instruct those who lack confident faith in the profound teachings,
spiritual qualities will not arise in their minds. These profound
instructions belong to the lineage of the transmission of blessings.
If faith and devotion are lacking, it is impossible for the slightest
qualities of experience and realization to appear in beings' minds.

If because of craving and avarice one is not generous to the cause
of the Dharma and of the teacher—however much wealth one may
possess—one will be powerless to loose the fetters that bind one,
namely, one's attachment to one's property. People like this are
unsuitable vessels for the teaching.

People of bad character and ignoble background are also unsuitable vessels for the teaching. It is as the Kadampa masters of the
past used to say, the mistakes of a disciple may be corrected, but
it is hard to correct a person's character. People of vile and ignoble
character have no appreciation for the Dharma, the teacher, and
the spiritual kindred. They neither respect nor esteem them. For
this reason, they are liable to turn against their teacher. The profound teaching should not be given to such people, for they are
unsuitable vessels.

People who are unable to overcome the shackle of assuming the
true existence of what are in fact the hallucinatory appearances of
this life are also improper vessels, and to them too the teaching
should not be revealed. On the contrary, these instructions should

be kept very secret, for such people have no chance of being able to practice them properly. Indeed, not only would there be no benefit, but it is likely that great harm would come to both the teacher and the disciple.

2. Those to Whom the Teaching Should Be Given

This is divided into two: the character of qualified disciples and the manner in which they should behave.

3. The Character of Qualified Disciples

> 3. Those of highest caliber, endowed with fortune,
> Are the proper vessels for the Great Perfection.
> They respect their teachers and possess great
>   knowledge.
> They are joyful and broad-minded,
> Faithful friends and generous.
> They are without ambitious thoughts
> And have but little clinging.
> They give up all preoccupation for this present life
> And are intent on winning their enlightenment.
> Endowed with faith and diligence,
> They are able to maintain the secret.
> These are those to whom
> The teachings should be given.

Fortunate beings are those with perfect karmic fortune; they are the best disciples. Those who are particularly apt as vessels of the Great Perfection are the fortunate people who have a particular respect for these teachings, their teacher, and the spiritual community. They must have a keen and quick discernment and a knowledge that enables them to absorb and take to heart the teacher's instructions. They are broad-minded and are able to assimilate the teachings. They are, moreover, cheerful and are long and faithful friends. They are pleasant and able to give whatever they have to the cause of the Dharma and their teacher. As it is said in *The All-Creating King*,

> They have great faith, samaya pledges, diligence,
> Compassion, joy, and weariness with worldly ways.
> They are not engrossed in many thoughts
> And are without attachment to their bodies,
> Children, spouses, servants, property.
> They offer all with confidence and joy.
> These qualities are signs of faith and pure samaya.
> On all such persons let essential teachings be bestowed.

Such disciples, moreover, are not proud and conceited. They are not filled with ambitious thoughts or a desire for greatness. They do not have much clinging to the appearances of this life. All these characteristics are essential for people who are suitable vessels for the teachings of the Great Perfection. *Awareness Self-Arisen* lists the requisite qualities as follows:

> Strong faith, great diligence,
> Deep knowledge, little clinging,
> Great respect, and practice of the Secret Mantra,
> Undistracted, free of all discursiveness,
> Pure samaya, and effort in the practice . . .

Those who are vessels for the teachings should also be able to turn away from the activities of this life and to give up the eight worldly concerns, leaving them behind like something lying dead on the road. Day and night, they should strive in the practice leading to enlightenment, like hungry and thirsty people yearning for food and drink. With unshakable faith, they should see their teachers as buddhas in person and constantly remember them with love. They should practice the instructions with a diligence that is neither too tense nor too slack—like archers drawing their bowstrings. Again we find in *Awareness Self-Arisen*,

> Considering your teacher with a deep and constant love,
> Be alert and yet relaxed in meditation.
> Act according to your teacher's words
> And with a pure samaya pledge,
> Behave harmoniously with others.

And,

> Act in harmony with others' feeling,
> Considering your teacher and the Tathāgata
> As the same, without a difference,
> For this is the true mark of a disciple.

In addition, one must be able to maintain secrecy and not speak of the profound and secret teachings to those who are unsuitable vessels. Again, it is said in *Awareness Self-Arisen*,

> Acting properly for your own sake,
> Keeping the entrusted secrets,
> Do not transgress the vajra teachings.

To bestow and set forth gradually the extraordinary teachings upon such fortunate disciples endowed with these special qualities is of the highest significance, for they are worthy vessels.

3. The Manner in Which These Disciples Should Behave

> 4. With presents they should please their teachers,
> And in a spirit of commitment
> They should wholeheartedly request instruction.
> When the teaching has been granted,

> They should practice it correctly
> And reach the level of exhaustion of phenomena
> In the fundamental nature.

Before they request the essential teachings, disciples who are suitable vessels in the manner that has just been explained should please their teacher with offerings and in numerous skillful ways. Then, without a care for this present life, they should promise to implement whatever secret and profound instructions their master will impart, practicing them with strong determination and perseverance even though it may cost them their lives. It is in this frame of mind that they should make their wholehearted request. It is said in *The All-Creating King*,

> If I receive these quintessential teachings,
> Of what importance are such worldly things to me?
> "If I receive them, every hardship I will undertake"—
> Give the teachings to the ones
> Who perfectly maintain this promise.

As this text says, in order to underline the greatness of the sublime teachings, disciples should make the mental commitment to offer such precious things as gold, their own bodies and possessions, and even their own life. And without any hesitation, they should offer all their property, great or small, house, land, and so on. And though they have no need of such things, teachers should accept these offerings, presenting them to the Three Jewels, thus allowing the disciple to accumulate merit. *The All-Creating King* declares,

> In short, you should present
> Your body and your life,
> No need to mention your belongings,
> Your livestock, and your wealth.
> And though they have no need for them,

The holy beings should accept them,
Offering them to the Three Jewels.

It is also said in *Awareness Self-Arisen*,

The master who bestows the pith instructions,
Should thus be served with offerings
Of body, treasure—all that is most rare.

And *The Word-Transcending Tantra* declares,

To masters who bestow instructions and transmissions
You should offer father, mother, uncle, your own eyes—
Your jewels, your children, treasures of your wealth,
Whatever you may love and cherish most.

Teachers should bestow all the profound instructions that they possess on qualified disciples such as these, protecting them with loving care. And for their part, the disciples should practice these teachings correctly, unconcerned for the things of this life, and with a strong and determined perseverance, they should be ready to put up with whatever hardships and difficulties might arise. In this very body, they should be able to progress to the sixteenth level called Unsurpassed Wisdom,[69] reaching the state of the exhaustion of phenomena in the dharmatā, the fundamental nature. They should, in other words, be able to achieve freedom in the ever-youthful vase body.

1. The Qualifications of the Teacher Who Bestows Instruction

**5. Teachers should be very learned,
Possessing all required qualities.**

Teachers who set forth the Secret Mantra should be richly endowed with great learning as well as an effortless love and compassion. They should not allow the samaya pledges, taken in the course of empowerment, to decline. Their minds should be liberated through their realization, and they should have both ability and skill in compassionately freeing the minds of others. All these requisite qualities they must possess in full. *Awareness Self-Arisen* has this to say about teachers who are able to bestow the pith instructions of the Luminous Great Perfection:

> They do not waver from the view;
> They give up all activities, outer, inner, secret.
> They enjoy an endless treasury of perfect qualities,
> Which are like precious jewels.

And we find also in *The Word-Transcending Tantra*,

> Teachers who are fully qualified
> Are themselves the source of perfect qualities
> And hold the ground of perfect buddhahood.

As this implies, such teachers must have themselves received the precious word empowerment of primordial purity, and they should observe the samayas of nothing to keep.[70] Thanks to their utterly pure view and meditation, they must have completely attained the level of the exhaustion of phenomena, the ultimate space-like fundamental nature. Finally, they should have compassion and the ability to establish others on the same level as themselves. These are all indispensable characteristics.

1. The Manner in Which the Teaching Is Bestowed

They should examine their disciples
And gradually bestow on them the key instructions.
But they should keep these teachings
From unsuitable recipients.

They should mark them with the seal of secrecy
And hide them with the seal of their entrustment.

Qualified teachers must properly examine their disciples to see whether they are suitable vessels. Then, gradually they should bestow on them the key points of instruction according to the mental acumen of the disciple concerned. If teachers fail to examine their disciples properly, their teachings will not be attuned to the mental capacity of the disciples. If they give profound teachings on the spur of the moment to whomever they may meet, the unsuitable persons who request such teachings will distort them and the blessing power of the teachings themselves will disappear. These and other mischiefs will occur. It is like when a vessel breaks: its contents are spilled. And even teachers of high realization should not give many profound teachings at the same time, disregarding their proper order in view of the capacity of their disciples. If one were to consume in a single day the food for a whole year, one's stomach would be incapable of digesting it. Likewise, even in the case of suitable vessels for the teaching, if disciples are not brought to maturity through the practice, the evil consequence of such a manner of transmitting the teachings will be that the disciples become impervious to them. In his text *An Examination of the Key Point of Timeliness*, Padmasambhava said,

> Not all at once but gradually
> The vessels should be scrutinized.
> The teachings should be given step by step
> And hidden, concealed, from those
> Who cling to this, their present life.

For fully qualified teachers, happiness and sorrow are the same, gold and earth are the same, and space and the hollow of the hand are the same. They have no need of worldly riches, but in order to emphasize the greatness of the sublime Dharma and as a means of examining the minds of their disciples, they must accept offerings.

When it comes to making offerings and paying homage, people who are suitable vessels, who are endowed with respect and devotion for the Dharma, will have no concern for their own persons or for their lives or possessions. They will devote themselves entirely to the profound Doctrine. Those who are unsuitable vessels, on the other hand, pay only lip service with fine words but will not devote themselves to the teachings. It is most important, therefore, that disciples be examined. It is said in *The All-Creating King*,

> Good disciples, once examined,
> Make requests with precious offerings,
> And thus their faith may be discerned.
> But those with pride and strong attachment,
> Whose care for others is not genuine—
> To them the All-Creating King is not to be revealed.

These teachings should therefore be kept very secret from those who are unsuitable vessels. They should not even be spoken of in a wind that blows in their direction. Commands should be given to the guardians of the teachings of the Great Perfection to place on them the seal of secrecy, the seal of treasure, the seal of concealment, the seal of mystery, the seal of entrustment, the seals of the enlightened body, speech, and mind. One should feel no inclination to explain the secret teachings to those who are unsuitable. One should not pronounce a single syllable to them. One should not put the texts into their hands. One must keep them secret.

Longchenpa declares that they must be sealed as secret teachings and withheld from the unsuitable. By contrast, they should indeed be taught to suitable persons, concealing them strictly with the seal of entrustment. As we find in *Awareness Self-Arisen*,

> The pith instructions of the Great Perfection
> Should not be poured into inferior and common vessels.
> If the essence meant for just the faithful few

Is poured into a bad or common cup,
It will be lost, and teacher and disciple both
Will fall down to their ruin.
These teachings should therefore be kept
From those of base, inferior mind.

1. The Essential Teaching That Is to Be Imparted

6. To the children of the teacher's heart,
The fortunate of high capacity,
Essential teachings, definitive in meaning,
Should be granted.

Here, Longchenpa is saying that the quintessential teachings of the secret and definitive meaning should be entrusted to fortunate disciples of the highest caliber, who are indeed the children of the teacher's heart. In the autocommentary, he divided this section into two parts: the actual teaching itself and a description of those to whom it should be given. The first of these is again divided twofold: first, a consideration of the ground nature established by the view (namely, awareness beyond the law of causation) and second, a description of the way in which the view is to be maintained through meditation. We will review these points in slightly more detail as follows.

Regarding the ground established by the view, Longchenpa quotes extensively from *The All-Creating King* and *The Lion's Perfect Power*. Here, awareness is shown to be beyond all action, whether positive or negative. It is beyond cause and result, benefit or harm. In particular, it can be said that in order to remove dangers on the path, the lower vehicles do of course teach the existence of virtue and nonvirtue. The reason for this is that [at this level] the authentic fundamental nature cannot be realized owing to a very strong clinging to the supposed reality of phenomena. Nevertheless, as far as the ultimate way of being of phenomena is concerned, virtue and nonvirtue are without true existence in the same way that the hallucinations appearing to someone suffering from a high fever are completely unreal. The teachings of Atiyoga, which transcend the principle of cause and effect, cannot be applied to the conventional level in the same way that [conversely] the example of a shoot emerging from a seed cannot be used to indicate the nature of space. Longchenpa demonstrates this very well with many citations taken from the tantra of *The All-Creating King*, and there is no need for me to discuss this matter further.

Now, with regard to the way in which the view is maintained through meditation, [we must advert to the fact that] awareness is the naked dharmakāya, which transcends cause and effect, virtue and nonvirtue. When one settles in the uncontrived state, leaving everything as it is, without in any way reflecting or thinking about primordial purity (the state of the exhaustion of phenomena that transcends the ordinary mind), one is in a state that is lucid in its natural luminosity, vivid in its empty luminosity, and even in its primordial luminosity. As one rests in this state without any manipulation or alteration, it remains even in its natural flow, lucid in its natural vanishing, free in its natural subsiding, clear in its natural purity, relaxed in its natural condition. It is a wide-awake, unbroken, all-pervading evenness within the relaxation and openness of the five sense doors. In this immensity, in this vast expanse, the continuity of mind, which stretches through the past, present, and future, is severed. There is nothing but a state of rest in an unceasing luminosity that is thought-free, naked, even, and all-embracing. There is nothing else. This is what Longchenpa describes in detail, citing various tantras: *The Mirror of Samantabhadra's Mind*, *The Six Expanses*, *The Blazing Lamp*, *The Union of the Sun and Moon*, *The Lion's Perfect Power*, *The Supreme Array of Studded Jewels*, *The Word-Transcending Tantra*, *The Heap of Jewels Tantra*, and *The Great Garuḍa's Power*. For fear of being excessively prolix, I will not elaborate on it further.

1. The Way in Which the Entrusted Teaching Is Implemented and the Benefits That Accrue Therefrom

> 7. And they in turn must not divulge to all
> This essence, which is ultimate and free from all
>   decline.
> They must keep it undiminished
> As the essence of their practice.
> If the secret door is compromised,
> Punishment is sure to come.
> Through misinterpretation,
> The essential teachings will recede.
> Disciples therefore must maintain the secret
> And keep their masters joyful company.
> They will reach within this very life
> The everlasting kingdom of the dharmakāya.

According to what was said above, after scrutinizing the minds of the disciples to establish whether or not they have the ability to practice these teachings, which are of such extraordinary depth, the master should impart the profound instructions to their fortunate disciples, those who are suitable vessels. And the latter should in turn put them into practice. Through realization they will free their own minds, and through compassion they will free the minds of others. That the victory banner of the quintessential teachings be held high without decline, those exceptional disciples, to whom the profound pith instructions have been entrusted, must implement them, cherishing them more than life itself. Most especially, if the disciples are fully qualified for such teachings, their masters must instruct them, giving them everything without omission, without hiding or concealing anything. It is said in *The All-Creating King*,

> The oral lineage that comes
> From the transmission of this discourse—

> To you who will uphold its essence
> Beyond all increase and decline,
> The All-Creating King is now entrusted.

As a means of examining the character of disciples endowed with fortune and in order to eliminate their attachment to worldly things, teachers must accept all the gifts that their disciples offer them—their bodies and possessions—bringing to the fore the greatness of the sublime Dharma. It is thus that the ties of attachment in the disciples' minds will be broken. The instructions must then be imparted in their entirety. As it is said in *The All-Creating King*,

> To free disciples from their clinging to the world,
> To test their character,
> The teacher must accept
> Their bodies and possessions.
> As for their capacity or otherwise,
> If they show the special signs of aptitude,
> They should be instructed
> In the quintessential teachings.
> To them the All-Creating King is given.

If, therefore, they meet with people who are fully qualified, the teachers must give to them the profound and quintessential instructions, thereby ensuring that the latter remain, without disappearing, for as long as this world lasts. But these profound teachings must not be given to those who are unsuitable. If, however, they are imparted to disciples who are proper vessels for them, the latter must in turn pass them on so that the teachings do not disappear and the lineage of the holders of the doctrine remains unbroken. And again, those who are the proper recipients of the teachings must not leave them indifferently aside; they must hold them dear as the heart of their practice. That the quintessential doctrine might remain in the world for a long time without vanishing, its practice must be repeatedly encouraged and beings must strive in it.

If, however, the secret teachings are carelessly divulged to those who are improper vessels, not only will this fail to serve one's own or others' benefit, but the teachings will be misunderstood and the evil action of abandoning the Dharma will ensue. As a result of this, one will have to wander for many kalpas in the lower realms. Both teachers and disciples will be severely punished by the ḍākas and ḍākinīs, and by the Dharma protectors of the Great Perfection teachings. Because of all the possible misunderstandings that place in jeopardy the survival of this quintessential doctrine, it must never even be spoken of in a wind that blows in the direction of those who are unsuitable. As *The All-Creating King* says,

> Spirits and nonhuman entities
> Will rain down obstacles.
> Ḍākinīs endowed with siddhi
> Will inflict upon both teacher and disciple
> Terrors and untimely death.
> Through misinterpretation
> Will the quintessential vehicle fade.
> Therefore spurn the company
> Of those who are inferior.

This is why the pith instructions should be withheld from those who are unworthy. They should, however, be given in their entirety to the qualified. If the latter attend their teachers lovingly and devotedly and in an ambience of joy, they will come, in this very life, to the ultimate and everlasting kingdom of the dharmakāya, which is like the wish-fulfilling tree, the jewel, and the abundant cow, bestowing all that is needed and desired. It is said in *The Word-Transcending Tantra*,

> As though from wishing trees and wish-fulfilling jewels,
> And from the cow that grants all one desires,

You will receive an excellence beyond all measure.
With this in mind, rely upon your teacher;
You will win the war against samsara.

A Concluding Statement of the Vajra Topic's Name

Here ends the word commentary on the fifth vajra topic on *The Precious Treasury of the Fundamental Nature*, which establishes with certainty the kind of people to whom these teachings may be given.

4. The Conclusion of the Treatise as a Whole

This part has five sections: a dedicatory prayer for the freedom of all beings in the three worlds, a dedicatory prayer for the spread and prosperity of this doctrine in the ten directions, the author of this work and the circumstances of its composition, an exhortation to rejoice addressed to the fortunate people of future generations, and the colophon of the author himself.

1. A Dedicatory Prayer for the Freedom of All Beings in the Three Worlds

> 1. This teaching has disclosed
> Directly, without hiding anything,
> The view of the sublime and secret
> Great Perfection.
> May it naturally and without effort
> Bring beings, leaving none aside,
> To freedom in the space of the primordial ground.

As these words declare, the sublime heart essence of the victorious buddhas of the three times, the most secret and unsurpassed teaching, more secret than the secret words of Dharma, the difficult key points of the view of the Luminous Great Perfection, is revealed and clearly explained in this faultless text. Nothing is hidden. It is like the sun rising in a dark sky. Thanks to this teaching, may all the beings of the three worlds without a single exception realize the primordial wisdom that is the very nature of their own minds.

May they gain freedom naturally and without the slightest effort in the ground expanse of Samantabhadra, the primordial lord, the great and natural state of Ati, the expanse of blissful, primordial wisdom.

1. A Dedicatory Prayer for the Spread and Prosperity of this Teaching in the Ten Directions

> **2. This teaching, which completely covers**
> **All the lower views,**
> **Is the very peak of all the vehicles,**
> **The vast space of the great garuḍa king.**
> **May this teaching of the Atiyoga,**
> **Superior to every other,**
> **Be spread in all the ten directions.**
> **May the banner of its victory be never lowered.**

The primordial wisdom of great, natural bliss covers in a single stroke the entire terrain of the conceptual, lesser views of the lower vehicles. Such is the profundity of the view of Atiyoga, the Natural Great Perfection. As it is said in *The Natural Subsiding of Characteristics*,

> The Atiyoga teachings are the peak
> Of all the other vehicles.
> Like Sumeru, they are the supreme summit,
> The greatest of the great,
> Samantabhadra's space-like mind.
> By their strength these teachings overwhelm
> The eight preceding vehicles.

Mount Meru, king of mountains, is higher than all the peaks of the four cosmic continents—overwhelming and dominating them all, including the seven encircling golden ranges. In the same way, this vehicle of the Great Perfection is the pinnacle of all the intellectually based tenets of the eight lower vehicles. It towers above them. And just as the great garuḍa, king of birds, soars in the sky above the higher and lower mountains of the world, dominating the entire earth, this highest of all vehicles reigns supreme above the views of the intellectually contrived tenets of the eight lower systems. Its view, superior to all of them, is the realization that samsara and nirvana are naturally pure. May the never-failing victory banner of this Atiyoga instruction and scriptural tradition fly above the three worlds of existence until this very kalpa dissolves into the void. Jamgön Lama Mipham has declared,

> The summit of the victory banner of the whole of
>   Buddhadharma
> Is adorned with the jewel of the luminous vajra essence.
> The banner of supreme victory
> Reigns on high in all the ten directions.[71]

In accordance with these words, may this profound, quintessential teaching embrace and spread throughout the ten directions and be victorious everywhere.

1. The Author of This Work and the Circumstances of Its Composition

> 3. Three classes, nine expanses
> All subsumed in the four principles.
> The final view of all their sixteen sections
> Is expounded in this *Precious Treasury*
> Of the Fundamental Nature,
> Which Longchen Rabjam Zangpo
> Has perfectly composed.

Generally speaking, the path of beings of great scope is divided threefold: the long path, the short path, and the swift path. Of these, the present text containing the pith instructions of the path of the Luminous Great Perfection belongs to the swift path. Now the swift path of the Great Perfection may be classified as follows. The six million four hundred thousand tantras of the Great Perfection may be condensed into three classes: the mind class, the space class, and the pith instruction class. And among these, the profound Heart Essence of the Vast Expanse[72] belongs to the secret pith instruction class. Moreover, the pith instruction class is further divided into four cycles: the outer, inner, secret, and the most secret unsurpassed. The present teaching belongs to the fourth of these: the most secret, unsurpassed cycle. To this belong the seventeen tantras of the Heart Essence and the tantra of the Wrathful Protectress of Mantra—eighteen tantras in all—as well as one hundred and nineteen pith instructions. These have been condensed into the Four Parts of the Heart Essence.[73] Of these, Padmasambhava's *Heart Essence of the Ḍākinīs* and Vimalamitra's *Secret Heart Essence* are the two "mother volumes," while the *Innermost Essence of the Ḍākinīs* and the *Innermost Essence of the Master*—both composed by the omniscient Longchenpa—are the two "child volumes."[74] All together, therefore, these are the four volumes, "mother and child," of the Heart Essence cycle. In addition, Longchenpa composed his *Profound and Innermost Essence*,[75] which is a summary of the other two *Innermost Essences*. The teachings in these texts may be summarized into instructions on trekchö,[76] which have to do with primordial purity, and instructions on *thögal*,[77] which deal with spontaneous presence.

In brief, the teachings of the Natural Great Perfection are subsumed in the outer mind class, the inner space class, and the secret pith instruction class. They are also gathered in what are referred to as the nine expanses: the primordially pure expanse of the ultimate nature; the spontaneously present expanse of luminous character; the expanse of unceasing manifestation; the expanse beyond causality, action and effort; the expanse utterly devoid of error and obscuration; the expanse of the primordially pure view and meditation; the expanse devoid of deliberate action, contrivance, and manipulation; the expanse of the seamless view; and the expanse in which phenomena subside there and then in their own nature.

The meaning of the teachings contained in these three classes and nine expanses is set forth in the present text by means of four principles: nonexistence, evenness, spontaneous presence, and single nature. This meaning is completely subsumed in these four immutable principles of the ultimate quintessence. Indeed, this text reveals the key points of these four principles in their entirety. Moreover, each of the four principles is again subdivided into four aspects. That is, the key points are revealed, essentialized, subsumed, and a clear conviction is reached concerning them. These sixteen sections expound and directly disclose the profound, secret, ultimate view.

This profound teaching demonstrates, in a quite uncontrived manner, the view of the fundamental nature of the Luminous Great Perfection. It is like a treasure house that satisfies every need and wish without exception. Thanks to this, we are able to actualize, in this very lifetime, the condition of the sovereign primordial lord. For this text explains the secret and profound method for attaining such a goal.

The Precious Treasury of the Fundamental Nature was composed by Longchen Rabjam Palzangpo, a yogi of the supreme and sovereign vehicle. He is crowned with the name Longchen, the "great expanse," because his view of ultimate reality and his meditation on it resemble a vast space similar to the sky itself. And it was well set forth—bequeathed as a legacy for his followers, the fortunate disciples who are its proper recipients.

1. An Exhortation to Rejoice Addressed to the Fortunate Beings of Future Generations

> 4. The final view that is contained
> In the five topics of *The Treasury*
> *Of the Fundamental Nature,*

> Is perfectly adorned with riches,
> Both profound and vast.
> It is made beautiful with the splendor
> Of its words and meanings.
> Let a host of fortunate disciples
> Take great joy therein.

The chakravartin, the wheel-holding monarch who reigns over the four continents of the universe, has in his possession a perfect treasure house that, supreme in every quarter, is replete with wealth and possessions that are immeasurable and glorious and is adorned with many a beautiful array. In the same way, the fundamental nature of phenomena or suchness, the matter of which the present text speaks, is essentialized in the treasure house of the spontaneously present vajra peak of Atiyoga, which is the pinnacle of the nine vehicles.

Within the five vajra topics, and with words that express these points, the ultimate view of validly established dharmatā, the ultimate quintessence, is clearly summarized. It is perfectly adorned with a prolific wealth of marvelous key points pertaining to the profound and vast meanings and is rendered beautiful by a splendid array of words and meanings. This text is like an inexhaustible mine of precious gems. It was left as a legacy for the fortunate beings of future generations and as the foundation and basis for the enjoyment of their every wish. Let this be for them a source of sincere and confident rejoicing!

1. The Colophon of the Author Himself

This concludes *The Precious Treasury of the Fundamental Nature*. It was composed by Longchen Rabjam, a yogi of the supreme vehicle.

Notes

Abbreviations

TPQ, Book 1   Jigme Lingpa and Longchen Yeshe Dorje, Kangyur Rinpoche, *Treasury of Precious Qualities*, translated by Padmakara Translation Group (Boston: Shambhala Publications, 2010).

TPQ, Book 2   Jigme Lingpa and Longchen Yeshe Dorje, Kangyur Rinpoche, *Treasury of Precious Qualities, Book 2*, translated by Padmakara Translation Group (Boston: Shambhala Publications, 2013).

1. Note that the Tibetan titles all contain the word *precious* (*rin po che*): *The Precious Treasury of Wish-Fulfilling Jewels* and so on. For the sake of brevity, and following the common practice among Tibetan scholars, we have systematically omitted this element in the English titles.

2. The possible exception to this rule is the brief explanations of certain aspects of *The Treasury of the Wish-Fulfilling Jewels (Yid bzhin mdzod)* composed by Mipham Rinpoche in connection with the edition he himself made of this text at the behest of his teacher Jamyang Khyentse Wangpo. Even though a few of these texts are elucidations of Longchenpa's meaning, they are not extensive commentaries in the sense intended here.

3. We know, for example, that *The Treasury of Tenet Systems* predates *The Treasury of the Dharmadhātu* (composed in Gangri Thökar), which quotes it.

4. While in Bhutan, Longchenpa built eight temple hermitages of which Tharpa Ling was the first and most important. Furthermore, in the fourteenth-century biography by Chödrak Zangpo, Longchenpa is said to have composed over 270 treatises, while Nyoshul Khen Rinpoche, in his *Marvelous Garland of Rare Gems*, raises this total to the vertiginous figure of 307. Most of these texts are said to have been composed during Longchenpa's exile, only to be lost on the journey home.

5. See Germano, "Poetic Thought," p. 24.

6. Respectively, *Yid bzhin rin po che'i mdzod* and *Grub mtha' rin po che'i mdzod*.

7. *Man ngag rin po che'i mdzod.*

8. Respectively, *Chos dbyings rin po che'i mdzod* and *gNas lugs rin po che'i mdzod*.

9. *Theg mchog rin po che'i mdzod* and *Tshig don rin po che'i mdzod.*

10. See TPQ, Book 2, p. 426n400.

11. See TPQ, Book 2, p. 205.

12. Ibid., p. 208.

13. In Tibetan, these stages are respectively, *gnad bkrol ba, 'gag bsdam pa, chings su bcing ba,* and *la zla ba.*

14. It should be noted that in *The Treasury of Precious Qualities,* Jigme Lingpa discusses the four samayas of nothing to keep in a slightly different order.

15. *gNas lugs rang 'byung gyi rgyud.*

16. *sNang sbyang.*

17. It is clear from the wording of the text that the author of the biography is referring to the well-known proverb that describes the beneficial effects of all connections, good or bad, with bodhisattvas: "If the connection is good, one gains buddhahood in a single life. If the connection is bad, samsara itself will have an end" (*rten 'brel bzang po tshe gcig sang rgyas/ rten 'brel ngan pa 'khor ba mtha' can*). See *Biography,* p. 54.

18. Treasure revealers have occasionally appeared in other schools, one notable example being the Fifth Dalai Lama.

19. The theoretical basis for the revelation of spiritual treasures and the manner in which this occurs has been discussed in great detail by Tenpa'i Nyima (1865–1926), the third Dodrubchen Rinpoche, in his *Las 'phro gter brgyud kyi rnam bshad nyung gsal ngo mtshar rgya mtsho.* See Tulku Thondup, *Hidden Teachings of Tibet.*

20. *Ye shes bla ma.*

21. *Nges shes sgron me.*

22. See TPQ, Book 2, p. 208.

23. This famous saying is often quoted. See, for example, Dudjom Rinpoche, *Counsels from My Heart,* p. 88.

24. See Tenpa'i Wangchuk's reference to the story of Atiśa and the two monks, p. 260.

25. See p. 272.

26. See p. 122.

27. That is, the realization of the union of appearances and emptiness, the

union of awareness and emptiness, and the union of luminosity and emptiness.

28. Pronounced *Neluk rinpoche'i dzö chejawa*.

29. Skt. *nāma*, Tib. *ces bya ba*. This is the traditional manner of indicating that the words in question are the title of a book.

30. See TPQ, Book 2, pp. 240–41.

31. A vajra is said to be impossible to cut, indestructible, truly existent, solid, stable, invincible, and unobstructible.

32. In the present context, this term refers to the samayas of nothing to keep. See TPQ, Book 2, pp. 205–8.

33. In the expression "Natural Great Perfection," the term *natural (rang bzhin)* refers to the fact that the "face" or "likeness" (*bzhin*) of ultimate reality, or dharmatā, is shown exactly as it is without modification or elaboration.

34. This final element simply corresponds to the practice in Sanskrit and Tibetan literature of placing titles at the end of the sections, chapters, or texts that they refer to.

35. The eight conceptual extremes are arising and cessation, permanence and annihilation, coming and going, and identity and difference.

36. This and the following paragraph are taken from the autocommentary to *The Treasury of the Fundamental Nature*.

37. That is, they are without intrinsic existence.

38. The following quotation, which in the Tibetan is said to be taken from the autocommentary to *The Treasury of the Dharmadhātu*, is in fact taken from the autocommentary to the present work.

39. One of the twenty-five principal disciples of Guru Padmasambhava.

40. See TPQ, Book 2, pp. 205–8.

41. A translator and minister of King Trisong Detsen who became a disciple of Guru Rinpoche. He is said to have attained the rainbow body.

42. See note 31.

43. *ngo bo'i rig pa*.

44. *thugs rje'i rig pa*.

45. Shabkar Tsokdruk Rangdrol (1781–1851) was a celebrated nonsectarian master of the Nyingma school and yogi of the Great Perfection.

46. See TPQ, Book 2, p. 256.

47. These factors are described here as impure because, compared with the Great Perfection, they belong to an inferior view.

48. The enumeration here differs from the list given in TPQ, Book 2, pp. 351, 447n660.

49. That is, whatever is born will die, whatever is high will be brought low,

whatever comes together will be separated, and whatever is accumulated will be dispersed.

50. The three impurities are clouds, mist, and dust.

51. The nine activities are: outwardly, the deluded activities of body, speech, and mind; inwardly, prostrations, prayers, meditative concentration, and so on; and secretly, all physical movement, utterances of speech, and thought processes.

52. The term translated here as "understood" is *chinlab* (*byin brlabs*), which normally means "empowered" or "blessed."

53. "Self" refers to inherent existence.

54. That is, perceiving everything but without focusing on anything in particular.

55. Here and later, spontaneous presence is referred to as "precious" in the sense that it was described as an all-providing, or wish-fulfilling, jewel in the first stanza of this section.

56. In this context, beings to be trained referred to as pure are the buddhas and the bodhisattvas on the grounds of realization. Those referred to as impure are ordinary beings who have not yet reached the path of vision. See TPQ, Book 2, p. 282ff.

57. See TPQ, Book 1, pp. 431–35.

58. See TPQ, Book 1, p. 391.

59. See TPQ, Book 2, pp. 238–39.

60. That is, without specific focus.

61. See TPQ, Book 2, p. 238.

62. This is a reference to the "five days of meditation" in which a "day" corresponds to the period of time a practitioner is able, while still alive, to remain in the state of luminosity. It is said that this experience can last for as much as five "days."

63. See TPQ, Book 2, pp. 240–41.

64. This is *rig pa 'bras bu cog bzhag*, the fourth of the four states of "leaving as it is" (*cog bzhag bzhi*).

65. The autocommentary to *The Precious Treasury of the Fundamental Nature*.

66. That is, "nyingtik" (*snying thig*), the teachings of the Great Perfection in their most essential and refined form.

67. *Mkha' 'gro snying thig.*

68. See *Root Stanzas on the Middle Way*, XV, 7. An account of the Buddha's conversation with Kātyāyana (Kaccāyana) is found in the *Samyutta Nikāya*. See Bikkhu Bodhi, *The Connected Discourses of the Buddha*, 544.

69. According to the Nyingma tradition, six levels or grounds, the result of

the practice of the inner tantras, are added to the usual ten. The sixteenth ground, titled Unsurpassed Wisdom (*Ye shes bla ma'i sa*), corresponds to the "ever-youthful vase body," the ultimate attainment of Atiyoga.

70. See TPQ, Book 2, p. 205.

71. This is taken from a prayer for the preservation of the Nyingma teachings *The Teachings Pleasing to the Dharma King* (*sNga gyur bstan pa'i smon lam chos rgyal dgyes pa'i zhal lung*).

72. *kLong chen snying thig.*

73. This is also referred to as the Four Parts of Nyingtik (sNying thig ya bzhi).

74. Respectively, *mKha' 'gro snying thig, Bi ma snying thig, mKha' 'gro yang tig,* and *bLa ma yang tig.*

75. *Zab mo yang tig.*

76. *khregs chod.*

77. *thod rgal.*

GLOSSARY

arising-subsiding	*shar grol*
awareness	*rig pa*
character (luminous)	*rang bzhin*
cognitive power/potency	*thugs rje*
creative power	*rtsal*
display	*rol ba*
equality	*mnyam nyid*
evenness	*phyal ba*
fundamental nature	*gnas lugs*
fundamental stratum	*rang mal*
hallucinatory perceptions	*'khrul snang*
luminosity	*'od gsal*
natural meditative absorption	*rang bzhin bsam gtan*
nature	*ngo bo*
nonexistence	*med pa*
open and unimpeded	*zang thal*
open(ness) and free(dom)	*grol ba*
ornament	*rgyan*
primordial openness and freedom	*ye grol*
primordial/primal wisdom	*ye shes*
self-experience of awareness	*rang snang*
single nature	*gcig pu*
spontaneous presence, spontaneously present	*lhun grub*
subjective mental experience	*rang snang*

to essentialize key points	*'gag bsdam pa*
to gain clear conviction	*la bzla ba*
to reveal key points	*gnad bkrol ba*
to subside	*grol ba*
to subsume key points	*chings su bcings pa*
ultimate reality, dharmatā	*chos nyid*

TEXTS CITED IN KHANGSAR TENPA'I WANGCHUK'S COMMENTARY

All-Creating King Tantra, *Kun byed rgyal po'i rgyud*
All-Illuminating Sphere Tantra, *Kun gsal thig le'i rgyud*
Autocommentary on the Treasury of the Dharmadhātu, *Chos dbyings rin po che'i rang 'grel* by Longchenpa
Confession of the Fourteen Downfalls of the Mantra, *sNgags kyi rtsa ltung bcu bzhi'i bshags sdom*
Direct Immediacy of Awareness, *Rig pa spyi blugs* by Garab Dorje
Examination of the Key Point of Timeliness, *Dus gnad brtags pa* by Guru Padmasambhava
Great Commentary on the Prajñāpāramitā in Eight Thousand Lines, *brGyad stong 'grel chen*
Great Garuḍa Tantra, *Khyung chen gyi rgyud*
Guhyagarbha Tantra, Tantra of the Secret Essence, *rGyud gsang ba snying po*
Heap of Jewels Tantra, *Rin chen spungs pa'i rgyud*
Illusory Net of Manifestations Tantra, *sGyu 'phrul drva ba'i rgyud*
Instantaneous Severance of the Three Times, *Dus gsum chig chod* by Garab Dorje
Lion's Perfect Power Tantra, *Seng nge rtsal rdzogs chen po'i rgyud*
Meeting the Three Kāyas, *sKu gsum thug 'phrad* by Garab Dorje
Mirror of Samantabhadra's Mind Tantra, *Kun bzang thugs kyi me long gi rgyud*
Natural Subsiding of Characteristics, *mTshan ma rang grol* by Garab Dorje
Oral Lineage, *sNyan rgyud*
Pearl Garland Tantra, *Mu tig phreng ba'i rgyud*
Precious Tala Sutra, *dKon mchog ta la'i mdo*
Root Stanzas on the Middle Way, *dBu ma rtsa ba shes rab*
Six Consciousnesses Overwhelmed, *Tshogs drug zil gnon* by Garab Dorje

Six Expanses Tantra, *kLong drug gi rgyud*

Supreme Array of Studded Jewels Tantra, *Nor bu phra bkod chen po'i rgyud*

Tantra of Auspicious Beauty, *bKra shis mdzes ldan chen po'i rgyud*

Tantra of Awareness Self-Arisen, *Rig pa rang shar gyi rgyud*

Tantra of Samantabhadra, *Kun tu bzang po'i rgyud*

Tantra of the Blazing Relics, *sKu gdung 'bar ba'i rgyud*

Tantra of the Great Victory Banner Never to Be Lowered, *Mi nub rgyal mtshan chen po'i rgyud*

Tantra That Embodies the Definitive Teachings of the Great Perfection, *rDzogs chen nges don 'dus pa'i rgyud*

Tantra without Letters, *Yi ge med pa'i rgyud*

Treasury of the Dharmadhātu, *Chos dbyings rin po che'i mdzod*

Union of the Sun and Moon Tantra, *Nyi zla kha sbyor gyi rgyud*

Word-Transcending Tantra, *sGra thal 'gyur rtsa ba'i rgyud*

BIBLIOGRAPHY

Bhikkhu Bodhi, trans. *The Connected Discourses of the Buddha: A Translation of the Saṃyutta Nikāya.* Somerville, MA: Wisdom Publications, 2000.

Germano, David. "Poetic Thought, the Intelligent Universe, and the Mystery of Self: The Tantric Synthesis of Rdzogs Chen in Fourteenth Century Tibet." PhD diss., University of Wisconsin, 1992.

Khangsar Tenpa'i Wangchuk. "rDzogs pa chen po gnas lugs rin po che'i mdzod kyi 'bru 'grel dpal ldan bla ma'i zhal lung kun mkhyen dgyes pa'i mchod sprin zhes bya ba." In *Khang sar bstan pa'i dbang phyug gi gsung 'bum*, vol. 4. Beijing: Mi rigs dpe skrun khang, 2005.

Longchen Rabjam. *The Precious Treasury of the Way of Abiding.* Translated by Richard Barron (Chökyi Nyima). Junction City, CA: Padma Publishing, 1998.

Nyoshul Khenpo. *A Marvelous Garland of Rare Gems: Biographies of Masters of Awareness in the Dzogchen Lineage.* Junction City, CA: Padma Publishing, 2005.

Tulku Thondup. *Hidden Teachings of Tibet: An Explanation of the Terma Tradition of the Nyingma School of Buddhism.* London: Wisdom Publications, 1986.

———. *The Practice of Dzogchen: Longchen Rabjam's Writings on the Great Perfection.* Boston: Snow Lion, 2014.

THE PADMAKARA TRANSLATION GROUP
TRANSLATIONS INTO ENGLISH

The Adornment of the Middle Way. Shantarakshita and Mipham Rinpoche. Boston: Shambhala Publications, 2005, 2010.

Counsels from My Heart. Dudjom Rinpoche. Boston: Shambhala Publications, 2001, 2003.

Enlightened Courage. Dilgo Khyentse Rinpoche. Dordogne: Editions Padmakara, 1992; Ithaca, NY: Snow Lion Publications, 1994, 2006.

The Excellent Path of Enlightenment. Dilgo Khyentse. Dordogne: Editions Padmakara, 1987; Ithaca, NY: Snow Lion Publications, 1996.

Finding Rest in Meditation. Longchenpa. Boulder: Shambhala Publications, 2018.

Finding Rest in the Nature of the Mind. Longchenpa. Boulder: Shambhala Publications, 2017.

A Feast of the Nectar of the Supreme Vehicle. Maitreya and Jamgön Mipham. Boulder: Shambhala Publications, 2018.

Finding Rest in Illusion. Longchenpa. Boulder: Shambhala Publications, 2017.

A Flash of Lightning in the Dark of Night. The Dalai Lama. Shambhala Publications, 1993. Republished as *For the Benefit of All Beings.* Boston: Shambhala Publications, 2009.

Food of Bodhisattvas. Shabkar Tsogdruk Rangdrol. Boston: Shambhala Publications, 2004.

A Garland of Views: A Guide to View, Meditation, and Result in the Nine Vehicles. Padmasambhava and Mipham Rinpoche. Boston: Shambhala Publications, 2015.

A Guide to the Words of My Perfect Teacher. Khenpo Ngawang Pelzang. Translated with Dipamkara. Boston: Shambhala Publications, 2004.

The Heart of Compassion. Dilgo Khyentse. Boston: Shambhala Publications, 2007.

The Heart Treasure of the Enlightened Ones. Dilgo Khyentse and Patrul Rinpoche. Boston: Shambhala Publications, 1992.

The Hundred Verses of Advice. Dilgo Khyentse and Padampa Sangye. Boston: Shambhala Publications, 2005.

Introduction to the Middle Way. Chandrakirti and Mipham Rinpoche. Boston: Shambhala Publications, 2002, 2004.

Journey to Enlightenment. Matthieu Ricard. New York: Aperture Foundation, 1996.

Lady of the Lotus-Born. Gyalwa Changchub and Namkhai Nyingpo. Boston: Shambhala Publications, 1999, 2002.

Lion of Speech: The Life of Mipham Rinpoche. Dilgo Khyentse. Boulder: Shambhala Publications, 2020.

The Life of Shabkar: The Autobiography of a Tibetan Yogin. Albany, NY: SUNY Press, 1994. Ithaca, NY: Snow Lion Publications, 2001.

Nagarjuna's Letter to a Friend. Longchen Yeshe Dorje, Kangyur Rinpoche. Ithaca, NY: Snow Lion Publications, 2005.

The Nectar of Manjushri's Speech. Kunzang Pelden. Boston: Shambhala Publications, 2007, 2010.

Practicing the Great Perfection: Instructions on the Crucial Points. Shechen Gyaltsap Gyurme Pema Namgyal. Boulder: Shambhala Publications, 2020.

The Root Stanzas on the Middle Way. Nagarjuna. Dordogne: Editions Padmakara, 2008. Boulder: Shambhala Publications, 2016.

A Torch Lighting the Way to Freedom. Dudjom Rinpoche, Jigdrel Yeshe Dorje. Boston: Shambhala Publications, 2011.

Treasury of Precious Qualities, Book One. Longchen Yeshe Dorje, Kangyur Rinpoche. Boston: Shambhala Publications, 2001. Revised version with root text by Jigme Lingpa, 2010.

Treasury of Precious Qualities, Book Two. Longchen Yeshe Dorje, Kangyur Rinpoche. Boston: Shambhala Publications, 2013.

The Way of the Bodhisattva (Bodhicharyavatara). Shantideva. Boston: Shambhala Publications, 1997, 2006, 2008.

White Lotus. Jamgön Mipham. Boston: Shambhala Publications, 2007.

The Wisdom Chapter: Jamgön Mipham's Commentary on the Ninth Chapter of The Way of the Bodhisattva. Jamgön Mipham. Boulder: Shambhala Publications, 2017.

Wisdom: Two Buddhist Commentaries. Khenchen Kunzang Pelden and Minyak Kunzang Sonam. Dordogne: Editions Padmakara, 1993, 1999.

The Wish-Fulfilling Jewel. Dilgo Khyentse. Boston: Shambhala Publications, 1988.

The Words of My Perfect Teacher. Patrul Rinpoche. Sacred Literature Series of the International Sacred Literature Trust. New York: Harper-Collins, 1994; 2nd ed. Lanham, MD: AltaMira Press, 1998; Boston: Shambhala Publications, 1998; New Haven, CT: Yale University Press, 2010.

Zurchungpa's Testament. Zurchungpa and Dilgo Khyentse. Ithaca, NY: Snow Lion Publications, 2006.

INDEX

appearances (*continued*)
  as mind, refutation of, 80–83
  nonexistence of, 15, 128–29
  not blocking, 33, 193, 195
  as primordial wisdom,
    essentialized, 44, 238–39
  recognizing nature of, 13, 117–18
  six ways of arising, 185
  as sole sphere of awareness, 41,
    224–26
  See also under emptiness; ground
apprehender and apprehended, 26,
  99, 167
  analysis of, 95–96
  within dharmadhātu, 79–80
  dissolution of, 215
  evenness of, 21–22, 23, 147–48,
    154, 155
  knowing and, 84
  primordial purity of, 162
  as self-arisen awareness, 47, 251–52
  transcending, 24, 157–58
Atiśa, 260
Atiyoga. *See* Great Perfection
awareness
  appearances and, 77–78, 116
  beyond causality, 7, 28, 91–94,
    173–75, 273–74
  beyond extremes, 43, 235
  characteristics of, 168
  creative power of, 83–85, 116, 153,
    157, 176
  direct realization of, 105
  evenness of, 25, 26, 161, 162–63,
    164–65
  and expanse, union of, 218
  inexpressibility of, 47, 252–53
  lack of awareness and, 254–55
  leaving as is, 240, 242, 243, 277n64
  nonaction and, 126
  recognition or nonrecognition of,
    41, 43, 224, 225–26, 233–34
  single nature of, 43–44, 45–46,
    235–38, 247–50
  sole wisdom in, 42, 229–31

as source of everything, 27, 168–69
See also self-experience of awareness

Bamda Thubten Gelek, xxvi
Beacon of Certainty (Mipham), xxx
Bhutan, xviii, xix, 285n4
Blazing Lamp, The, 274
bliss
  as awareness self-cognizing, 138
  in mind, 24, 25, 158, 160, 162–63
  presence of, 9, 32, 103, 188, 189, 254
  resting/remaining in, 12, 105, 107,
    114, 115
  as supreme absorption, 11, 110–11,
    198
body
  attachment to, 266
  breaking seal of, 214, 215–16,
    288n62 (*see also* death)
  ease in, 25, 160, 161
buddha fields, 42, 143–44, 182–83,
  231
buddhahood, 87
  beyond extremes, 138, 209
  at time of death, 217–19, 221–22
  unfabricated, 105–6
buddhas, 183–84, 225–26, 229
  as enlightened mind, 234
  minds of, 30, 45, 188–89, 230, 244,
    245
  self-experience of, 231

calm abiding, 112, 220
causal vehicles, 17, 135–36. *See also*
  lower vehicles
causality, xxiv, 68, 92, 123
  clinging to, 49, 258, 260
  nonexistence of, 15, 128–29
  purpose of teachings on, 15, 32, 124,
    188, 189–90
  transcending, 14, 17, 120–21, 122,
    134–36
certainty. *See* conviction
childish beings, 8, 9, 16, 96–97,
  102–3, 132–33, 189

cleverness, trap of, 101–2, 126
clinging, 16, 132–33
  to causality, 49, 258, 260
  evenness and, 23, 152, 153–54
  to lesser vehicles, 49, 258, 273
  naturally unfettered by, 25, 163
  perception without, 159
  to present life, 271
  to self, 156–57, 288n53
  subsiding of, 240, 249, 252
cognitive power/potency
  creative power of, 83–84
  ignorance and, 211
  as luminosity, 81–82, 111, 218
  as nirmāṇakāya, 192, 205
  as spontaneous presence, 36, 182, 185
commentaries
  on Longchenpa's works, xvi–xvii, 285n2
  word and meaning, distinctions between, xv–xvi
compassion, objects of, 16, 132–33
concentration, 288n51
  in causal vehicles, 36, 203
  conceptual, 123, 129, 137
  on dharmatā, 243
  of natural resting, 39, 220–21
  river-like, 111
  of spontaneous presence, 35, 200
Confession of the Fourteen Downfalls of Mantra (Sūra), 262, 263–64
confidence, 92, 114, 162–63, 191
consciousness
  evenness of, 25, 160–61
  indivisible instants of, 94, 95, 148, 238, 252
  as primordial wisdom, essentialized, 44, 238–39
  See also six consciousnesses
conviction, 19, 142–43
  about appearances, 34, 196
  about apprehender and apprehended, 47, 251–52
  about awareness, 47, 252–53

about causality, 16–17, 28, 133–35, 173–75
  in dharmatā, 12, 112–13
  in dissolution, 38, 214–16
  in evenness, 28, 172–73
  in four extremes, transcending, 16, 130–31
  importance of, 39, 219–22
  in nonexistence, 38–39, 216–17
  in objects of compassion, 16, 132–33
  in phenomena is beyond names, 18–19, 139–42
  in phenomena's exhaustion, 47–48, 253–56
  in phenomena's nature, 10, 11, 46, 106–7, 108, 109, 250–51
  in self-cognizing awareness, 17, 137–39
  in spontaneous presence, 36–39, 207–8, 212–14, 222–23
  yogic, 9, 100–101
crystal sphere, 30, 179–80, 202, 237, 248

death, 217–19, 221–22
delusion, 154, 155, 162, 211, 249
dharmadhātu, 109, 139
  inseparability from, 128
  mind and object in, 79–80
  and primordial wisdom, inseparability of, 231
  resting/dwelling in, 25, 161, 188
  sole wisdom of, 230, 233
dharmakāya, xxii, 65, 92, 215
  actualizing, 68
  appearances within, 90, 99
  display of, 12–13, 114–16
  dissolution in, 38, 212, 213, 214, 216, 217
  merging with, 104–5
  recognizing, 34, 196
  as sole sphere, 42, 226, 227, 255
  spontaneous presence of, 36, 203
  See also three kāyas

Secret Heart Essence, 258, 288n66
Secret Mantra, 262–64
self
  clinging to, 78, 97
  distorted belief in, 130–31
  misapprehending, 193–95
  nonexistence of, 163
  śrāvaka view of, 260
self-experience of awareness
  appearances as, 78, 90, 115, 116, 157
  cognitive acts as, 136–38
  as enlightened mind, 38–39, 216,
    217
  five elements as, 195
  nonexistence and, 9, 13, 100–101
  recognizing, 214, 215
  spontaneous presence and, 35,
    36–37, 182, 201, 207–8
sense faculties, 24, 25, 158, 159, 163,
    199, 274, 288n54
sense objects, 21, 44, 147, 148, 151,
    161, 240, 241
Serta Larung Gar, xvii
Seven Treasuries (Longchenpa),
    xviii–xx, 61–62, 285n3
Shabkar Tsokdruk Rangdrol, 113,
    287n45
single nature, xxv
  of ground, 43, 232–33, 254
  of luminosity, 44, 238–39
  of phenomena, 41–42, 224–26,
    226–27, 238–39
  of primordial wisdom, 45–46,
    247–50
single taste, 25, 105, 162, 163, 168
six consciousnesses
  dissolution of, 38–39, 216–17
  as empty, essentialized, 33–34,
    195–96
  relaxation of, 24, 33, 158–60, 193,
    195, 243–44
*Six Consciousnesses Overwhelmed,
    The* (Garab Dorje), 146, 170, 182,
    205–6, 211
Six Expanses Tantra, The, 108, 121,

145, 197, 201, 209, 210, 240,
    241–42, 243–44, 274
six migrations, 16–17, 29, 42, 133–34,
    177, 228
space examples, 136
  for awareness, 7, 10, 28, 43, 91–92,
    107–8, 175, 233, 234
  for enlightened mind, 5, 6, 34,
    76–77, 85, 198–99
  for primal purity, 37, 209
spontaneous presence, xxiv, 68, 245
  action and, 32, 188–90
  as all-supplying treasury, 31,
    184–86
  of appearances, 22, 67, 150
  effort and, 31–32, 186–88
  eight doors of, 185
  five sense doors and, 33–34, 196
  groundlessness of, 29, 177–79
  inconceivability of, 36–37, 207–8
  leaving as it, 34–35, 198–99
  nature of, 29, 175–76
  outer and inner, blending of,
    38–39, 216–17, 221
  phenomena within, 254
  as primordial, 32, 190–91
  as ultimate ground, 37–38, 212–14
  unwavering concentration of, 35,
    200
  See also under three kāyas
śrāvakas, 259–60
suchness, 8, 26, 32, 67, 96, 128,
    134–35, 164–65, 190–91. *See also*
    dharmatā
*Supreme Array of Studded Jewels
    Tantra, The*, 139, 274
Śūra. See *Confession of the Fourteen
    Downfalls of Mantra*
symbols, 22–23, 113, 151, 152

Tai Situ Changchub Gyaltsen, xviii
tantra, ten elements of, 17, 28, 122,
    135, 136, 149–50, 174
Tantra of Auspicious Beauty, The,
    211

view
  introducing, sealing, essentializing,
    195
  loss of one's conduct in, xxxii
  of natural state, 120, 287n47
  through meditation, 274
  transcending, 6, 87, 89, 90–91, 92
Vimalamitra, 282
virtue
  awareness as core of, 100
  beyond causality, 16–17, 133–36
  fabricated, 10, 105, 106
  in nonexistence, 14, 123
  transcending, 7, 14, 91–94, 95–96,
    120

Way of the Bodhisattva, The
  (Śāntideva), 259
wisdom. *See* primordial/primal
  wisdom
Word-Transcending Tantra, The, 199,
  229, 231, 245–46, 269, 270, 274,
  277–78

Yingrik Drubpa Rinpoche, xv
yogis
  awakening in present life, 217
  certainty of, 12, 18, 112–13, 137–39
  free of action, 32, 187–88
  of great secret, 15, 127–28
  realization of, 8, 96, 97–98, 131
Yudra Nyingpo, xxv, xxix